THE
FOOD
AND
BEVERAGE
MANAGER

Paul Cullen

HOSPITALITY
P R E S S
MELBOURNE

Hospitality Press Pty Ltd
38 Riddell Parade
PO Box 426
Elsternwick, Victoria 3185
Australia
Telephone (03) 9528 5021 Fax (03) 6528 2645

The Food and Beverage Manager

First Published 1997. Reprinted 2001

National Library of Australia
Cataloguing-in-publication data:

Cullen, Paul, 1954—.
    The food and beverage manager.

    Bibliography.
    Includes index.
    ISBN 1 86250 459 8.

    1. Food service management. 2. Restaurant management.
    I. Title.

647.95068

Designed and typeset by Lauren Statham (Alice Graphics)
Edited by Frances Wade (Wade's Distractions)
Printed by Pearson Australia Demand Print Centre
Published by Hospitality Press Pty Ltd (ACN 006 473 454)

THE
FOOD
AND
BEVERAGE
MANAGER

CONTENTS

PREFACE

The trade of innkeeping has a history almost as old as civilisation. In the earliest centuries of commerce, when cultures began to make contact with each other—often across vast distances—to swap silver for silk, furs for salt and spices for gold, the innkeeper was already there to provide food, lodging and safe shelter for travellers. Long before restaurants existed, or anyone had flown in an aeroplane, traders relied on inns, hostelries and stables to provide a meal, a bed and rest from the hard business of travel.

In these days of fax machines, transcontinental flights and teleconferencing, much has changed and much has stayed the same. Though instant communications have made the world much smaller, somehow people travel more than ever, whether for business or for entertainment. Their expectations have risen to include conference facilities, spa pools, valet service and fine restaurants, but they still look to hotels to provide them. We modern hoteliers still have this in common with medieval innkeepers: it is our business to provide hospitality, comfort, food and drink for weary travellers at any time of the day or night.

The hotel industry has grown so large that it is now a major contributor to the economy of nearly every country on earth, and indeed the leading hotel companies were among the first to become 'multinationals'. It is a complex, demanding and highly professional business, calling on the skills of market analysts, financial planners, architects, designers, trainers and personnel managers. Yet, however complex and far-reaching this industry becomes, it is important to keep a clear eye on the fundamentals of the business we are in. We provide our customers with accommodation, food, drink and service so that they, in turn, can get on with their own business or pleasure.

Every modern hotel can be thought of as having three essential divisions: Front Office (which includes reservations, reception, porters, accounts and record-keeping), Housekeeping (which provides clean, attractive guest rooms and public areas and runs the laundry and guest services) and Food and Beverage (which includes bars, restaurants, banquets and convention facilities). Other departments, such as Human Resources (Personnel), Engineering, Administration and Finance are essential to the smooth and profitable running of a large hotel, but the three basic operating departments—Front Office, Housekeeping and Food and Beverage—are those in direct contact with the customers: our guests.

Each one of these departments is a large business in itself. The Housekeeping department may employ a hundred staff or more in a large property. The Front Office operates 24 hours a day, with a formidable array of electronic data storage, retrieval and communication systems. The Food and Beverage department may operate several independent bars, restaurants and banquet rooms, ranging from a poolside snack bar to a conference centre for 1000 delegates. Each of these departments necessarily has a manager in charge of planning, operations, staffing and quality control. This book is written to explain the demanding role of the Food and Beverage Manager.

A note on the use of language

To avoid the artifice of sentence rearrangement, or the repetitive use of 'he or she', the author asks that the reader take every instance of the word 'he' or 'his' to include the feminine gender as well. This is borne out by the facts in many hotels around the world, where women occupy top management positions in every department. Even that last bastion of chauvinism, the Chef's office, may now be occupied by a woman or a man.

CHAPTER ONE

FOOD AND BEVERAGE MANAGEMENT

The role of the Food and Beverage Manager in a modern hotel

What are your responsibilities, and how is your performance measured?

Understanding how the Food and Beverage department works with, and relies upon, the other operating departments of the hotel, particularly the Rooms division and Front Office

Management structure

A large international hotel is a complex organisation, which relies on hundreds of skilled people to deliver the services required by a sophisticated clientele. At any given moment, guests may be using their rooms, telephoning overseas, ordering a bottle of wine in the restaurant, enjoying a swim in the pool, and arriving at the front desk exhausted from a long overseas flight. Without well-organised and well-trained staff working in a dozen different locations, the hotel could not cope effectively with the multiple demands made upon it.

The first step is, of course, organisation. To accomplish a difficult task, you must break it down into component parts and assign responsibility to staff qualified to handle them. At the top of the organisational tree in a large hotel is the General Manager, whose responsibility it is to ensure that the whole operation runs smoothly, successfully and profitably. He or she must delegate authority to department heads, who will in turn assign jobs to experienced managers and supervisors. The traditional organisational chart looks something like Figure 1.1 (see page 2).

You should be aware that there are as many possible organisation charts as there are hotel companies, and that even within the structure of a multinational hotel chain there will be local variations on this arrangement. Some hotel companies, embracing a fashion for 'flat management structure', may even have eliminated such titles as Rooms Division Manager and Food and Beverage Manager; but old habits die hard in the industry, and the traditional arrangement of responsibility generally emerges even when the names have been changed. This is because the basic division of work in a hotel has not altered significantly in decades. The kitchen, for instance, is necessarily run by a qualified and experienced Executive Chef, who is able to communicate professional instructions to the kitchen crew. Likewise, a Front Office Manager (FOM) will usually have come up through the

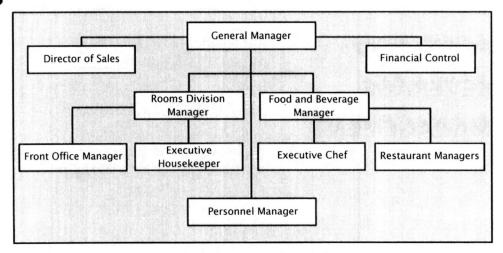

Figure 1.1   The senior management in a large hotel

ranks in reception or reservations, and will possess a high degree of skill with computer systems and guest relations. The FOM will be able to solve problems quickly and train staff effectively, and so emerge as the 'natural' leader of that department. Changing a title, or the lines on a wall chart, will not significantly alter the dynamic of the group.

Personalities will also play a part in the real organisation of a particular hotel. The Executive Chef may have more experience than the Food and Beverage Manager, and so take on a greater role in menu planning and design, perhaps reporting directly to the General Manager. The Rooms Division Manager may have a stronger background in Housekeeping than in Front Office, and so rely upon the FOM for greater than normal involvement in decision-making. Even general managers have their strengths and weaknesses, according to their own career paths in the hotel business. This sort of compensatory arrangement is not unusual. In fact, when responsibilities and strengths blur across traditional departmental lines, a team-based, entrepreneurial joint effort can often achieve real excellence.

A professional hotel staff is, however, built from the ground up. There is no benefit in having a multi-skilled management team if the porter on the front door is not polite to guests, or the cocktail bar staff do not know how to mix a Martini. There is no substitute for experience, the saying goes, and it remains true, even in the era of fashionable management theories. It may be useful to train a table server in inter-personal communication skills, but if you are unable to show him how to open a bottle of wine, you will have some difficulty managing the department in which he works. Thus the traditional career path that leads a table server to train in the service bar, to supervise on banquets, to manage a restaurant and eventually take promotion to Food and Beverage Manager is a sound one. Alternatively, a kitchen hand may qualify as a chef, proceed to *chef de partie*, be promoted to Executive Chef, then cross over to Food and Beverage management. In either case, the new manager will have to acquire some skills from the other side of the passe, but will build on a solid foundation of technique and experience gained at ground level.

The Food and Beverage department

The responsibilities of the new Food and Beverage Manager (known in hotel jargon as the 'F&B') are many. He or she will be directly in charge of the restaurant managers, the banquet team and the bar supervisors, and will liaise closely with the kitchen, in order to provide top-quality service, food and beverages for the guests in-house and for patrons using the public areas of the hotel. Most modern hotels will have at least two, and more frequently three or four, restaurant 'outlets' on the property. Each of these must be provided with a service bar. In addition there may be a cocktail bar, nightclub or entertainment lounge, as well as informal café or snack bar outlets, often at the poolside. Room service in a four- or five-star property will be expected to supply a full range of food and beverages to the guest rooms, and mini-bars must be replenished regularly. Function and conference facilities may range from a private dining room for a small group up to a major conference centre for hundreds of delegates. Theme functions may involve full stage equipment for entertainers or speakers, and the department may be called upon to cater for special events outside the hotel.

The Food and Beverage Manager will also be responsible for the planning of new restaurant or bar outlets, for the preparation of yearly budgets and forecasts, and for the purchase and renovation of operating equipment in the kitchens, restaurants and bars. Another important part of the job is overseeing the purchasing, receiving, storage and distribution of supplies for the various operating departments. The Food and Beverage Manager will also be required to liaise closely with Front Office, Housekeeping, Engineering, Sales and Administration in order to maintain a smooth flow of information and co-operation and will, of course, eventually report directly to the General Manager.

This may at first glance seem an insurmountable task, but in fact it is done every day in large hotels around the world. The whole relies on its parts, and it is here that the Food and Beverage Manager's skill is really put to the test, for unless he or she is an able manager of people, and capable of bringing together a willing team, then the task will indeed be too much to handle.

Attributes of a successful Food and Beverage Manager

Experience

It is essential that you know what you are talking about. Nothing so undermines the effectiveness of a manager as the perception that his staff know more about what they are doing than he does. You will have gained certain skills and experience from your working background, but you must be willing to learn the skills you need to effectively supervise. If you have not got the experience, you must get it. If your background is restaurant service, you may need to put on an apron and help plate up a few banquet meals. If your background is in the kitchen, you will need to spend some time on actual table service in order to understand what a table server has to do. If your weakness is in the theory of management, be prepared to read textbooks, attend courses or take advice from more experienced managers. Weak managers shy away from areas they are unfamiliar with; effective managers plunge in to learn the things they need to know.

Knowledge

The hotel business is changing constantly, as is the environment in which it does business. You will need to keep up with current trends in restaurant and menu design, be aware of changes in hotel law, industrial relations and trade regulations and keep well-informed in the world of wine and food. You will almost certainly subscribe to several trade magazines, and use a library to improve your in-depth knowledge of the hotel industry. When the demands of the job require new knowledge (of accounting practice, for instance, or of market research) you will have to know where and how you can obtain it. It is not enough to wait for news to come to you— you will have to seek it out.

Presence

The special quality that sets a good manager apart is a subtle combination of appearance and grooming, voice control, the ability to remain calm in stressful situations, and a genuine interest in people. This goes deeper than simply wearing a well-pressed suit. A professional hotelier maintains a degree of dignity, even in the most informal situations. This is not to encourage snobbishness or conceit—quite the opposite. People will look to you for answers and assistance, be they staff or guests. They will respond best to someone who is taking them seriously, and will look to you the next time they need direction. Beware of the temptation to be flippant, rude or coarse in speech, whatever the provocation. Each time you slip in the presence of staff or guests, it will cost you more dearly than you realise.

Encouragement of staff

Faced with a very complex job, with thousands of variables, you are going to need a large number of people to help you do it. If your staff are not entirely with you, then you may work 100 hours a week and still never have confidence in your department. If, on the other hand, you are able to recruit, train and encourage good people, then you will be investing time and effort in an organisation that becomes easier to run by the week. Your ability to inform, to enthuse, to cajole and reward your staff will in the end be the deciding factor in whether you are personally successful or not. Managers who complain frequently about their own superiors are admitting their inability to cope with the demands of an organisation. Managers who complain about the inefficiency or laziness of their own staff are not managers at all.

Endurance

The punishing schedule of the professional Food and Beverage Manager is little understood by anyone outside the industry. There is nothing unusual about having to do a twelve- or fourteen-hour day, starting with a tour group breakfast at 7.00 a.m. and finishing with a banquet dinner that lasts long into the night. This will make extreme demands on your family and your social life outside the hotel. Your ability to pace yourself, to keep going, to remain alert and personable when other people are running out of steam, will distinguish you as a professional. You will need to keep in a reasonable state of physical fitness, avoid alcohol completely while you are working, and be able to bounce back after a few hours' sleep.

Manners maketh the man (or woman)

Formal good manners, which took a holiday during the last generation, are back in style, and nowhere more intensely than in the world of hotels. Knowing when to open a door for a lady (and when not to), how to introduce a bishop to an air vice-marshal, and when to call on the after-dinner speaker, are not silly bits of useless information. To the professional hotelier, they are vital pieces of working knowledge. Your use of exceptionally good manners at all times will enable you to soothe a ruffled guest, charm a colleague into co-operation, or recover faultlessly from a disaster. If manners were not on the curriculum when you were at school, you will need to study them. Several modern guides to good behaviour are available. *A Guide to Modern Etiquette*, by Ita Buttrose (Mandarin, Australia, 1990) is a good introduction.

How your performance is measured

Running the Food and Beverage department of a large hotel is a business, and a big business at that. You may be responsible for a yearly turnover that runs into millions of dollars. You are employed as a department manager in order to guarantee that the enormous amount of money invested is invested wisely, and that it returns a profit. In the end, it will be your ability to control costs and return profits that marks you for promotion to a larger property or to general management. Contrary to the opinion of most accountants, it is not careful measuring, counting and record-keeping that turns a profit—it is the application of entrepreneurial flair. But the 'bean-counting' is useful as a means of keeping score, if you know how to interpret the figures. We shall discuss details in later chapters, but you should be aware of the main indicators.

Food cost

Food cost is a joint responsibility shared by the Purchasing department, the Executive Chef and the Food and Beverage Manager. This is an indication, expressed as a percentage, of how much has been spent on food supplies for each dollar received in restaurant income. A 30% food cost means that for one dollar in sales, 30 cents was spent on raw materials. Food cost will vary significantly across a spectrum of food service outlets. A fine dining room, for instance, may find a food cost of 40–45% acceptable, but in banquets anything higher than 25% must be considered a problem. The figure is arrived at by dividing the total amount spent on food by the total revenue derived from it, and multiplying the result by 100.

$$\text{Opening stock} + \text{purchases} - \text{closing stock} = \text{usage}$$

$$\frac{\text{food usage (July)}}{\text{food revenue (July)}} \times 100 = \text{food cost percentage}$$

Beverage cost

Here it will be your responsibility to juggle several different factors to achieve a profitable result. The size and range of the beverage inventory, the buying methods used, the level of standardisation achieved and the system used for requisition and distribution will all affect the bottom line. Beverage cost will also vary considerably according to the type of outlet, be it a drive-in bottle shop, a poolside cocktail bar or a fine dining room. The same calculation is made as for food cost. The total beverage purchase cost is divided by the beverage revenue, and the result multiplied by 100 to express a percentage.

Labour cost

A significant amount of your budget will be spent paying the people who work for you. In this case, separate figures will be generated for food preparation (kitchen staff), food service (restaurant managers, supervisors, casual and full-time table staff) and bar staff. This cost is controlled by rostering, and the result is calculated in the same way as food cost. The total wage bill for a week's operation is divided by the total revenue for that department in the same period.

$$\frac{\text{Labour cost (coffee shop)}}{\text{July revenue (coffee shop)}} \times 100 = \text{labour cost percentage}$$

Staff training

Training is an investment in quality of service and product. It is not a sideline, a second thought or an annoying obligation. You will be responsible for establishing and running a successful training plan for all the staff in your department. This not only improves individual skills, but also grooms people for advancement from entry-level jobs to supervisory roles and eventual management. An organised, continuous and visible system of staff training is the mark of a healthy organisation. In a larger property, the Personnel department may assist in this program, but the final responsibility for results lies with you.

Staff turnover

Your ability to retain skilled staff is a measure of your own management ability. Each new employee hired represents a significant investment of money and time in recruitment, screening, induction and training. If this employee leaves a few weeks later, then you will have spent a considerable amount of money for no return, and be forced to spend yet more on a replacement. People stay in demanding jobs for a variety of reasons, most of which can be controlled by a skilled manager. A sense of participation, an atmosphere of enthusiasm and professionalism, frequent recognition of achievement and a clear path for advancement are all major reasons why a staff member will stay with a particular hotel. Your role as manager is to create this atmosphere in your department and maintain it.

Customer response

The hotel business is tremendously competitive, and customers are always ready to try something else if they are not satisfied with the level of quality and service received for the money spent. Repeat custom is difficult to acquire, and easy to lose. The outcome of a major tour-company contract can hinge on the quality of the breakfast service received that morning. A hotel restaurant that does not anticipate and plan for changes in food fashion, that does not effectively promote itself, or that allows standards to slip when times are very busy or very quiet, will quickly be left behind by the competition. An empty restaurant invites criticism; a full one speaks for itself. You will be judged by your ability to attract business and to retain it.

Working with the other operating departments

The restaurants, bars and function facilities of a hotel do not operate in a vacuum. A hotel is a very large machine, with a great number of moving parts. The support provided by other operating departments can contribute greatly to the success of your department, but you will also have an obligation to work with other managers to ensure the smooth running of the whole. Competition between departments for budget, prestige or influence is almost always counter-productive. Far more can be achieved by working together than by pulling in opposite directions.

Administration

Your direct superior is likely to be the General Manager, and it will be to this person that you report. You may also be called on to attend executive committee meetings, budget meetings, conference planning sessions and policy review meetings. In each of these roles you will be expected to have solid facts at your disposal, and a clear understanding of what your department can and cannot profitably do. You may expect to field questions about suppliers, stock levels, staff training programs, food promotions, equipment shortages, sales figures or any one of a dozen other subjects that apply to your department. It is essential that you be well-informed, honest and fair-minded when discussing problems or shortcomings within your responsibility. Your practical, problem-solving attitude to challenges will reflect well on your ability to manage. Back-biting, scheming, prevarication or accusation have no place in the professional manager's repertoire. Blaming your own subordinates for mistakes or failure is like the kiss of death: if you are not running your department, then who is?

Keep in mind that the General Manager is not the only person on the Administration staff. Cordial relations with the General Manager's secretary, for instance, will improve your access to that office when you need it. You may need a report from the Accounts department, a quick fix to a payroll problem, or fast distribution of a memorandum. In each case, your good manners, approachable nature and polite requests will significantly improve your chances of getting what you need when you need it. You will return the favour by listening when the payroll clerk asks you to get your departmental time sheets in promptly, or the accountant asks you to have a word with your cashiers about the legibility of their writing. There is no one in a hotel whom you can afford to ignore or dismiss—spanners can be thrown into your works from any direction.

The Controller's office or the Finance department will normally produce the financial statements, including your departmental profit and loss, food, beverage and labour costs reports. You should be aware that these reports are only as accurate as the information upon which they are based, so you will build a good relationship with the staff in this area to ensure that they are getting accurate, timely information and are aware of any unusual circumstances that may affect your results. (A large stock purchase of house wine, for instance, would distort your beverage cost figures, unless it were correctly entered in the system.)

Engineering

When the wheels fall off your dessert trolley, the ceiling in the restaurant springs a leak, or the air-conditioning in the cocktail bar refuses to work, you are going to need help. Whether you wait an hour or a fortnight for the job to be done will depend, in part, on the relationship you have built up with the Engineering department. Maintenance engineers have the fairly thankless task of repairing or putting back together the multitude of things that can be broken in, or fall off, a 300- or 400-room building. Make sure that when they do a job for your department they are thanked, preferably by you.

You can improve your standing with the engineers and maintenance staff if you see that the damage inflicted on the building by your own crew is minimal. This may involve teaching a kitchen hand how to use a piece of machinery correctly, instructing the maître d' on the finer points of the air-conditioning system or simply asking your staff not to slam doors. Look around your department with the same care you would use to inspect a new car. If you can discover something while it is still a minor problem, you will make the job of fixing it much easier than if you had let it become a major one.

Timing helps, too. Since most of the maintenance staff are daytime workers, the time to tell someone about the broken chair in the dining room is at nine o'clock in the morning, not at five in the afternoon, when you are just about to open for service.

Obviously, if one of the maintenance crew or their family should come into the hotel as guests in the restaurant or to a function, you will go out of your way to see that they are made welcome and well looked after.

Housekeeping

The Housekeeping department covers almost as wide an area of responsibility as the Food and Beverage department (the Executive housekeeper would likely say more). In addition to maintaining and cleaning every one of the guest rooms every day, housekeeping staff also maintain the public areas of the hotel in a pristine and presentable condition. This department looks after all the hotel's laundry and uniform supply (whether it is done in-house or sent out to contract cleaners) and provides the hundreds of pieces of table linen, bar linen, kitchen towels and cleaning cloths used in food and beverage areas daily. Carpet and window cleaning will be done to a regular schedule, and special cleaning jobs will be undertaken after a large function or a special event. Housekeepers will cater for dozens of special requests from house guests, from warming a baby's bottle to sponging a wine stain out of an evening dress.

You cannot operate efficiently without the support of the Housekeeping department. You will rely on them for many of your supplies; the queue of table servers, bar staff and chefs lining up every afternoon for uniforms and linen will become a familiar sight. However, as vital as these supplies are to your department, they are not the principal workload of the laundry—guest linen comes first, and in much larger quantity.

You and your supervisors can help expedite things by maintaining a small, standard stock of linen in each restaurant or bar. Restaurant tables should always be left set at the end of a night, so that there is no desperate demand for tablecloths in the afternoon; if banquet rooms can be preset for the following day, they should be. Presenting the linen room with a forecast of the linen that will be required over the next ten days will also help to smooth over any coughs and sputters in the system.

Effective communication with the Executive Housekeeper is essential. Whether you agree on regular meetings or simply call into the office every few days, you will need the flow of information that comes back on linen usage and condition, priorities for scheduled cleaning and problems arising.

The Housekeeping department is often overlooked as a source of forecasting information. Certain patterns of guest movement (a large tour group checking out late, for instance) can have a dramatic effect on the workload in your restaurants. It is worthwhile checking the information you have against the latest Housekeeping forecasts to get a more accurate idea of what your guests are likely to do.

Sales

As the banquet sales office has a specialised function, and as it is normally included within the administration of the Food and Beverage department, we will discuss it in a later chapter. The larger, corporate Sales department is usually headed by a Director of Sales, who may employ several sales executives and a clerical staff. Their job is to sell the hotel's services and facilities to a wider, often international, clientele. The Director of Sales (or Sales Manager) will negotiate contracts with tour companies, incentive travel companies, airlines, inbound tour operators and individual corporations, in order to guarantee long-term business for the hotel.

The food and beverage component of these negotiations will obviously concern you closely. Once locked into a contracted price for particular meal rates, you may be obliged to sell at that price for twelve months, regardless of fluctuations in the actual cost of supplies or labour. Your aim is to get the highest possible price for your services. The Sales Director's aim is to get the contract signed. These two aims are not always in concert.

It is important that you are able to put forward a realistic estimate of the cost of providing the various food and beverage services that may be included in these contracts. To this end, you must be able to marshal your facts. Recorded results on profitability and food and labour cost for the last twelve months will help you to put your case. You must also have an accurate idea of what the competition is charging, since to win a victory for a high price, and then lose the contract to the opposition, is no victory at all.

One area of keen concern to the Sales department is the issue of quality. Though your department may serve a thousand meals of fine quality to a particular corporate client over the space of months, it is unfortunately your mistakes that show up on the comment forms. Tour companies, in particular, regularly sample the opinions of clients at the end of a tour. Customers are asked to specify any faults or weaknesses in the performance of the hotel properties they stayed in, and to rate them in comparison with one another. It is in these comment forms that we learn of the cold cup of coffee, the inattentive table server, the crowding at breakfast or the taste of the mushroom sauce. Often, there has been no complaint made at the time. The guest simply said nothing until someone asked him to comment.

Clearly, your position will be badly undermined if the Director of Sales has to cope with a long string of complaints coming back from a particular company. If your hotel gains a reputation for problems, it can be almost impossible to reverse this perception, since people are much more likely to report faults than they are to write glowing testimonials. This can easily lead to losing the contract, since the competition is always ready to promise better results and a comparable price.

Therefore, you must ensure that an effective quality assurance program is in place in all your operating departments. Further, you can build a groundswell of support by offering corporate or tour guests a genuine, warm welcome when they arrive and throughout their stay. Flexibility and a 'can-do' attitude will also endear your hotel to tour leaders, who are powerful moulders of guest opinion while in-house.

Front Office

You will work more closely with the Front Office than with any other department in the hotel, save the Kitchen. Take an early opportunity to establish a good relationship with the Front Office Manager, because the flow of information back and forth between Food and Beverage and Front Office is vital to the smooth operation of the hotel. From breakfast charges on early morning check-outs to the last balance of the last till from the cocktail bar, your staff will be in constant contact with Front Office, and relations between the two departments must be cordial.

Front Office staff are often the first to greet guests on arrival, and can set the tone for the guest's entire stay. A guest who receives a pleasant welcome and a smooth check-in will soon afterwards breeze into your restaurant, looking forward to a good meal. Guests who have had a bad time at the front desk may already be in a hostile mood when your restaurant manager greets them at the door. Reception staff are also a key part of your sales effort, since they will frequently be asked for details on restaurant menus, bar opening times, special events and promotions.

The duties of the Front Office, aside from the cordial reception and efficient check-in of guests, include the reservations system, the telephone switchboard, guest billing and special charges, the accurate transmission of messages, night audit and the hotel computer system. This involves the acquisition, storage and distribution of information—much of it vital to the planning of your own operations and staffing.

The Front Office can provide you with details of guest arrival patterns, special diets, meal arrangements for tour groups, function facilities requested, and incentive and corporate groups. Its reservations system will enable you to forecast demand for weeks and months in advance. Daily reports generated by the night audit department will provide you with valuable data on average checks, food and beverage sales breakdowns, performance against the past month or the past year, total revenue and hotel occupancy. Aside from the sales figures recorded by your own cashiers in the bars and restaurants, there is no better source of information on what happened yesterday, what is happening today, and what will happen tomorrow.

With such a large amount of information to handle, and so many demands for that information, the Front Office has its hands full answering hundreds of queries daily from guests, tour companies, corporate clients and the other operating departments of the hotel. It is also taking in new information hourly as group numbers change, arrival times alter and special requests are made. Therefore, you must not rely solely upon the reports already circulated by the Front Office, but must be willing to get into the system in order to find out what you need to know. This may involve spending an hour a week with the reservations department, updating details on group bookings, or checking in with the Front Office Manager regularly to review projected occupancy figures for the months ahead. You will find an enormous amount of information to help you run your department efficiently, if you are willing to do a bit of leg-work.

Be aware, too, that this information flows in two directions. If your cocktail bar is offering a happy hour from 5.00 to 6.00 p.m. every evening, it may be useful to tell guests about it when they arrive in the mid-afternoon. If your seafood grill is the best in town, then the reception staff should feel confident about recommending it and have at least a passing knowledge of what is on the menu. If the opening time of the pool bar has changed, or the fine dining room is booked out for a special function, then it is vital that the front desk staff and the switchboard operators know about it, because they are the ones likely to be answering questions. Once again, you cannot rely on a half-hearted memo, buried in a pile of other memos. You must promote your department's services actively, and if that means standing at the front desk explaining what is on to the desk clerks, then that is what you must do. Point-of-sale cards, promotional leaflets, sample menus and the like will also help to get your message across.

Concierge

In a larger property, the Concierge Desk is the centre for a range of different services, from baggage handling and transfers to tour bookings, dinner reservations, theatre tickets, car parking and more. The Concierge and staff (porters, bellhops and drivers) are in constant contact with guests, and will frequently be asked for recommendations. They should be fully aware of the range of food and beverage services offered in-house, and up to date on any special events, menus or promotions that you have planned.

It is traditional for the maître d' or restaurant manager to keep a table or two in reserve, so that a late booking from the Concierge can be accommodated in a pinch. It is essential that the Concierge Desk be provided with a copy of the room service menu, and be familiar with its contents.

Security

Operating food and beverage outlets involves a great deal of cash handling and the movement of valuable items of equipment and stock, particularly alcoholic beverages. Though operational security (till procedure, stock requisition and so on) is your responsibility, you will also need help from the hotel's Security department to ensure that safe storage remains safe, that cupboards and doors are properly locked, and that effective measures are in place to prevent pilferage.

Your bar staff have certain obligations under the law to prevent the service of alcohol to patrons who have already had enough to drink, but inevitably some customers will become intoxicated. Occasionally you will have reason to call on Security to help with a guest who is suffering from a temporary loss of decorum and needs assistance.

The Security department will sometimes be the first line of response for a guest who has become ill, for a suspected fire or break-in, or for any one of a dozen other emergencies that can occur in a large hotel. As with every other department, it will profit you to make good contact with Security, and understand how your staff can make their job easier.

Kitchen

The working relationship between the Executive Chef and the Food and Beverage Manager is so vital to the success of the department that it cannot be overestimated. Your understanding of how a professional kitchen works is a basic qualification for your job. Therefore, we shall assign an entire chapter to it.

CHAPTER SUMMARY

The modern international hotel is a complex machine, capable of doing many things simultaneously and providing food, drink, entertainment and lodging to its guests. In order to accomplish these things efficiently, the operation of the hotel is broken down into several departments. The largest of these are Housekeeping, Food and Beverage and Front Office. Each of these departments is run by a manager who will oversee a staff which includes section managers, supervisors and workers.

The Food and Beverage Manager will be responsible for the operation of all restaurants, bars, room service and function facilities within the hotel, and may be called upon to arrange outside catering as well. He or she will normally report to the General Manager.

Qualifications for the job include an excellent working knowledge of professional food and beverage service, long experience in hotel operations, the ability to motivate and encourage staff, a commitment to high standards of professional behaviour, and considerable endurance. The Food and Beverage Manager will be fully conversant with the importance of cost controls, staff training and retention, and effective promotion.

The Food and Beverage department must work in concert with all the other departments of the hotel, and have a clear understanding of the jobs they do to ensure the smooth running of the whole. The Food and Beverage Manager will work to build strong links with each of these departments, to ensure co-operation and to avoid conflict.

REVIEW QUESTIONS

1 What are the three principal operating departments in a large hotel?

2 One important attribute of the professional manager is 'presence'. What does this mean?

3 Your performance as a Food and Beverage Manager is judged according to several criteria. One of these is staff turnover. How can you control this?

4 Food cost, labour cost and beverage cost are usually expressed as percentages. Give the formula for calculating a cost percentage.

5 Detailed information on restaurant revenue, average check and other trading figures are obtained from which department?

6 You are appointed Food and Beverage Manager in a medium-sized hotel. Relations between your predecessor and the Engineering department were less than cordial. How would you go about correcting this?

CHAPTER TWO

THE PROFESSIONAL KITCHEN

The structure and operation of the hotel kitchen

Building a professional relationship with the Executive Chef and designing systems that ensure a smooth mesh between food preparation and service

How menu design affects operations

The role of the Chef

In any restaurant, whether independent or attached to a hotel or club, the kitchen is the source of the goods your customers have come to buy. The reception may be charming and the décor sensational, but if the food is not well prepared and promptly served, you will have problems. A sensible Food and Beverage Manager realises that getting the best from the kitchen is every bit as important as getting the best from the service staff. Unfortunately, some managers in the industry still have a sort of 'upstairs–downstairs' mentality that imagines the person who wears a suit to be somehow superior to the chef who wears a white jacket and apron. Nothing could be more foolish.

Professional chefs study and practise for three, four or five years to gain their basic qualification. This is quite as long as others may work to gain a degree in hotel management, accountancy or civil engineering. After this first qualification, chefs will go on to study more, often moving through several hotels or restaurants to widen their experience. Like all professionals, qualified chefs are proud of their accomplishments, and will not take kindly to condescension, or to inexperienced managers stepping on their toes. Modern hotels demand that chefs be talented, creative, responsible and consistent. If you still labour under the misapprehension that all chefs are temperamental, flighty and prone to throwing pots around the kitchen, you are long overdue for a change in your thinking.

The classical kitchen

The French chef Auguste Escoffier worked in partnership with Swiss hotelier César Ritz to establish some of the world's finest hotels in the early years of the 20th century, and became internationally famous as the greatest chef of his generation. Escoffier's great accomplishment was not his cooking, since this was no more than a standardisation of the French *haute cuisine* in which he had been trained. His real gift was for organisation, and the systems he devised for running a hotel kitchen are still in use today. In Escoffier's day, there were many celebrated European chefs who could prepare brilliant dishes. It was Escoffier's ability to produce three hundred brilliant plates, one after the other and without variation, that made him a leader in his profession. Escoffier's books on kitchen management will still be found on the shelves of any serious professional today.

To understand the professional kitchen, you must understand the hierarchy of chefs, and the way in which responsibilities for hundreds of different tasks are distributed. The classical kitchen looked something like Figure 2.1. The Executive Chef (or *Chef des Cuisines*) ruled a large staff (*brigade de cuisine*) who were divided into sections. Each section was run by a section head (*chef de partie*), who was a qualified tradesman with years of experience. The Executive Chef was assisted by a *sous-chef* (literally, 'under-chef'), who delegated for the Chef on his day off. Each *chef de partie* had one or more assistants (*commis de cuisine*) who might be apprentices or qualified cooks. In addition, a small army of kitchen hands and stewards was employed to do the hundreds of hours of preparation, cleaning and setup that were required in the days before automatic dishwashers, deep-freezers and prepared foods became commonplace.

The principle behind this organisation still applies in restaurant and hotel operation today: to do a very large and complex job, it is necessary to break it down into its component parts and delegate the responsibility. To create hundreds of meat, vegetable, fish and farinaceous dishes, as well as dozens of sauces, garnishes, soups

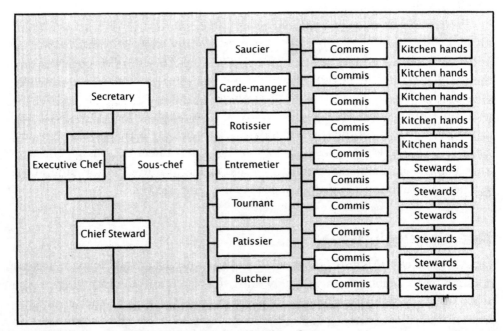

Figure 2.1 Traditional kitchen organisation chart

and desserts for complex menus in multiple restaurants, all on the same night, you must be organised.

Escoffier's principle was easy to understand, but almost revolutionary in his day: he suggested that all the sauces be made in one sauce kitchen and all the pastries in the pastry shop. One chef would be in charge of everything to do with fish; another would look after all the savoury dishes that were served cold. When a dish was made up of more than one type of food (a fillet of beef with a mushroom sauce and a pastry garnish, for instance) then it would be assembled, just before it was plated, from ingredients provided by each section of the kitchen. This may seem obvious to the modern hotelier, but before Escoffier, the practice was for each cook to dabble about, making whatever ingredients he needed to assemble his masterpiece, regardless of what the chef on the next bench was doing.

This 'classical' kitchen organisation depended on a ready supply of young cooks willing to put up with long hours and low pay, in order to learn from highly-skilled master chefs. It also relied on a large staff of unskilled workers to hand polish hundreds of pieces of silverware, burnish heavy copper pots and peel bushels of potatoes by hand. Though some of these elements remain (particularly in the rarefied atmosphere of the Michelin three-star restaurants of Europe), in most professional kitchens times have changed.

The modern kitchen

The world was a different place in 1890 when Escoffier and Ritz opened London's Savoy Hotel, which was then the largest and most luxurious in the world. Labour was cheap, food supplies were strictly seasonal, and electric refrigeration was almost unknown. Tinned foods were available, but were still very expensive and regarded with popular suspicion.

Wages have been climbing steadily for most of the time since then, so that it is no longer possible to employ large numbers of people in hotel kitchens if we wish to operate at a profit. Even if hotels could afford it, our training colleges and hotel schools would be hard pressed to supply enough properly trained young chefs to satisfy the enormous demand from an expanding tourism industry. Where food supplies are concerned, better transportation and frozen storage have made it possible to obtain food products from many countries all the year round.

One effect of these changes has been to increase our reliance on sophisticated technology and prepared (usually frozen) foods. Today, a chef can choose from hundreds of high-quality prepared foods packaged ready to cook. It no longer makes sense to handle raw potatoes—to peel, cut, blanch and store them—when excellent quality frozen 'French fries' can easily be bought in. A modern thermostatically-controlled, steam-equipped, fan-forced electric oven can perform miracles compared to the grimy, coal-fired stoves of Escoffier's day. Prepared foods can be handled with fewer people, not all of whom need to be skilled tradespeople.

The shape of kitchens has changed: we now require much larger areas for frozen and chilled storage, and less for basic vegetable preparation. In smaller kitchens, the butchery, bakery and pastry shops have disappeared altogether, since these items are now bought in ready to use. More thought is given to sanitation and food handling safety, with movable equipment, drained floors and improved ventilation. Cooking equipment is generally smaller, more efficient, and given to more than one use.

Staffing levels have changed dramatically. In a kitchen that might once have employed fifty chefs and apprentices, these days twenty may do the same job. They are more highly paid and work in better conditions and for shorter hours. The days of the 'split-shift'—when cooks were required to work breakfast and lunch, take a short break in the afternoon and then return for dinner service—are numbered, as most establishments reconcile themselves to the eight-hour shift and the five-day week.

In the organisation chart of a modern kitchen, the number of sections has been much reduced. The chain of command is generally simpler, with fewer grades of seniority and fewer sections (see Figure 2.2).

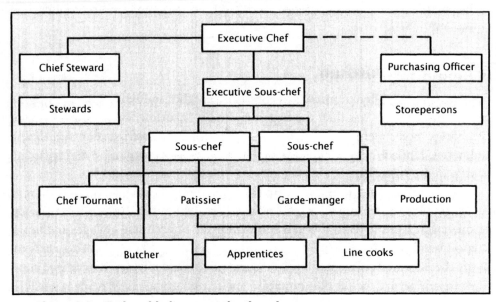

Figure 2.2 Modern kitchen organisation chart

The Executive Chef

The Executive Chef is responsible for the overall management of the hotel or restaurant's kitchens, including staffing, training, menu development (usually in association with the Food and Beverage Manager), banqueting design and execution, quality control and purchasing (often with the help of a purchasing officer). One hundred years ago, the *Chef des Cuisines* was a master artisan, capable of passing on his advanced skills in food preparation and presentation to his *chefs de partie* and apprentices. These days, the Executive Chef is a business manager in the true sense of the phrase: he or she is responsible for achieving maximum profits from food operations by increasing turnover, minimising costs and preventing waste. It is not unusual, in a large hotel, for the Executive Chef to control an annual operating budget that runs into millions of dollars.

The Executive Sous-chef

This position was created to meet the needs of large hotel and convention centre kitchens, where the demands of supervising a large staff and multiple food service outlets, which often operate 24 hours a day, make it necessary to have a senior kitchen manager on duty at all times. The Executive Sous-chef assists the Executive Chef with all duties, generally takes an active role in planning and operates with full authority to make decisions and implement them. The Food and Beverage Manager's working relationship with the Executive Sous-chef is every bit as important as his relationship with the Executive Chef.

The Head Chef

In smaller kitchens, the chef in charge will be a working cook, with responsibility for one or more sections of the kitchen in addition to her duties in staffing, ordering, menu planning and training. When a working head chef is employed, the owner or Food and Beverage Manager is expected to take on more clerical and administrative duties, such as payroll, purchasing or menu design.

The sous-chef

The sous-chef is in charge of practical kitchen operations, under the supervision of the Executive Chef. The sous-chef's duties will often be 'hands-on', including hot and cold food preparation, banquet preparation and service, apprentice training and staff rosters. In a large kitchen there may be several sous-chefs, supervising separate shifts or restaurants. In a smaller kitchen, the sous-chef may be in charge of one or more sections and stand in for the Head Chef on days off.

The Chef Tournant

Usually the senior of the *chefs de partie*, the chef tournant moves from one section to another, replacing those section heads on days off or holidays. The chef tournant must be familiar with every section, other than the pastry shop, where the assistant pastry chef is in charge on days off and holidays.

The pastry chef (*chef patissier*)

This is a separate profession from that of cook: the pastry chef has been extensively trained in bread-making, pastry-cooking, dessert preparation and the making of sugar decorations, chocolates, specialised gâteaux and wedding cakes. A large pastry kitchen or 'shop' may employ several bakers and pastry-cooks to prepare all of a hotel's requirements for Danish pastries, fancy breads, croissants, cakes, gâteaux and decorative pieces.

The garde-manger

This *chef de partie* is responsible for the preparation of all meats and seafoods served cold, including pâtés and terrines, cold sauces, garnishes, salads, canapés and cocktail sandwiches. The chef garde-manger pays particular attention to banquet work, including cold food displays, ice and butter sculptures and so on. In some kitchens, the garde-manger may be responsible for the supply of breaded (crumbed) meats, stuffed chicken breasts and other partially-prepared items.

The production chef

The modern 'production' kitchen combines several sections of the 'classical' kitchen: *rotisseur, entremetier, poissonnier* and *saucier*. The production chef is responsible for all the basic sauces, roasted meats, starches, vegetables, soups and the like. These will be passed on to the restaurant line cooks for finishing and plating. The production chef will also prepare banquet foods and, occasionally, staff meals.

The butcher

Small kitchens may buy in most of their meats and poultry ready-dressed, sometimes in portion-control cuts for more accurate costing. Larger kitchens will find it more economical to employ a butcher to dress out primal cuts, trim them, portion them and store them for use by the production kitchen and the line cooks.

The line cooks

These are cooks assigned to a particular restaurant, who will prepare foods to order. The 'hot line' will prepare grills, sautés, deep-fried foods, vegetables and pasta dishes. A 'cold line' will supply individual salads, cold entrées, sandwiches and some desserts. The point at which the service staff collect the prepared foods is called the passe. During very busy times, either the sous-chef or the restaurant manager may stand at the passe to expedite orders.

The commis chefs

These are the assistant chefs, who may be assigned to any one of the sections. Some will be qualified cooks, who have yet to be given responsibility for an entire section. Others may be apprentices, working towards their qualification in professional cookery or hotel management.

Filling the roles in a smaller restaurant

A textbook chart can only be a general approximation of how things work in the real world, but it is useful to study the diagram in Figure 2.2, because each of the jobs described must be done, however small the food and beverage operation. Clearly, it would be ridiculous to appoint an executive sous-chef in a kitchen with just four staff. However, someone will have to stand in for the Chef on days off, and if not an executive sous-chef, then who? The role of purchasing officer in a large organisation is a crucially important one (as we shall see when we examine cost and controls in later chapters). Even in a small restaurant, though, the telephone calls must be made, the orders placed and the records kept. If there is no purchasing officer, there must be a clear assignment of these duties to someone else in the organisation. If a position is to be dispensed with altogether (if there is no pastry chef, for instance), then allowance must be made in cost projections and budgets for the higher cost of buying in the products from outside suppliers.

Establishing the working partnership

Like many sections of a busy hotel, the professional kitchen is an exercise in controlled mayhem. In the hotel business it is difficult to predict exactly when the greatest workload will occur, and it is impossible to postpone work until some other time. Particularly in the restaurant, the customers want their meals and service *now*—not when it is convenient for the hotel to provide them. Every professional hotelier has experienced the 'rush' caused by an unexpected number of guests arriving all at once and demanding immediate attention. Nor is this a rare occurrence: it happens all the time in our business.

In the kitchen, many demands will be made on chefs working very quickly, in hot conditions, listening to shouted orders and handling tools that are very hot, sharp, slippery, or a combination of all three. It is no wonder, then, that concentration can lapse and tension run high. If the Executive Chef and the Food and Beverage Manager have done their jobs well, if co-ordination between kitchen and service is well practised, then the restaurant will cope with the rush and the customers will be satisfied. If any part of the system is weak, it will show up under the strain. Problems may develop, but this is absolutely not the time to discuss how they should have been prevented. The customer is the first priority in such a situation, and kitchen and restaurant staff must work together to expedite service. How well this works is the acid test of the relationship between the Executive Chef and the Food and Beverage Manager.

To establish a successful working relationship, it is important to remember that these are two people who have not (in most cases) arrived where they are by the same route. The Executive Chef will have had long training and experience in professional cookery, sometimes to the exclusion of anything else. The F&B may have risen through the ranks from table or bar service to supervisory level, then to restaurant management and so on. Either one or both may have studied hotel management at tertiary level. In smaller properties, where the owner or General Manager takes on the responsibilities of the Food and Beverage Manager, it is possible that one side of this partnership has had little professional experience in food preparation and service while the other has had a great deal.

Introducing yourself

If you are new to the organisation you will have many things to think about, but it is advisable to pay particular attention to your first visit to the Chef's office. Since you will be working together closely, it is important that you introduce yourself in a pleasantly neutral tone, with all your senses tuned to reception rather than broadcast. This is not the time to announce that you have sweeping new plans for food and beverage service in all the restaurants, and that you have already worked out all the details. Instead, you will listen, ask questions and generally try to get an early appreciation of how things are arranged, who really runs the show and what relationships are already in place.

You will pay very careful attention to the way the kitchen and restaurant staff work with each other during busy service. You will observe the state of sanitation, safety, equipment use and maintenance in the kitchen and in the restaurant. You will study the menu carefully, and learn how the items listed are actually prepared, by whom they are prepared, and how long they take. You will make many notes. (Avoid doing this while standing in the kitchen—write down your impressions over a cup of coffee in the restaurant.) You will not air any opinions about how things are done until at least two weeks have passed. Above all, you will spend most of your time on the floor, not in your office. Everything you are finally responsible for happens here: in the restaurants, on the loading dock, in the banquet rooms, in the bars and in the kitchen.

Introducing a new Chef

If you are the one greeting a new Executive Chef, you will be similarly pleasant and neutral at the start. You will certainly help the new Chef by introducing him to all the staff, supervisors and managers by name, and by conducting several tours of the building during the first week (not all at once—take it in stages). You will invite the Chef to lunch, so that he can see at first hand how the restaurants operate. You will encourage the Chef to spend plenty of time in the restaurants, for the same reason. You certainly will not recite a list of the failings of the Chef's predecessor. (Being rude about the ex-Chef is no way to gain the confidence of the new one.) You will watch, discreetly, how the new Chef goes about his job, and how well he gets on with other staff. If the Chef demands that all the menus be changed immediately, you will agree, but gently suggest that the two of you discuss it thoroughly after he has had a few weeks to settle in.

Common goals

The object of the co-operative relationship between service and kitchen is to provide the customer with the best possible quality of food and service, according to the standards of the hotel or restaurant. To this end, the Food and Beverage Manager and the Executive Chef work together. It is their job to set quality standards, design systems that ensure these standards are adhered to, train staff and monitor results.

Setting quality standards

High quality, in food service, does not necessarily mean the most expensive or rarest ingredient available. It means that the expectations of the customer are met, or exceeded, with every meal served. If the customer expects a simple, inexpensive dish served quickly, then quality is measured by how well this is done. If the customer has good reason to expect the finest food available, served in surroundings of considerable luxury, then those expectations must be met. Obviously, the first step is to decide what standards you wish to offer, and whether they are achievable with the facilities, equipment, staff and pricing structure you are working with. There is no sense promising the last word in *haute cuisine* if the only tools you have are a barbecue grill and an apprentice chef. If your restaurant is located within a five-star, international class hotel, it will not be enough to offer steak sandwiches served on paper plates.

Achieving consistency

The most popular and profitable restaurants are those in which customers can rely on getting the same value for money, quality of food and service as they enjoyed on their last visit. To this end, you will work with the Executive Chef to prepare standard presentations and recipes for every dish on the menu. Photographs are very useful here, so that staff can easily refer to a picture of what the dish should look like. A wall chart of photographs, placed near the passe, will help cooks and service staff alike to remember exactly what should be served, and what cutlery, crockery, condiments and extras should be served with it. The Executive Chef should be encouraged to prepare standard written recipes for every sauce, soup, dessert and prepared food on the menu, including the name of each ingredient, the weight or portion required, and a method of preparation. These 'recipe cards' will be important tools for achieving consistency, and invaluable for costing and purchasing control.

Another method that will prove useful is the 'cook-off'. This involves having the restaurant chefs prepare a sample of every dish on the menu at one time, so that service staff and managers can taste, ask questions and discuss the standards required. This is an obvious necessity whenever a new menu is introduced, but a wise Food and Beverage Manager will also recognise its usefulness when a menu has been in place for some time (say, 4 to 6 months), or when customer complaints indicate that standards have slipped. The cost, in materials and staff time, will be negligible compared with the damage that may be done without it. Work out an agreement with the Executive Chef for an automatic 'cook-off' for new or special menus, and regular reviews at given intervals. You will ensure that you, your restaurant manager, maître d', supervisors and service staff are all present at the agreed time.

Docket control

A frequent source of friction between the service and kitchen staff is the standard of docket writing. If abbreviations are to be used for menu items (such as S/STK for sirloin steak), then you must ensure that everyone knows and uses the same abbreviations for each dish, and for cooking instructions (for example, R = rare, MR = medium rare, and so on). You should work with your restaurant managers and supervisors to see that an effective training program is in place for all food and beverage staff, and that the accuracy and clarity of written dockets is monitored in the restaurant, not in the kitchen. It is essential that dockets note the time the order was placed, either manually or by means of a time-stamp in the kitchen.

Verbal orders, called across the passe to the cooks, are notoriously inaccurate and difficult to control. This system may have limited application in a fast food or 'short order' kitchen, but it is seldom used in a full service restaurant.

Electronic ordering is a system by which table staff enter orders on an electronic keyboard, or with a hand-held scanner and a bar-coded menu. The orders are then printed out in the kitchen for preparation. While this is an effective and speedy method of handling orders, you must be aware that accuracy is in the hands of the table server, and a good training program is just as important for electronic systems as for manual systems.

In the interests of honesty, it is essential that all dockets be numbered and accounted for, and that no food be passed from kitchen to service without a docket.

Expediting

In peak periods it may be useful to have someone remain on the passe, expediting orders. This role is normally taken either by a restaurant supervisor or by a sous-chef, but in exceptional circumstances the Executive Chef or Food and Beverage Manager may step in. The purpose of an expediter is to retain a measure of calm control over the orderly dispatch of various dishes, even in the midst of a hectic rush. The expediter takes the written order from the table server or the printer, calls out the order to the cooks, then places it in a queue, using a docket board or docket wheel. When the dishes are plated up for a particular table, the expediter will check that the order is complete, and that it is picked up by the right table server. The expediter may remind the cooks of the next table coming up, and advise the service staff of the anticipated delay, so that they do not have to spend unnecessary time in the kitchen waiting for orders. The job obviously calls for someone with a good memory and a cool head. An expediter is often called for in banquet service, particularly when a choice of dishes is offered to guests. It is useful to discuss this with the Chef in advance.

The effect of menu design on operations

The menu is, at a minimum, a list of products which you offer to your customers. The menu is much more important, though, than a simple list. Your choice of menu dictates many operational decisions:

- the overall style of the restaurant
- your competitiveness in the restaurant market
- the level of skill required from service staff
- the level of skill required from kitchen staff
- the amount of inventory carried
- the dining room and kitchen equipment required
- minimum sales volume required.

It is no small matter. In the next chapter we will discuss the marketing and cost control aspects of menu design, but you should also be aware of the impact your choice of menu can make on the relationship between service and kitchen operations. It is vital that the menu be a joint effort between the Executive Chef and the Food and Beverage Manager. It is wise to seek opinions from supervisors and managers in both areas, and from the purchasing officer. In some properties the owner or General Manager will have preferences, and in the case of a franchised restaurant or a chain, there may also be constraints placed upon you by a central organisation.

Overall style

The menu will dictate, to some extent, the clientele the restaurant attracts and the average check you may expect to achieve. The menu you work out with the Executive Chef should be appropriate to the market you wish to reach. There is no point in offering a complex dish that requires tableside cooking in a casual brasserie, nor will a frozen, pre-cooked chicken portion be acceptable in a sophisticated à la carte dining room.

Competitiveness in the market

Few things change faster than fashions in food, and if your restaurant operation is too slow to react to these changes you will rapidly lose market share to your competition. If wood-fired pizzas and Mediterranean cuisine are the current fashion, then you must consider including these in your menus and in your calendar of scheduled food promotions and festivals. Keep in mind the need for flexibility and timely change before you commit equipment, training and resources to a narrow menu. A handsomely fitted out salad bar may be adapted to other uses; an expensive piece of equipment for making doughnuts may not. Discuss with the Chef exactly what is needed to produce a given item.

Level of skill: service staff

If a menu calls for guéridon cooking or other tableside preparation (slicing smoked salmon, for instance, or assembling desserts), then you will obviously be committed to finding, training and retaining staff who are able to perform these duties to a professional standard. Other demands on service staff may not be so obvious: a decision to include Australian native ingredients in a menu requires that the table servers be familiar with these ingredients and be able to explain them well to customers. If you include Asian specialities on a menu, it is not enough to assume that your customers will know what is being offered. Your service staff must be familiar with names, correct pronunciation and ingredients. Be aware that some dishes (such as rack of lamb or whole spatchcock) may take some time to cook, and will make particular demands upon the service staff. It should not be presumed that a fast turnover, low average check environment means a correspondingly low level of training. Often the opposite is the case, as the well-organised training programs developed by chains such as McDonald's and KFC demonstrate.

Level of skill: kitchen staff

However attractive a particular menu item may be, it is only worth considering if there are enough trained kitchen staff to produce it reliably. It is not uncommon to take advantage of one chef's speciality, only to lose that chef six days after the menus are delivered from the printer. A sensible manager considers the average degree of difficulty in the menu and matches it to the average level of skill across the whole kitchen brigade. Some menu choices will require kitchen staff to be present in the restaurant (omelettes prepared to order, or a luncheon carvery). The Executive Chef must be able to retain staff with the appropriate guest-contact skills and presentation. Work with the Chef to determine exactly how long it takes to make the dishes you are considering, and what level of difficulty is involved. It may be easy to make four portions during a quiet time of day. How will things go if 40 portions are ordered during the peak service period?

Inventory

It is important in the early stages of menu planning to consult the purchasing officer, if there is one in your organisation, or the suppliers themselves. What ingredients are readily available? Are there any seasonal fluctuations in supply or price? Is there only one supplier, or can competitive bids be obtained from several suppliers? Note carefully all the ingredients that will be required, including condiments, essential seasonings and garnishes. If the product is bought in partially prepared, could it be done in-house in an emergency? With the Chef, determine whether the new menu item will increase overall inventory levels, and if there are any special shelf-life or storage considerations.

Restaurant and kitchen equipment

A good Food and Beverage Manager has a healthy suspicion of any menu item that requires the purchase of new equipment, especially if the equipment is specific to that particular dish. At the best of times, it is difficult to achieve sufficient sales to make an item profitable. When you have to calculate in the cost of special equipment, you will need strong evidence to suggest that buoyant sales will justify the expenditure. A quick look around the store-rooms of any large city hotel will reveal a collection of fondue sets, kebab swords, brandy warmers and other dusty relics that never made a profit for anyone other than the agent who sold them in the first place. Even menu items that do not require new equipment may call for a reassignment of refrigeration space, cooking equipment, storage shelves, crockery or cutlery. Work this through carefully during the planning stages of the menu.

Minimum sales volume

Unique dishes, unusual ingredients and local specialities will always appeal to the creative chef and food service professional. These may create interest in a new menu, enhance a restaurant theme or take advantage of a local product. (Dishes prepared with vine leaves in a wine-growing region would be an example.) This kind of creativity and innovation is essential to keep your restaurant in line with popular trends and ahead of the competition, but if you choose to do something you must do it well. Be careful of unusual dishes that read well on the menu, but are unlikely to sell enough portions to earn their keep. A char-grilled crocodile steak with native plum sauce may be a great dish for flavour and presentation, but if you can only sell twelve portions a month, then quality and consistency will suffer in the long run. It is better to create a new and interesting presentation of a standard item (a fillet steak or breast of chicken, for instance) than to rely on the novelty of an expensive and difficult-to-get ingredient with limited customer acceptance. A menu item should hold its place only if you can demonstrate an acceptable minimum sales volume and a reasonable contribution to the profitability of your operation.

CHAPTER SUMMARY

As a professional Food and Beverage Manager, you are expected to have an excellent working knowledge of the modern kitchen, including its design, organisation and function. You must understand why a kitchen is laid out the way it is, and how changes in diet, food fashions and the labour market have affected kitchen design. You must understand the organisation chart of the kitchen brigade, and the role of each person included in it.

Much of your daily work will be done in co-operation with the Executive, or Head, Chef of your hotel or restaurant kitchen. Establishing a professional, cordial and effective working relationship with the Chef is an essential part of your job. The best way to achieve this is to understand and respect the Chef's responsibilities, and to make it clear that you intend to work in concert with, rather than in opposition to, the kitchen. You also will be aware that it is just as important to have a good working relationship with the Chef's second-in-command and with the section leaders.

You will work with the Chef to set standards of quality and presentation, and use a variety of different methods to ensure that you achieve the consistency of product that retains and returns customers. You will understand the strains placed upon the organisation by an unexpected rush, and how kitchen and service can effectively cope with these demands.

Many organisational problems can be avoided by a wise choice of menu. You will be aware of the wider effects of particular menu choices on kitchen layout, equipment and operations. When planning a new menu with the Chef, you will consider the level of skill required, the reliability of supply, the ease of preparation and the profitability of each item.

REVIEW QUESTIONS

1 In a modern kitchen brigade, what is the role of a sous-chef? Of a *chef de partie*?

2 What does the garde-manger, or larder section, do?

3 When, and why, would an 'expediter' be required?

4 Give three methods by which an order can be conveyed from the customer to the kitchen.

5 Choices made in menu design affect many aspects of a restaurant operation. Give at least five examples.

6 Describe how the level of skill of the service staff might influence menu design.

CHAPTER THREE

THE MENU

Identifying the various types of menus, and understanding how each is designed to meet a particular market

The classical menu and modern improvements

How to choose a range of menu items and encourage upselling

Design, layout and typography of the printed menu

Suiting your clientele

We have seen how the choices made when writing a menu have a great impact on kitchen and service operations. The menu has an even greater impact on your customers. The menu is the one part of your restaurant operation that every customer sees, and it may define your restaurant or food service outlet in several ways. First, it should establish who you are aiming at: are you looking for young people, families, business patrons, shoppers or in-house guests? It will determine who your competition is, since customers will naturally tend to compare like with like, measuring your performance against that of other restaurants with a similar style and prices. It will strongly influence customer buying habits (presuming that it is attractively and intelligently laid out) and it will, of course, determine your profitability, if you have the product mix and pricing right. Because the menu is so fundamental to the successful operation of a restaurant, it pays to study in detail the theory behind writing good menus. The basics are simple: a menu should be suitable to the style of restaurant, it should be easy to read and understand, and it should help generate profits.

Menu types

The fast food menu

Fast food restaurants account for a large part of the total food service market, for the very good reason that they are often cheaper and more convenient for consumers than buying food and preparing it at home. Fast food menus are clear, simple, easy to read and have a narrow price spread (the range from the most expensive to the cheapest item). Photographs, either on illuminated signs or on bright table-top menus, play a big part in selling the product. Fast food restaurants operate on narrow margins; therefore consistency, accurate portion control and high sales volume are critical to maintaining profitability. An observant food service professional can learn a great deal from fast food operations. Note the use of signature names (Big Mac™, Whopper™, Original Recipe Chicken™) to promote product familiarity. Note the encouragement given to customers to order inclusive meals (for example hamburger, fries and soft drink) either by 'special offer' prices (slightly less than the sum price of the individual items), or by prompting ('What kind of drink would you like with that, sir?'). New product promotions are frequent, to prevent customer boredom with a static menu.

The buffet menu

This popular and growing section of the restaurant industry may not seem, at first glance, to have a menu at all. A buffet restaurant offers customers a large selection of foods from a self-service bar, at an all-inclusive price per person. Yet the most successful operations in this sector of the market also offer customers very detailed and attractive menus of extras, side dishes and beverages, designed to increase the average check. The menu, and associated advertising, will often describe the most attractive dish offered on the buffet ('All the Prawns You Can Eat', 'Ice Cream and Dessert Bar'), then use a well-designed menu to encourage the customer to add value to the main attraction.

The café menu

The European-style café, or brasserie, is an increasingly popular format in Australia and New Zealand, as customers respond to the convenience of all-day dining, flexible menus and menu choices that reflect fast-changing fashions. Menu items are well described, with plenty of information about the ingredients ('Fresh Tasmanian Ocean Trout') and the method of cooking ('Wood-Fired Oven Pizzas'). Menu presentation tends toward the modern and artistic. Individual prices for each item are the norm, including side dishes of vegetables, wines by the glass, specialty breads and so on. The basic menu may be supported by blackboard daily specials, or by spoken descriptions from service staff. In this section of the market, it is vital that the Food and Beverage Manager stays very well informed on restaurant and food trends, and tries to anticipate them.

The à la carte menu

Traditionally, the à la carte menu is the full list of every dish available from the restaurant kitchen, with individual prices for each item. In practice, it has come to mean the full, or normal, menu, to distinguish it from set menus or specials. The à la carte menu may be classical or modern in style, and should include a full range of entrées, soups, main courses, vegetables and desserts. The presentation should be in keeping with the style and customer base of the restaurant; for instance, in a family restaurant, a children's section should be included. In a restaurant catering for a business clientele, it is important to provide for the customer who wishes to impress or entertain by including a few expensive luxury items, such as fresh cray-fish or special dishes prepared at the table-side. A stylish city restaurant with a young, sophisticated, fashion-conscious crowd would offer a range of different cooking styles, including Asian, Mediterranean and Middle Eastern dishes.

The table d'hôte menu

These days more commonly known as the 'set menu' or 'daily menu', the table d'hôte menu implies a limited number of choices offered for an inclusive price. In France, this is referred to as the *prix fixe* menu. Whichever term is used, the principle is the same: a set number of courses (usually entrée, main course and dessert) for a fixed price. Within each course, there may be one or more choices (for example, a soup or a salad for the first course). The table d'hôte menu can be used to promote quick service (some of the dishes, at least, will be prepared in advance), to attract customers on price alone (the dishes are carefully chosen within a certain cost range), or to accommodate the requirements of a tour company or other large group, who wish to know the total bill in advance. Care should be taken with a table d'hôte menu to ensure that customers do not get the impression that they are being offered second-class food or service. The dishes should be properly described, and as many choices offered as may be allowed by the constraints of time and cost. Small items served 'free', such as breadsticks, after-dinner mints, an aperitif or a glass of wine, may increase the perceived value of a table d'hôte meal, and are simply costed into the inclusive price of the meal.

The menu dégustation

This translates into English as the 'tasting menu'. The principle is similar to that of a table d'hôte menu, in that a set number of courses are offered for a set price. The emphasis, however, is not on speed or economy, but on the virtuosity of the chef. The menu dégustation is intended to showcase the skills of the kitchen by serving several courses (as many as seven or eight) in small portions, so that the customer can taste the full range of the restaurant's specialities. There are not normally any choices within courses; rather the chef decides what to serve, and in what order. It is presumed that the dishes tasted should be available on the full à la carte menu, unless the menu dégustation is a special seasonal menu or prepared by a guest chef. Prices for a menu dégustation may be quite high, and will sometimes include particular wines by the glass, chosen for their fine match with certain dishes. Obviously, a great deal of attention must be paid to this kind of menu by the kitchen and by the restaurant staff, to ensure that the restaurant presents its best effort.

The promotional or seasonal menu

It is a regular custom, particularly in larger restaurants, to run special promotional menus at various times of the year. These may tie in with a particular festival or holiday (such as Chinese New Year, Christmas, Oktoberfest or Bastille Day) or with a theme (Thai Food Festival, Indian Buffet or Seafood Buffet, for instance). The new menu provides an opportunity for temporary decoration of the restaurant in keeping with the theme, it creates staff interest in new or unusual foods, and it offers some variety to the restaurant's regular customers. An advertising campaign may serve to attract custom, and to keep the restaurant's name in the public eye. Editorial coverage in local media is easy to obtain when a special menu is seen as news. A seasonal menu may be offered as a supplement to the à la carte menu, as an inclusive table d'hôte menu, or as a buffet. It is worth the effort to chart out the coming year, paying attention to holidays, national days and special events, any of which may provide keys for special promotions.

The ethnic menu

With rising interest in cooking styles and foods from other countries, ethnic restaurants and ethnic menus are increasingly popular with people who like to dine out. These menus require particular care from the Food and Beverage Manager who wishes to take advantage of their attraction. Authenticity is extremely important to a sophisticated dining public, so there is little point in promoting, for instance, a Thai menu unless the restaurant can call upon chefs who know the cuisine very well and are experienced in preparing it. Accuracy is also vital, so it is essential that the names, spellings and descriptions of all dishes be carefully checked before printing, preferably by a native speaker of the country from which the cuisine comes. Service staff must be fully trained to understand the ingredients, the cooking methods and the style of service required for unfamiliar dishes. This applies not only to Asian or Middle Eastern cooking but also to European, American and English menus, where an error in preparation or description can be all the more embarrassing if presented to a customer familiar with the cuisine.

The children's menu

Demographics is a term used to describe the study of geography, ages, income levels, spending habits and family compositions of a given population. Demographics are of vital importance to the hotelier or restaurateur, because they give a picture of the possible customers in the area. The fastest-growing sector in the food service industry in Australia and New Zealand, demographically, is that which serves families dining out together. A sensible Food and Beverage Manager will understand this, and provide for the needs of children when designing a restaurant menu. Children have relatively simple tastes and a short attention span, and require entertainment if their parents are to enjoy a meal and return. These needs are easily met with special children's placemats, giveaways and menus. If restaurant staff are trained to be welcoming and accommodating to families with children, the restaurant will enjoy the tremendous repeat custom that children can generate.

The banquet menu

Banquets should be an important and profitable part of almost any restaurant operation, and in a large hotel banquets may account for a large part of the total food and beverage sales. Banquets may be served on the premises or at some outside location, such as a garden party or a wedding reception. Banquet menus may be divided into two main types: the set menu and the buffet. In each case, it is important to give customers the impression of luxury and abundance, so that the set price per head is seen to be good value for money, while still offering lavish hospitality to the guests. Banquet menus should be carefully written to ensure that several price steps allow customers to choose, without embarrassment, how much they wish to spend in total. They must also be carefully costed, since banquet menus change less frequently than restaurant menus. Prices must have a sufficient margin of profit to allow for fluctuations in raw material and labour costs.

Writing the menu

Having given careful thought to the type and style of the menu to be presented, and the practical considerations involved in its production, the Food and Beverage Manager can set about designing it to achieve the three principal goals: suitability, ease of use and profitability. The following points should be kept in mind:

- **Time available** If the market you are aiming at demands a well-presented meal served within an hour, you will not include dishes with long cooking times or complicated service. Consult with the Executive Chef to get a realistic estimate of how quickly each dish can be produced. Conversely, if the market demands elegant, relaxed dining, allow for gentle spacing between courses and well-paced service of wine, desserts and liqueurs.
- **Suitability** The menu should match the style of the restaurant. Consider what your customers are most likely to want, and give it to them. If the restaurant is elegant and expensive, then the menu should reflect this in its content and appearance. If quick, casual and friendly service is the key, make sure the menu suits this style.
- **Ease of reading** Take professional advice on layout, typography, printing and colour schemes so that your menu makes it easy for customers to understand, and to order, what you are offering. Be sure to test sample menus under actual

restaurant conditions (such as by sitting at a table with normal restaurant light-ing level, accompanied by someone who has not read the menu before).

- **Demographics** Be sure that you understand the profile of the customers you are seeking to attract. If your audience is responsive to fast, uncomplicated family dining at reasonable prices, then provide it and advertise it as such. If you are aiming at a business clientele, make sure you understand what is important to the business customer, and adapt the menu to suit. If you cater for overseas visitors, find out what their expectations are and design your menu with these in mind.

- **Competition** Keep in constant touch with what is happening in the restau-rant market: monitor trends, compare prices, watch advertisements and talk to customers about what interests them and what is new. You will visit the com-petition regularly and keep abreast of the trade press, trade shows, food maga-zines and food writers, overseas trends and the local media.

- **Local specialities** A good menu will take advantage of any local produce, seafood, cooking style or ingredient that attracts interest and attention. If, for instance, Queensland mud crabs or Tasmanian apples are local specialities, they should appear in one form or another on your menus. Failure to feature local products only gives away ground to your competition.

- **Language** If a significant number of your customers speak or read a language other than English, then it is obvious that you will provide a more comfortable reception if you can offer menus in their own language. An ability to cope with more than one language is the mark of a professional restaurateur, and can generate repeat custom. Take care to have translations professionally prepared and typeset, and then have them checked by native speakers before printing. Take extreme care when using 'menu French' to be sure that the names of the dishes, sauces and garnishes are accurate and correctly spelled or, better still, avoid using French altogether.

- **Product mix** Review the number and type of dishes to be included on the menu before layout begins. Are there enough choices for the customer who wants a quick, light meal? What about the health-conscious guest, or the vege-tarian? Are there luxury items for customers who wish to indulge themselves or their guests? Are there too many choices, complicating production and slowing down service? Refer to sales analysis data from previous menus to determine what sells and what does not.

- **Price spread** This is the difference between the most expensive dish on the menu and the cheapest. It should be calculated by category (main courses, entrées, desserts). In general, the price spread should not exceed a factor of 2. That is, if the cheapest main course is $11, the most expensive main course should not be more than $22. A much narrower price spread may be called for in certain styles of restaurant.

- **Price rises** Avoid too-frequent or clumsy price changes. Over-written menus call attention to increased prices, but high printing costs may delay lifting prices for too long. Check carefully that food costings are tested and accurate, and that they will absorb seasonal fluctuations. Avoid changing prices and menu content at the same time; it calls attention to the increases, and may cause customers to look elsewhere.

Menu content

When you write an entire menu without consultation, there is always a danger of including, however unconsciously, only those dishes that are attractive to you. Remember that what you are writing is for your customers, many of whom have different eating habits from yours. The purpose of the menu is to sell food and drink to the general public, not to provide the management with the sort of lunch they enjoy most. Take a wide sounding of opinions from your staff regarding what customers ask for and what dishes are popular, and check which dishes are profitable. Compare these opinions carefully. The Executive Chef may like the idea of offering a whole roast prime rib of beef from a carving trolley in the restaurant. The maître d' may point out that there is not enough room in the restaurant to move a trolley about, and that fewer guests are ordering red meat these days. One of your restaurant supervisors may suggest that asparagus hollandaise is very popular when offered as a special. The purchasing officer may remind you that asparagus is only available at a reasonable price for a very brief season of the year, making it a poor choice for inclusion on the à la carte menu.

In the past, formal dinners served at hotels and restaurants were major events, calling for elaborate preparations and even more elaborate menus. When we read about banquets given in the 18th century, we may be staggered at the number of dishes and the number of courses offered, but it is important to remember that these meals were served in a style more similar to a buffet than to the plated, individual portions we are accustomed to today. Even a relatively simple modern buffet may have several dozen 'courses' on offer, but no one expects a guest to eat a plateful of every dish placed on the buffet. When 'Russian service' became fashionable in Europe in the latter part of the 19th century, it was a great novelty to be served an individual portion, carried straight from the kitchen by a waiter, not least because there was a good chance that the food might still be hot.

In the restaurant industry, there is still much disagreement about what constitutes a 'classical' menu. There are great differences, for instance, between the English arrangement of courses and the French or Italian practice. If you have several staff who have been trained in different countries, this can lead to foolish arguments about the 'right' way to lay a table or organise a menu. There are two points to keep in mind.

First, there is no such thing as a 'classical' menu that provides an unchanging model of how things should be done. Fashions in menus have changed constantly since restaurants and hotels first opened. Less than 100 years ago, it was normal to arrive at the dinner table to find all the food laid out at once, and it was considered polite to eat only those dishes that happened to be near you, regardless of whether they were sweet or savoury, lukewarm or cold. English menus long resisted the 'Russian' fashion for plated food, and stuck firmly to using the platters, tureens, salvers and sauce boats of the family (silver) service.

Second, the new influences of Mediterranean, Japanese, South-East Asian and Middle Eastern cookery on modern restaurant menus make it difficult to comply with the traditional Anglo-French menu arrangement. A Chinese formal dinner *ends* with soup; bread has no place on the Thai or Japanese table, yet is an essential in a Middle Eastern or Italian meal.

A modern version of the English 'classical' menu may look something like this:

Hors d'oeuvres

Soup (hot or cold)

Entrée (of light meat, seafood or pasta)

Fish course

Meat course

Vegetables

Dessert

Cheese and fruit

Coffee

Petits fours or chocolates

This simplified version of the traditional English formal dinner may still be called for when writing a special menu for a grand occasion, but more often one or more of the courses will be combined with another, or dropped altogether. The bare essentials of this arrangement are still to be found in the familiar soup–main course–dessert of the table d'hôte. If a frozen sorbet is served as a palate refresher, it should be presented between the fish course and the meat course. A green salad is usually offered with the meat course in the English manner but this varies considerably, since Americans are inclined to eat their salad at the beginning of the meal while the French prefer it at the end. In France, the order of the cheese and dessert courses would be reversed. In Australia and New Zealand, the habit is to follow the English pattern, unless the menu is written to a particular theme (such as an Italian menu with antipasto, pasta, meat, vegetable, salad, dessert, cheese and fruit).

Designing an à la carte menu to suit modern fashions and eating habits requires more ingenuity. Your intention should be to offer as many different types of food as the kitchen can reliably produce, so that the menu caters to a wide range of tastes. At the same time, you will keep an eye to the profitability of what you sell, and take every opportunity to increase the average check. If we keep these things in mind, then the menu begins to look a little different.

Hors d'oeuvres

Literally translated, this means 'outside the works', and originally meant a collection of side dishes or savouries set around a grand platter, rather like the small accompanying dishes served with an Indian curry. Hors d'oeuvres have almost vanished from the modern restaurant menu, but they live on in the form of cocktail snacks, or appetisers, on the banquet menu. They may also be served as 'teasers' in the cocktail bar, encouraging guests to stay on and order another drink. In fine dining restaurants, one may still find appetisers (tiny portions of savoury foods served before the order is taken) or intermezzos (palate cleansers, often a frozen sorbet) served without being specifically ordered.

Soups

Soups are attractive first courses, because they are perceived as light (although some soups may be quite hearty and filling). Chilled fruit or vegetable soups are good sellers in hot weather and conversely, chowders and thick bean or pulse soups will do well during a cold season. Be aware of the main course possibilities of soups like the Thai *tom yam*, Japanese *udon* or Chinese *won ton mein*. Present these in special large bowls to be eaten with chopsticks and spoon, and price them just below the average main course. They can be very popular and profitable additions to the menu.

Entrées

This term, for a small serving of a savoury dish that leads on to the main course, can cause some confusion with American guests, who refer to the main course as the entrée. They use the alternative name 'appetiser' to describe the first course, and this usage has started to appear on some Australian and New Zealand menus. The range of possibilities is enormous. These dishes can be divided into cold and hot entrées.

Cold entrées

Seafood is essential, so prawns, squid, mussels or marinated fish should be considered. Fresh oysters are almost a necessity, especially in areas where they are harvested. Terrines, pâtés, marinated vegetables and compound salads may also be used. If meats are offered, it is customary to concentrate on white meats (Italian *vitello tonato*, for instance), poultry or charcuterie (terrines, pâtés and smoked or cured meats, usually pork).

Hot entrées

Again, seafood is extremely popular, so small fillets of fish, shellfish, octopus and the like may be successful, especially if they are cooked in different styles (say grilled, pan-fried, deep-fried and steamed). Hot entrées include meats, and this may be an appropriate place on the menu for offal meats such as kidney, sweetbreads, brains or tongue. Grilled meats (especially from a char-grill) in the form of kebabs or brochettes are popular entrées. Creamed dishes, such as chicken and mushroom vol-au-vents, are not as popular as they once were, though they may still prove useful on banquet menus.

Pastas

Pastas, and related farinaceous dishes such as polenta, gnocchi and rice noodles, have taken on a role of their own; so that they are now more commonly listed on the menu in a separate section, rather than with the hot entrées. This indicates their place somewhere between an entrée and a full main course, and menu pricing should reflect this. Customers who do not want a full three-course meal may order a pasta dish with a soup or another entrée. While pasta dishes would seem to be very profitable, be aware that the cost of filling the bowl may only be a small part of your overall costs, and fine pasta dishes frequently require expensive garnishes or ingredients to make them attractive.

Main courses

Seafood

Take some care when designing the menu to offer enough choice in this important menu section. You should be looking for a variety of ingredients (shellfish, fillets, whole fish), a variety of cooking styles (baked, grilled, stir-fried, steamed) and a variety of flavours (spicy, plain, Asian, Mediterranean). The first step is to determine what seafood ingredients you can reliably buy at realistic prices, then discuss preparation styles with the Chef. Seafood is rapidly overtaking red meat as the main course of choice for many customers.

Vegetarian dishes, light meats and poultry

Without listing a hundred dishes on the menu, it is important to offer some well-chosen alternatives to the fish-or-steak main course. A stuffed chicken breast, pork cutlet, escalope of veal or portion of duck will provide for those customers who want neither red meat nor fish. Offer at least one or two savoury dishes without meat or seafood, keeping in mind that many of your customers will be (at least occasional) vegetarians.

Red meats

A well-grilled sirloin steak is still the heart of a good meal for many, especially if your clientele includes a high proportion of males, or business people, or both. Offering four or five different cuts, such as T-bone, fillet, sirloin and rump, is wasteful unless the restaurant specialises in steaks. It is better to offer two or three different garnishes with one type of steak. Be cautious with roasted meats such as prime rib, since the potential waste, in cooking and in unsold portions, can easily wipe out any potential profit.

Specialty dishes

Many restaurants, especially in the United States, have made very successful business out of 'specialty' dishes such as broiled lobster, BBQ ribs, chilli con carne and the like, which are heavily promoted by advertising. The aim is to establish your restaurant as the only place to go for a certain dish. This is by no means restricted to fast food restaurants, and if there is a particular food product for which your locality is known (such as farmed Atlantic salmon in Tasmania, Queensland mud crab in Cairns or spring lamb in Victoria), it may be worth considering this approach. Specialty items may be featured in display boxes on the menu, promoted by means of table tents, or displayed in the restaurant (wood-fired ovens or char-grills, for instance). Note that in menu English, the word 'specialty' is an adjective ('specialty dishes') and the word 'speciality' is a noun ('the Chef's speciality').

Side dishes and salads

Most customers will use the average price of your main courses to judge the 'value for money' they see in a restaurant. While an increase of two or three dollars on the average main course may push the perceived bracket from 'reasonable' into 'fairly expensive', customers will often spend as much and more on a good selection of side dishes without complaint. Intelligent use of side dishes can increase your average check without pushing the menu into the next price bracket. Side dishes can be much more interesting than plain French fries, green salad and garlic bread. If a certain dish is already on the menu as part of a main course (such as spätzle, polenta, ratatouille or coleslaw), make sure that it is also available as a side dish. This will not only increase sales, but will also improve turnover and freshness in the kitchen. A plain 'green salad' may sell, but individual salad ingredients (roasted capsicum in olive oil, grilled eggplant, pickled vegetables, fresh rocket or mesclun) will often sell better as side dishes.

Desserts

A good Food and Beverage Manager recognises that desserts can be some of the most profitable items on the menu, and does not tack them on as an afterthought. There is always some customer reluctance to overcome; guests may see desserts as an unnecessary indulgence—as 'too much' or 'too fattening'—but if they did not want to buy them, cake shops, ice-cream stores and bakeries would not be doing such good business. What all of these have in common is a keen sense of display. Desserts will sell themselves, if they are well presented and the customer can have a good look at them. In some restaurants a dessert trolley will be wheeled to the table, and this is an effective sales tool. An even more effective method is a dessert display located near the entrance to the restaurant, so that diners have a luxurious dessert in mind even before they start their meal. Remember that children seldom leave a restaurant without having dessert, so make your dessert list attractive to them, too.

Cheeses and afters

Cheeseboards are often listed on the menu, particularly in restaurants where bottled wine sales are high. (The cheeseboard is a suitable accompaniment for finishing up a good bottle.) However, these are seldom profitable sales for the restaurant, when the cost of keeping garnishes, dried fruits and six or seven cheeses, as well the cost of labour, is taken into account. A recent trend is to list single cheeses (for example, King Island Brie, Gippsland Blue) with fresh fruit (figs, grapes, melon) as individual dishes on the dessert menu. Chocolates, after-dinner mints or petits fours may be served with coffee at the end of the meal in more expensive restaurants. Since they are not charged for, remember that they must be included when calculating overhead costs.

Upselling the menu

The jargon word 'upselling' was coined to describe the role the service staff have in determining your average check. A good table server can recommend side orders, extra beverages or desserts in such a way that customers order more than they would if you simply relied upon a written menu. Upselling the customer gives direct and immediate results: a more satisfied customer, a better sale for the restaurateur and, quite possibly, a better tip for the table server.

Though upselling, or suggestive selling, is not technically a part of menu design, we can certainly write menus that make upselling easier. In restaurants, as in so many other organisations, making a thing easy to do greatly increases the chances that it will be done.

If the menu has an acceptable price spread (that is, the most expensive main course is no more than twice the price of the cheapest), it will be easier to move the customer from a cheaper dish to a more expensive one—the steps are smaller.

If a speciality of the house is enticingly described (for example, roast prime rib, chilli crab, fresh local crayfish) on the menu or on a table tent, it will be easier for the table server to sell it. A good list of side orders—such as spicy potato wedges, Mediterranean grilled vegetables, hand-cut coleslaw and fresh pita bread—at reasonable prices (15 to 20 per cent of the average main course price) will encourage customers to order more. On the same principle, quality wines available by the glass and interesting non-alcoholic drinks (cranberry juice cocktail, iced mint tea) will also make upselling easier. The customer may be tempted to try a glass of a good local wine at $4, but would resist buying the full bottle at $24.

Effective menu upselling is, of course, more than a matter of listing things on the menu. It depends greatly on the selling skills of the service staff. This ability must be encouraged and developed, often in the face of initial reluctance. Some service staff are simply shy or inexperienced and will resist upselling, feeling that they will embarrass themselves or the customer. They will do no more than write down what the customer orders, offering no advice or suggestions. In some operations, particularly fast food restaurants, this problem is addressed by training the server to ask a rote question ('What would you like to drink with that, ma'am?') at some point in the transaction. This is better than no upselling at all, but in a full service restaurant we need more.

Staff should be trained and encouraged to talk to the customer about the various choices offered on the menu. To do this, they will need to know how the dishes are prepared, where the ingredients come from, what they look and taste like and which items go well with each other. At regular intervals, all the principal dishes on the menu should be prepared and presented at staff tasting sessions. The chefs should be asked to explain the cooking methods and ingredients, specifically noting local products, unusual ingredients or methods of preparation. The bar manager or wine waiter might be invited to comment on suitable matches of wine and food, giving specific examples from the wine list. The more knowledge your table staff have about the product they are selling, the easier it will be to pass this on to the customer.

Other service staff will resist the very idea of upselling. You may hear the comment: 'The customers know what they want; why should we push them into ordering more?' The truth is, customers do not know what they want until someone tells them what is available. The written menu does only part of the job; it is up to the order taker to explain what a dish looks like, what comes with it, the portion size, what ingredients it contains and what it goes well with. Even the most reluctant table server could hardly refuse to tell a customer who is allergic to seafood whether today's soup has any shellfish in it. If they are willing to tell a customer what *not* to order, then why not be willing to recommend what they *should* order? The customer who is encouraged to order a little more than absolutely necessary will leave the restaurant with a feeling of abundance and repleteness. The customer who has ordered too little will only remember a meagre and unsatisfying meal. Which one of these customers is more likely to return?

Finally, a healthy spirit of competition can be harnessed to increase sales. It is easy enough, with the help of a cashier or an electronic register, to track sales for each table server over the space of a week. Dividing the dollar value of the sales by the number of customers served will give an average check figure for the week. Posting a weekly chart of the top three sellers will encourage friendly competition. The top seller for the month might be rewarded with a discounted meal for two in the restaurant or a good bottle of wine. The cost to the operator will be more than offset by the extra sales generated.

Menu design

When you begin to consider what the menu will actually look like, what colours it will be printed in and what size it should be, you move out of the domain of restaurant operations into the highly specialised realm of graphic design. Here it is important to take good advice, because printing is a painstaking, expensive and very final process, which will commit you to certain decisions for some time. First, it is worth remembering that there are several types of non-standard menus:

- Blackboard menus, including handwritten variations such as menus written on mirrors or windows, have the advantage of being cheap, easily changeable and visible at all times. These are suitable for the casual atmosphere of a brasserie or a café, for a seafood restaurant (in which the fish available may change between lunch and dinner) or for very small restaurants where the menu is written according to what was available at the market that morning. This style of menu requires attention to keep it accurate and presentable, and someone on staff who can do attractive hand-lettering. As it conveys a casual, breezy atmosphere, it is unsuitable for more elegant or luxurious restaurants. Many mid-range operations use a combination of printed à la carte menu and handwritten daily specials board.
- Placemat menus are less common than they once were, though they are still used for children's menus and may include games or puzzles to keep very young customers amused. The placemat menu is making something of a comeback, as good photography and slick graphics become more common, especially in low-cost family restaurants. Laminated placemat menus must be kept scrupulously clean, or be single-use disposables.
- Illuminated overhead menus are frequently used for fast food restaurants and for situations in which customers will order at a counter and carry their food to a table. The customer can browse through the menu while waiting to be

served. Layout and pricing are carefully considered and back-lit photographs feature attractive illustrations of the foods offered. For the independent operator, generic food photographs are available from graphics companies that specialise in this area. These provide an affordable alternative to expensive professional food photography.

- Daily menus printed in-house are quite common in better restaurants, and this option is much less trouble than it used to be, with the advent of sophisticated desktop publishing programs for small office computers. With a laser printer these programs can produce very acceptable results, especially if the printing is done on special, coloured stock that has already been overprinted with the restaurant or hotel logo, or a trademark design. However, there is a danger of producing amateurish, poorly presented and sloppy results if the menu design is left up to secretarial staff who have no training or experience in layout or graphic design. High-quality desktop publishing programs are expensive (in the range of $1000 to $2000) and require skilled operators. The advantages of being able to produce, and quickly change, menus in-house may outweigh these disadvantages.

The great majority of menus are of traditional format: a one- or two-page display printed by offset lithography on heavy card or paper, which may or may not be enclosed within a permanent cover. There are hundreds of variations on the card stock used, the layout, the typefaces chosen, the colour, the use of illustrations and inserts and, of course, the content. Once the F&B decides to commission a new menu, he or she can be swamped in endless decisions about design, methods of printing, print runs, finishes and so on. However confusing this may be at first, it is vital to have a sound understanding of how the process works, since the menu is such an important part of the restaurant's operation.

The printed menu

If we keep in mind the job the menu has to do, we have somewhere to start. The menu should suit the style of the restaurant, it should be clear and easy to read, and it should generate profitable sales. Practical considerations, such as how long the menu is expected to last, may also affect early decisions.

Many professional restaurateurs keep collections of favourite menus, gathered from other restaurants and hotels over a period of years. Specialist industry magazines in the UK and USA feature collections of the best menus and best food service advertisements produced in a given year. Your advertising agency or printing firm should be able to provide you with samples. The idea is to choose a few examples of a suitable style for your restaurant. You may like the typeface used in one menu, the card stock used for another, and the layout chosen for a third. Collect these together so that you can discuss ideas with your printer or advertising agency.

Advertising agencies provide a total service, including advice on the design of the menu, the various methods of printing, the costs involved and so on. An agency can also help you to maintain a cohesive theme or style for all the company's advertising, brochures, menus and stationery. To choose an agency, it is important to check references from other companies, to look carefully at the style of the agency's work, and to agree on specific charges, commissions and deadlines. No agency should be given a 'blank cheque' to produce what is required, since you will be charged for creative time and ideas, not simply for finished products. Having chosen a suitable agency, you will be relieved of many of the technical decisions entailed in producing a menu.

If there is no agency involved, you will have to deal directly with a printing firm. Again, it is important to seek references and to look at samples of each company's work before choosing one to do the job. You should not ask for a quote until you have discussed in detail exactly what the printing firm will do for you. Will they supply the design expertise and the artwork, or simply print from 'camera ready' artwork that you supply? If you agree to supply artwork, you must understand that the printer's staff will duplicate exactly what you give them, and cannot be held responsible for errors, sloppy design, poor typography or other faults. If they are doing all or part of the artwork for you, you will be supplied with 'proofs' at some stage before the menu goes to print. These must be very carefully checked (preferably by several people) for errors in spelling, layout, pricing or accuracy. Once you have returned these proofs (with any corrections carefully noted) then you have accepted the finished product and will be obliged to pay for it, even if an obvious error is later discovered. The printer will show you examples of different card stocks and give advice on lamination, coating, colour matching and prices. You will discuss the size of the print run, keeping in mind that larger print runs may be more economical per unit, but will also commit you to using the menu for longer.

Layout

Whether the layout of the menu is handled by an advertising agency or by the printing company's staff artist, you must have a clear idea of what you want to achieve. Where you put an item on the menu, and what sort of typeface you choose, can have a very real effect on sales. How the specials will be highlighted and side orders listed are Food and Beverage decisions, not printing decisions. Research has demonstrated some very clear patterns in the way people read menus, and how they react to what they see. Be innovative with your menu by all means, but refrain from breaking the basic rules of graphic design.

In Figure 3.1, the single-page menu is read in much the same way a customer might read a magazine article or an advertisement. Our eyes are conditioned by habit to scan a page in a particular sequence, and the position of a given item on a page will have a lot to do with how effectively the message gets across. The eye normally travels from the top left of a page to the bottom right, then lingers just above the centre. It is here that the main courses should be listed.

In a double-page menu (see Figure 3.2 on the next page), the pattern is much the same, except that the 'dead areas' are larger, and concentration tends to rest on the right-hand page. We can still use all areas of the printed page, but must take care to use boxes, highlights, graphics or larger typefaces to attract the eye. The menu should look balanced, from top to bottom and from side to side.

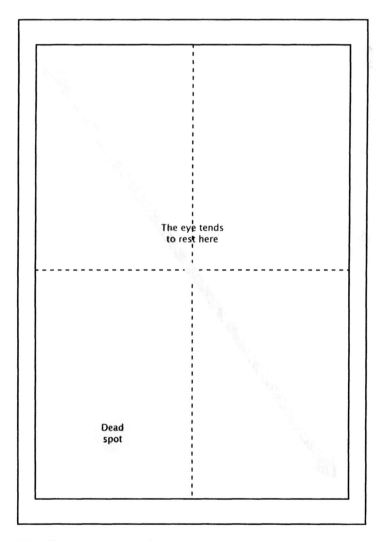

Figure 3.1 Single-page menu layout

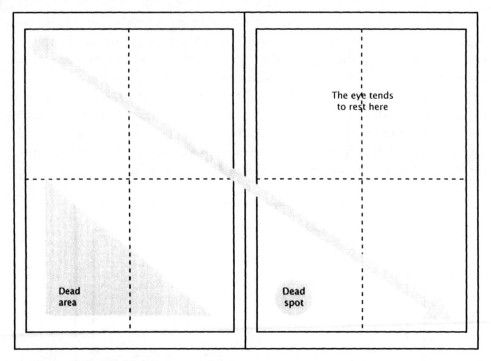

Figure 3.2   Double-page menu layout

The choice of typeface is important, since it is essential that your customers can easily read the menu under normal lighting conditions in the restaurant. Check the legibility of samples while sitting at the darkest table, in the evening. Have several people do this before you decide on a typeface and size. Type fonts are classed as serif (as in this text) or sans-serif (as in this example). Serif faces are generally more legible. Avoid gothic, script, fancy or unusual fonts, since reading comprehension falls away rapidly with these. Avoid overuse of capital letters for the same reason. Type size is measured in points. Anything smaller than 12 point type is unsuitable for a legible menu. The use of boxes, shaded areas, illustrations and photographs can liven up the printed menu, and make good use of areas that would otherwise be 'dead' to the eye.

CHAPTER SUMMARY

The content and physical appearance of your menu will affect the way your customers use it. The basic rules are that a menu must be suitable for the style of the restaurant, that it must be clear and easy to read, and that it must encourage profitable sales. A menu that is poorly written or presented will cost dearly in terms of lost sales, lost profits and customer dissatisfaction. Since the Food and Beverage Manager is principally responsible for the production of this important tool, it is vital that you understand the choices available to you.

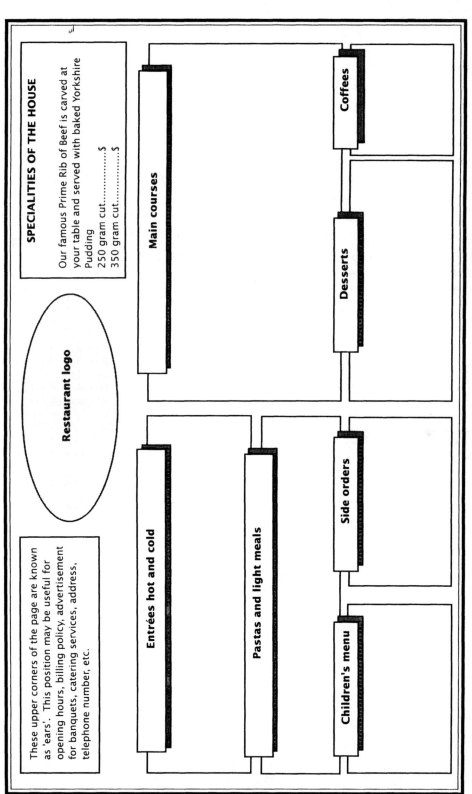

SPECIALITIES OF THE HOUSE

Our famous Prime Rib of Beef is carved at your table and served with baked Yorkshire Pudding
250 gram cut............$
350 gram cut............$

Main courses

Coffees

Desserts

Restaurant logo

Entrées hot and cold

Pastas and light meals

Side orders

Children's menu

These upper corners of the page are known as 'ears'. This position may be useful for opening hours, billing policy, advertisement for banquets, catering services, address, telephone number, etc.

Figure 3.3 A simple menu layout for a middle-range family restaurant, coffee shop or café. Note the use of position, highlighting and boxes to catch the eye and retain attention. Typefaces are clear and readable, and the effect is balanced.

First, we consider what type of menu best suits the food service operation. This could be anything from a sophisticated à la carte menu to a quick-service buffet. Which type you choose will depend on the resources and facilities available, the kind of people you are seeking to attract, the presence of competition and changes in food fashions and eating habits. Professional Food and Beverage Managers keep themselves informed of new developments in the industry and try to keep a step or two ahead of the competition.

The menu content should offer a good range of cooking styles, ingredients, portion sizes, familiar dishes and innovative creations in each of the menu sections. These dishes should be chosen with the customers' likes and prejudices in mind, since it is the customers who will be making the buying decisions, not the staff or management of the restaurant. Care should be taken to include menu items from each of the traditional courses of the 'classical' menu, and to keep an eye on nutritional balance and practical service considerations. A good restaurateur understands that a printed menu does only part of the job. Staff must be trained and encouraged to 'upsell' the customer for a better result.

Once menu type and content have been decided, the appearance and layout of the menu must be considered. You may seek advice from professional designers or layout artists, but should still retain overall control of what the menu will look like. It will help to be familiar with the basic principles of graphic design and with the mechanics of printing, as well as the alternatives to a standard printed menu.

REVIEW QUESTIONS

1 What are the three fundamentals of a successful menu?

2 Define the following: à la carte menu, table d'hôte menu, menu dégustation.

3 What are demographics, and how do they influence menu design?

4 Give the courses of a modern 'classical' dinner menu in correct order.

5 What is menu 'upselling'? How can it be encouraged?

6 Give some reasons for, and against, using an advertising agency to prepare restaurant menus.

CHAPTER FOUR

MENU PRICING

Menu calculations

Standardising recipes and food cost, and the difference between cost-as-purchased and cost-as-served

A comparison of various methods of setting menu prices

Price sensitivity and the psychological aspects of pricing

Monitoring results and menu engineering

A careful balance

In this chapter, we shall examine how prices are determined for a variety of menu items. Setting the right price is not simply a matter of checking to see what the competition is charging, or adding a set margin of profit on top of your costs. Pricing is a sensitive exercise in balancing the going market price, the perceived value, an acceptable contribution rate and an allowance for cost increases.

In order to monitor how well the customer is responding to your choice of menu offerings and the prices you have set, it will be necessary to collect information. If you monitor sales accurately and regularly, you will be able to measure the success or failure of these decisions, and make timely changes to improve results. Sales analysis is the best tool available for sensible planning and forecasting. If you know what has happened in the past, you have a reasonable chance of predicting what will happen in the future.

Terminology

To begin, it is useful to learn a few terms used to discuss menu pricing:

cover The setting for a single meal, or the service of one meal. Thus we can say a restaurant is set for 120 covers (there are 120 seats ready to be used), or that we served 120 covers at breakfast this morning (120 individual meals were ordered and paid for). One guest, eating breakfast in the restaurant and returning for dinner, would account for two covers.

pax A jargon word used in the hotel industry to mean 'number of people'. Thus 'twelve pax' means a dozen people, either for accommodation or meals. The term comes from the airline industry, where it is used as an abbreviation for 'passengers'.

average check This is a calculation to determine how much money is spent, on average, by each customer who dines in the restaurant. In its simplest form, it is the total revenue from one day of trading, divided by the number of covers served. This number may be more useful if it is further broken down by meal period (breakfast, lunch or dinner), by food or beverage sales, or by type of menu (such as set menu, à la carte menu or promotional menu).

sales analysis Collected information on how many and what kinds of products have been sold, used to determine how your customers are reacting to the product mix and pricing. This information will allow you to calculate profit margins, monitor costs and plan changes for your next menu and may be collected daily from handwritten dockets. A more efficient method is to use the detailed records stored in an electronic cash register or computerised billing system.

gross profit This is the sales price of a particular menu item, less the cost of the raw materials that went into it. Note: this is not the same as the contribution margin.

contribution margin A mathematical calculation that tells you how much profit is made on a particular item each time you sell one. Simply put, it is the sales price less the food and labour costs. This margin 'contributes' to offsetting overhead costs and providing a net profit.

Standardising costs

If the sales price of a given item is to be based, at least in part, on the cost of that item, then you will obviously need to know what that cost is. This is not as simple as it looks. If you want to know the cost of a bottle of mineral water, you could simply ask the supplier or check the most recent invoice. If you want to know the cost of a loaf of bread, however, you will need to specify what sort of bread you are talking about. Is it the sliced white loaf, the French stick or the German rye bread? Of course, your customer will not be eating the whole loaf, but only two slices from it. If that is the case, how many slices are there in a loaf, and how much does each slice cost? If the loaf of bread has a very short shelf-life, so that you cut two slices and then have to throw away the rest of the loaf, should you charge for the two slices, or the whole loaf?

When training a new bartender to prepare a Singapore Sling, you would not give him instructions to pour 'as much as you think is right' or 'whatever the customer asks for'. You would specify the amount of liquor to be served, the exact ingredients in the cocktail and which garnish is to be used. Precise measurement would allow you to calculate precise costs. There is no reason to do things any differently when serving food, so we will apply the same method to determining food cost.

The standard recipe card

The key is the standard recipe card. This is an index card or computer file that des-
cribes the menu item, the ingredients that go into it, the portion size, the garnish,
the method of preparation and the yield. It is prepared jointly by the Chef, the
purchasing officer and the Food and Beverage Manager. The Chef provides the
materials, recipe and method. The purchasing officer provides accurate measurement and pricing. The F&B uses this information to set quality controls and menu
prices. A standard recipe card must be prepared for each item listed on the menu,
and for such things as bar snacks, complimentary fruit baskets, staff meals and so
on. Serving food without knowing what it costs is just the same as instructing the
bartender to 'pour whatever you like'.

MENU ITEM: *Breakfast Muffin, Plain*		Date checked: 7/8/97		
Ingredients		Price	Per	Ext
1020 g	Sugar, granulated white	1.09	kilo	1.11
25 g	Salt	0.24	kilo	0.01
120 g	Honey, blended	2.80	kilo	0.34
680 g	Cake margarine (Trend)	2.75	kilo	1.87
11 each	Whole eggs, large	2.55	doz	2.34
1020 mL	Milk	1.07	litre	1.09
1870 g	Baker's flour, plain	0.90	kilo	1.68
85 g	Baking powder	9.45	kilo	0.33
Method: Cream sugar and margarine, beat in eggs. Add dry ingredients, mix by hand. Portion @ 40 grams in muffin sheets. Bake at 220 degrees for 15 minutes. Cool on wire rack.		**Total cost**		$8.77
		Yield		120
		Portion		2 ea.
		Portion cost		$14.6

Figure 4.1   A standard recipe card

In the example (Figure 4.1), we want to know the cost of a serving of breakfast
muffins, which are offered on the breakfast menu. The muffins are also included in
the Continental breakfast, along with coffee, croissants, toast, preserves and orange
juice. The Executive Chef advises that this recipe has been tested several times, to
ensure that the product quality is acceptable and the method of preparation is correct.
The purchasing officer brings along a small electronic portioning scale with a capacity
of, say, 2 kilograms, accurate to 1 gram. In the pastry kitchen the Chef, or one of
her staff, prepares the recipe in the normal way; but in this case, the purchasing
officer checks the weight of each ingredient as it is used. The muffins are portioned out, and sample portions are weighed before baking. When the muffins are

ready, the purchasing officer counts them to determine the recipe yield and enters the information on the card.

The next step is in the purchasing office, where the ingredients are checked against the most recent invoices to determine an accurate cost. If the most recent price for granulated white sugar was $27.25 for a 25-kilogram sack, then a kilogram of sugar must cost $1.09 ($27.25 ÷ 25 = $1.09). The recipe calls for 1020 grams, so the cost can be calculated easily ($1.09 × 1.020 = $1.11). Now the cost is entered on the card, and we go on to the next ingredient. When all the ingredients have been costed, we can add up the values for a total recipe cost. The total recipe cost is divided by the number of portions the recipe yields (note there are two muffins to each portion or serving), and we have a standard cost for a serving of plain muffins.

Finally, the Food and Beverage Manager can use an appropriate formula to determine the possible range of prices that might be charged for a serving of breakfast muffins. Various other factors (such as competition, perceived value and contribution rate) will be considered before a final price is determined. The standard cost of muffins will also be used to determine the cost of a Continental breakfast, since muffins are a part of it.

There are pitfalls in this process of preparing standard recipe cards. First, the information gained will be useless unless it is accurate. That means that the testing, measurements and costings must be done exactly, using accurate scales and recent prices. It is not enough to guess or approximate: there will be enough of that in later calculations based on these original figures. Some managers will not bother to go through this process, believing that it is too much fuss, or a waste of time. This is the sort of manager who spends most of his time shuffling papers in an air-conditioned office, wondering why the figures are not as good as they used to be. When the kitchen staff, receiving clerks and service staff see the Food and Beverage Manager down in the kitchen measuring, weighing, calculating and recording, it creates (by example) the idea that accuracy, precision, care and quality control are habits that the hotel or restaurant values, and it will encourage others to do the same. There is nothing in a restaurant so contagious as carelessness and a 'near-enough-is-good-enough' mentality. Once entrenched, these habits are extremely difficult to shift.

Second, the standard recipe cards must be updated every time they are used for a new menu price calculation. Ingredient prices must be checked against recent invoices, and altered if necessary. A movement of two or three cents in the price of flour may not have much effect, but the price of fish, green vegetables, fruits or imported goods can swing wildly over a space of six months. Any standard recipe that has not been checked for method and yield within the past six months should be tested again for accuracy. Recipes tend to drift and adapt in a busy kitchen, and you will be wasting your time if you cost a new menu based on old methods or old prices.

Third, be aware of the difference between weight as purchased and weight as served. If the restaurant purchases whole green tiger prawns in 12 kg boxes at $18.50 per kg, and the recipe calls for 200 g of shelled, head–off prawns, then some extra tests and calculations must be made. First, determine if there really are 12 kg in a carton. (This should be checked on delivery.) Next, weigh out 1 kg of prawns, defrost them and ask the Chef to prepare them in the way the recipe requires. Save the waste and weigh it. Weigh the finished, clean prawns and ask the Chef to select the proper portion (whether by number of prawns, cup or handful), then weigh that. Now you are ready to calculate the real price of green prawns:

Original weight of green tiger prawns	1000 g
Price per kg as delivered	$18.50
Weight of shell, heads, trimmings	480 g
Clean weight of prawns	520 g
Portion size	200 g raw
Price as served	$7.12

$18.50 ÷ 520 g = 0.0355c per gram
0.0355c × 200 g = $7.12

If you had simply calculated 200 g of prawns at $18.50 per kg, you would have believed a portion was costing you just $3.70. The real cost, almost twice that, could only be determined by measuring the ingredients after preparation.

In another case, it may be necessary to measure an ingredient after cooking. Take the example of a roast lamb roll, served at lunchtime in the carvery. The Executive Chef will indicate how much roast lamb should be carved to fill the roll, and train the cooks accordingly. To determine the cost of the meat, we will have to measure several stages in the process. First, how much does the meat cost as delivered? Second, how much is trimmed before cooking? Third, what is the weight loss from cooking? Finally, what is the weight of a portion of cooked meat? Here, the difference between the first price and the last can be dramatic:

Leg of lamb, bone-in, as purchased	2120 g
Price per kg	$4.80
Cost as delivered	$10.18
Trim weight (bone, fat, scraps)	640 g
Ready-to-cook weight	1480 g
Weight after cooking	1110 g
Portion size	150 g
Number of portions per leg	7.4

We can already dismiss the actual purchase price: after trimming and boning, we only had about 1.5 kg of lamb to put in the oven. Cooked to medium-to-well-done, the meat lost 25% of its weight during the cooking. When we cut it into 150 g portions, we were left with less than a full portion, which we could not sell. Now we can calculate the real cost of the roast lamb roll: purchase price ($10.18) ÷ saleable portions (7) = meat cost ($1.45) + roll, butter, gravy ($0.95) = true portion cost ($2.30). Note that the left-over portion could conceivably be used for something else, but if we want to be accurate about the costing we must regard it as waste, since there is no guarantee that we can sell it.

If lamb was to be used in other dishes, it might be useful to know the cost of boneless leg, ready to cook. ($10.18 as delivered yielded 1.48 kg after trimming. $10.18 ÷ 1.48 kg = $6.88 per kg.) If you wanted to know the cost of cooked roast lamb, you could easily calculate that, too ($10.18 as delivered ÷ 1.11 kg yield after cooking = $9.17 per kg).

Compound dishes

Once you have prepared a series of standard recipe cards, you will have begun to build up a database of cost information that you will use to calculate the true cost of the various items on your menu. (This, incidentally, is a suitable job for a small desktop computer, but it is not necessary. You can do quite an effective job with a boxful of index cards.) If a parsley and lemon garnish is standard with poached or steamed fish on your menu, you need only do a simple test to determine how many wedges an average lemon yields, and how many garnishes are picked from a standard bunch of parsley. In future, you may add a given garnish cost to compound recipes (that is, those with several prepared items in them), without having to weigh each sprig of parsley. Keep in mind that these costs should be checked for accuracy every six months or so.

Say we wish to serve a bakery basket with a room service breakfast, and the basket includes one croissant, one muffin and two pieces of toast. We have determined that one portion (two pieces) of plain breakfast muffins costs 14.6 cents; therefore, one muffin must cost 7.3 cents. Provided we have already done a yield test and an accurate costing on croissants and toast, then we can simply add up the individual costs to arrive at the compound cost of the bakery basket.

Since vegetables are highly seasonal, it makes sense to use whatever is in good supply at a good price. Many hotels and restaurants will average the cost of a serving of vegetables over a period of six months, to give a figure that can be used interchangeably for any main course served with vegetables. This can be an acceptable practice, as long as the chefs do not develop a sudden enthusiasm for snow peas, Jerusalem artichokes and oyster mushrooms, which can easily add two or three dollars to the cost of a main course. If a salad bar is provided with all main courses, then a separate costing must be done for the ingredients consumed from the salad bar over the space of a week. This aggregate cost is then divided by the number of main courses sold in the same period.

Cost of materials used for the salad bar in one week = $475
Number of main courses served = 218.
$475 ÷ 218 = $2.17 average cost per cover

Setting the menu price

Any sensible Food and Beverage Manager will want to get the highest possible price that is acceptable to the customer for the food and drinks sold in the establishment. The actual price should be based on the cost of the ingredients plus labour plus overheads, plus allowances for a number of other factors. We might consider the price the competition is charging, the amount of risk involved in selling that particular item, the volume that we can reasonably expect to sell, and the level of profit we consider necessary. There are several methods used to determine the menu price, each of which yields different results. It is not enough to settle on one basic margin or mark-up, as the following examples will demonstrate.

Before we can begin, we need to estimate the labour and overhead costs. These are best taken from historical data, that is, last year's trading figures if they are available. In the case of a new operation, cost forecasts may be taken from a similar operation (in size, menu type, location and price level) and from the manager's own experience. Let us look at an example, a large licensed hotel in a capital city (Table 4.1).

Table 4.1 Trading figures (food)—Central City Hotel

	$	
Sales last year	3 450 000	(100%)
Food purchases	1 207 500	(35%)
Labour cost	1 242 000	(36%)
Overheads	586 500	(17%)
TOTAL COSTS	$3 036 000	(88%)
OPERATING PROFIT	$414 000	(12%)
No. of covers served (B, L, D)		276 000
Average check		$12.50
Average labour cost per cover		$4.38
Average overhead cost per cover		$2.13

Equipped with an average labour cost per cover ($4.38), an average overhead cost per cover ($2.13) and the results of our food cost calculations, we can now experiment with a few different methods of setting the menu price. Let us imagine that we want to introduce three new menu items, a crabmeat salad, a main course pasta dish with bacon, mushrooms and white wine, and a breast of chicken with seafood sauce. We have tested the recipes to find raw food costs of $6.15, $2.10 and $4.15 respectively.

Food cost percentage method

When a new menu item is introduced, the raw food cost is simply divided by the average food cost percentage to reach the selling price:

Crabmeat salad	$6.15 ÷ 0.35 = $17.57
Mushroom pasta	$2.10 ÷ 0.35 = $6.00
Chicken breast	$4.15 ÷ 0.35 = $11.85

The problem here is that, by using simple arithmetic, we get a very wide price spread on our menu. If the pasta with bacon and mushrooms costs only $2.10 to produce, the selling price must be $6.00. Yet the crabmeat salad at $17.57 will be read as nearly four times as expensive (see the notes on psychological aspects of menu prices below). Customers will be 'driven' to the bottom end of the menu, and profitability will suffer.

Competitor's price method

Having canvassed the local competition, we are concerned that we must meet the price offered by another restaurant, or lose customers. We decide to match their prices, and hope for the best:

Crabmeat salad	$12.50 – $12.66 (labour + overhead + food) = $0.16 loss
Mushroom pasta	$8.50 – $8.61 (labour + overhead + food) = $0.11 loss
Chicken breast	$11.50 – $10.66 (labour + overhead + food) = $0.84 profit

Clearly, this is not a very satisfactory result. By allowing the competition to set our prices, we are forced to accept a loss on sales. The more successfully we capture customers at this price level, the more money we will lose.

Straight mark-up method

A colleague suggests that we try a straight mark-up of 200%. That is, if the raw food cost is $1.00, then we will add 200%, or $2.00, to reach the sale price. This mark-up is intended to cover the raw food cost, plus the overheads and labour. This method yields the following prices:

Crabmeat salad	$6.15 + 200% = $18.45
Mushroom pasta	$2.10 + 200% = $6.30
Chicken breast	$4.15 + 200% = $12.45

Here the price spread is slightly narrower, but still above the recommended 1:2 ratio. The gross profit is also fairly erratic: after taking away the food cost, we are left with a gross profit of $12.30 for the crabmeat salad, $8.30 for the chicken breast and $4.20 for the pasta dish. If the average labour cost plus overhead cost is $6.51, we can see that we will be making a loss every time we sell a dish of pasta.

Food cost plus labour cost plus overhead cost method

Here we decide to add the three principal costs together. The food, labour and overhead costs combined should provide us with a price we can live with:

Crabmeat salad	$6.15 + $4.38 + $2.13 = $12.66
Mushroom pasta	$2.10 + $4.38 + $2.13 = $8.61
Chicken breast	$4.15 + $4.38 + $2.13 = $10.66

This method achieves a much tighter price spread. The labour and overhead costs should be covered, but there are still some problems. First, there is no allowance made for profit. Second, crabmeat is more perishable than pasta (and thus carries an increased risk of loss). There is no allowance for this, or for the volume of sales we expect for each dish.

Contribution method

This method allows for labour and overhead costs, expressed as a percentage of the sales price. It also builds in the desired profit from trading, to guarantee a return on investment. An adjustment is made to allow for the relative perishability of the ingredients, the difficulty of preparation and the anticipated volume of sales.

Labour cost (36%) + overhead cost (17%) + profit (12%) = 65%
Sales price (100%) – 65% = 35%, which must be the food cost:

Crabmeat salad	$6.15 ÷ 0.35 = $17.57	sales price $15.95
Mushroom pasta	$2.10 ÷ 0.35 = $6.00	sales price $9.50
Chicken breast	$4.15 ÷ 0.35 = $11.85	sales price $12.95

We now have a price spread within the recommended range of 1:2. The relative values of the main courses are acceptable, yet we are not forced into unprofitable sales. Because we have built in all our operating costs and our anticipated profit, we can alter the contribution margin to allow for variables.

The crabmeat salad, which has a high food cost, is also highly perishable and is labour-intensive. Still, the market demands that we have a crabmeat salad on the menu, so we make some adjustment to the contribution margin (what is left after subtracting the food and labour costs). In the first column, we see that the contribution margin for a crabmeat salad would be $7.04 ($17.57 sales price minus $6.15 food cost and $4.38 labour cost). This is more than enough to cover our overhead cost and desired profit margin, but we judge that sales may be slow at this level, increasing the danger of wastage. If we accept a slightly lower contribution ($5.42) for each dish sold, then we can live with a lower menu price, encourage better sales and increase turnover to prevent wastage.

The mushroom pasta has a low food cost, but the contribution margin is not high enough if we set the price according to that alone. Here we can afford to increase the contribution slightly and still keep the pasta dish as the leading low-cost main course. We can test the figures at a sales price of $9.50:

Food cost (as tested)	$2.10
Labour cost (average per cover)	$4.38
Contribution (per item sold)	$3.02

The contribution margin at this price is 31.7%, slightly more than our budgeted average 29% (17% overheads plus 12% profit). However, we judge that the pasta will still sell readily at this price, as the cheapest main course. Volume should be high and wastage low, making this a profitable item.

The chicken dish is a good middle-of-the-road performer. We believe the market will stand a sales price of $12.95 for this dish. After subtracting the food and labour costs, we are left with a contribution of $4.42 for every meal sold, or 34%. We will monitor sales carefully to check our results, and still have room to increase or decrease the price as required.

Price sensitivity

It will be obvious that very few customers sit down to study your menu with a pocket calculator in hand. Most of our buying decisions are based on perceived value (what we *think* a thing is worth), on relative pricing (if it is more expensive, it *must* be better) and on unconscious rounding-off of figures (there is less *perceived* difference between $4.29 and $4.79 than there is between $4.89 and $5.39). It pays to keep these subliminal perceptions in mind when setting prices across a whole menu.

First, consider how prices are written on the menu. Some restaurants have experimented with writing out the price, for example 'Twenty-two dollars and fifty cents', and this may be appropriate in a very sophisticated restaurant where prices are not really part of the buying decision. However, like the now outdated 'ladies' menu' without any prices at all, the applications are very limited. At the other end of the scale we have the $1.99, $3.99 style of pricing, which may be perceived as cheap or downmarket. If the price is the deciding factor in a customer's decision to purchase (for instance, if there are two competitive fast food restaurants next door to each other, offering complete chicken dinners to take away) this may be justified; but again, the applications are limited. Curiously, $9.90 is not seen as cheap, but rather as keen pricing. It is the terminal digit that affects our judgement.

Most food service operations will have to list their prices on the menu and should choose their numbers carefully. If there is likely to be significant movement in a given price (as in the case of fresh fish or highly seasonal vegetables), then avoid printing the price on the menu. Over-writing or masking of old prices calls attention to increases, and may affect sales. It is better to use a card insert in the menu, or quote daily prices on a blackboard menu. Do not use the phrase 'market price' unless today's market price is clearly posted and visible to the customer: you will suffer loss of sales because the customer is not willing to risk embarrassment by asking how much the market price might be.

Be aware of the unconscious psychological effects of particular numbers. When we read a series of numbers, we tend to give the first figure dominance. That is, we see .65, .62 and .68 as 'about 60 cents', but .71 as 'about 70 cents', even though the difference between .62 and .67 is actually greater than the difference between .68 and .71. Longer figures are seen as more, so the difference between $9.95 and $10.05 is seen to be more than the difference between $9.50 and $9.95. We tend to round off figures in our heads, often in larger jumps than might be expected:

$1.40–$1.79 is rounded off to $1.50.
$1.80–$2.49 is rounded off to $2.00.
$2.50–$3.99 is rounded off to $3.00.
$4.00–$6.99 is rounded off to $5.00.
$7.00–$13.99 is rounded off to $10.00.

If the price spread within a menu category exceeds a factor of two, the customer tends to buy at the low end, which may not be what you want them to do. Specialities of the house are usually exempt from this perception, so if your restaurant features a fine but expensive item, you may safely price it outside the normal range without affecting sales of your mainstream menu—but be careful to make it clear that this is a speciality of the house. You can painlessly add perceived value to a dish by writing an effective description on the menu, explaining why the dish is special or unusual.

Monitoring results

All the care you have put into selecting dishes, calculating prices and printing attractive menus will be wasted if you do not monitor the results of your decisions. It is not what you think will happen that determines profitability, it is the actual buying decisions made by your customers. However irrational those buying decisions may seem at times, no restaurateur can afford to ignore what his customers are telling him. Fortunately, collecting the raw data has been made much easier in recent years by the introduction of electronic cash registers and computerised billing systems. If anything, the Food and Beverage Manager is probably faced with more raw data than he or she can sensibly use. The trick is to know which numbers are important and which are not.

The average check calculation is based on the total sales for a given period, divided by the number of covers served. That is, if sales for a given breakfast service were $758.50, and 82 covers were billed, then the average check for that breakfast service is $9.25 ($758.50 ÷ 82 = $9.25). If the Continental breakfast was priced at $7.50 and the full buffet breakfast at $12.50, we might reasonably conclude that roughly half the customers chose the Continental breakfast and less than half chose the full breakfast, with the difference made up by a few à la carte orders. This can be confirmed by looking at the department sales records. If the cash register is programmed with PLUs (price look-ups), and the cashier is trained to use them, then we can track how many of each type of breakfast were actually sold. If the records show, over a period of weeks, that the Continental breakfast is far more popular than the full buffet, then we might make a cautious increase in the price of the Continental breakfast, or consider reducing the price of the full breakfast. The intention is to achieve a higher average check. Since the overhead and basic labour costs are the same, whether a customer spends $7.50 or $12.50, then obviously a higher average check will provide a better contribution and a more profitable operation.

Let us take a look at the results after one week of trading with the new items on the lunch and dinner menu. For the purpose of the exercise, we shall ignore other sales and concentrate only on the three items we costed out (Table 4.2). Note that it is not necessarily the item with the lowest food cost percentage that shows the best results. Even though the pasta has a food cost of only 22.1%, the contribution per sale is just $3.02. Though it is clearly a popular dish with 44.2% of total items sold, it only contributes 33.6% of the net profit. Conversely, the crabmeat salad has a high food cost (38.5%), but the contribution is a healthy $5.42 for each dish sold. This item accounts for only 16.8% of total items sold, but contributes 22.9% of our net profit. Neither is volume a reliable indicator of profitability: the chicken dish sold 50 fewer covers than the pasta, but still contributed a higher amount to cover our overheads and return on investment.

Table 4.2   Sales results for three menu items

Item	No. sold	Revenue $	% sold	Food cost %	Contri- bution $	Net profit $	% profit
Crabmeat salad	160	2 552.00	16.8	38.5	5.42	867.20	22.9
Mushroom pasta	420	3 990.00	44.2	22.1	3.02	1 268.40	33.6
Chicken breast	370	4 791.00	39.0	32.0	4.42	1 635.40	43.4
TOTAL	950	11 333.00	100.0			3 771.00	100.0

It is this combination of cost, volume of sales and contribution margin that pro-vides the important information we need to make changes to the next menu. Any given menu item can be classed as a dog (low sales, low contribution), a plough-horse (high sales, low contribution), a puzzle (low sales, high contribution) or a star (high volume of sales, high contribution). Each one should be dealt with in a particular way.

Menu engineering*

Armed with accurate information taken from sales records, purchasing figures, standard recipe tests and financial reports (which should include labour cost figures and overheads), we can make intelligent management decisions about what stays on the menu, what is dropped and what is changed.

- **Dogs** Menu items that have a high food cost, are difficult to prepare, do not sell well and (at the best of times) do not contribute much to your overall prof-itability, should be the first to go. These are often the same items that present problems with quality control, storage or availability. These items are taking up staff time and menu space, without providing an adequate return. If the dog is a borderline case, with reasonable sales but a low contribution, consider reducing the portion size, cutting the food cost by substituting less expensive ingredi-ents, relocating the item on the menu or raising the price. Try changing the name of the dish, the accompaniments or the garnish to stimulate sales.
- **Plough-horses** These items are reliable performers that contribute to your overall profitability not because the contribution margin is high, but simply because you sell a lot of them. An example might be a wood-fired pizza, a pasta

* Menu engineering is a term, coined by Michael Casavana and Donald Smith, to describe a mathematical model that compares volume, contribution and cost of each dish on a menu, and then categorises it as a 'star', 'puzzle', 'plough-horse' or 'dog'. A simplified version is given here. For a very clear and concise explanation of the menu engineering concept, see *Cost Management for Profitable Food and Beverage Operations* by Morrison, Ruys and Morrison, Hospitality Press, 1994.

dish, a speciality of the house or a fast, popular luncheon dish. These are important items on your menu, because most of your customers see them as good quality at an attractive price. Alter these with great care, and pay attention to the first signs of a falling-off in popularity. You may consider packaging plough-horses with other items, such as pizza, salad and a glass of house wine at a set price, in order to increase the average check.

- **Puzzles** When a menu item provides a good contribution but seems to be difficult to sell, there are several avenues you can try. First, determine whether the problem item has a high food cost, has a limited shelf life, or is difficult to prepare or to serve. If this is the case, consider dropping it from the menu and replacing it with a more popular item. If the item is relatively easy to prepare and serve, consider highlighting it on the menu to achieve better sales volume. The problem item may be encountering resistance at the price you have set. Try reducing the price slightly to see if you can stimulate an increase in sales, converting it into a star.

- **Stars** It is in your interest to sell a lot of star items, since the contribution level is high and customers obviously like what they are getting. Make sure your quality controls are stringent, to ensure consistency of content and presentation. You may promote star items to specialities of the house with table tent cards, by highlighting on the menu or by external advertising. Test the perceived value of a star item by increasing the price slightly, while monitoring sales volume closely. If you have more than one food outlet, try running the star item in another venue to test demand, but be careful not to undercut sales in the main venue.

When a price increase becomes necessary, either to improve contribution or to pass along increases in food costs, labour costs or overheads, tread carefully. Look at the menu overall, rather than concentrating on a single item. If the price of fresh crayfish has risen, but the crayfish on your menu is already encountering some sales resistance at the existing level, consider raising the prices of several other items slightly to compensate. Do not be tempted to apply cost increases across the board, raising everything by the same percentage or dollar amount. Remember that food cost is just one element in the calculation, and that contribution is the most important factor in determining profitability. Price increases should not generally exceed 5% on a single menu renewal, and can be usefully timed to coincide with public announcements of CPI increases, federal or state budget increases and the like. Customer acceptance of price increases has been shown to be best when prices remain stable through four to six visits, and it is important to raise prices within a perceived bracket ($4.70–$4.95) before jumping into the next bracket ($4.95–$5.20).

CHAPTER SUMMARY

Writing a menu is a complicated process, but pricing that menu is even more complex, and more important, if the Food and Beverage Manager is going to achieve a profitable operation. Too often, prices are set by what the competition is charging, by unsupported hunches or by guesswork. It is essential, in any kind of professional food and beverage service, to determine exactly what your costs are, and then to apply sound business principles to arrive at a price.

The first step is to measure costs accurately, and we might start with the cost of the raw materials that go into a particular dish. Before that cost can be measured, however, we have to decide exactly what goes into the dish, and standardise the recipe by writing it down. Then we must measure how that food is processed before it reaches the customer's plate. There is usually a significant difference between the price of the raw ingredient as purchased and the prepared, or cooked, food ready for assembly.

Having determined an accurate food cost, we can then turn to estimating labour cost, overhead costs and an adequate return upon investment. Adjustments are applied to allow for volume of sales, perishability, contribution and price spread to reach a workable menu price. These careful calculations, based on recorded results and realistic forecasting, are known as 'menu engineering'.

REVIEW QUESTIONS

1 Whole salmon is purchased at $13.50 per kg, then filleted, cooked and served as a main course. Calculate the real food cost per portion of salmon from the following data:

Whole salmon as purchased:	3.5 kg
Trimmed weight of fillet:	2.5 kg
Portion size, uncooked:	180 g

2 What losses can be expected when processing a bone-in leg of lamb for service as a sandwich filling?

3 A new salad bar introduced in the restaurant has been well received, but it is difficult to determine an exact cost, since the ingredients vary from day to day. How would you measure the real food cost?

4 Why is it necessary to record sales data? What methods are available to do this?

5 Based on the following results obtained after a month's trading, categorise the menu items listed as 'dogs', 'plough-horses', 'puzzles' or 'stars'.

Item	No. sold	Revenue $	% sold	Food cost %	Contri- bution $	Net profit $	% profit
Burger	1 120	10 024.00	11.7	32.5	1.67	1 870.00	6.0
Pasta	2 567	20 407.00	26.9	23.2	1.73	4 441.00	14.2
Steak	4 220	56 649.00	44.1	34.1	4.16	17 555.00	56.2
Fish	1 653	24 712.00	17.3	41.0	4.45	7 356.00	23.6
TOTAL	9 560	111 792.00	100.0			31 222.00	100.0

6 Based on the same data, answer the following questions:
  a What is the average check?
  b What are the menu prices of the four items?
  c What is the overall net profit percentage available to offset overheads and provide a return on investment?

CHAPTER FIVE

DESIGN AND EQUIPMENT

Designing restaurants for safety, customer satisfaction and efficient service

Analysis of traffic flows and floor plans for kitchen and restaurant

Equipment requirements and table plans for restaurants and banqueting

Restaurant décor, furnishings and operating equipment

The role of design

Every professional Food and Beverage Manager could provide a list of the design faults in his establishment, which he would put right if it were feasible or economical. All too often the layout, equipment and facilities will have been designed by a firm of architects, who are very well qualified to design buildings but have little experience of operating them. While it may not be possible to move the four walls or rearrange the fire exits, it is still within the scope of a Food and Beverage Manager's job to see that the facilities are used in the safest, most efficient and intelligent way. To do this, you will need a sound knowledge of how work patterns, traffic flow and equipment layout can affect successful operation.

Safety

The first consideration to be taken into account is the safety of your staff and customers. It is not uncommon for safety to be put into a mental box along with hygiene, first aid and fire drills: things which are regarded as worthy, but boring, compared to the much more exciting business of planning a food promotion or selecting the new wine list. It is always remarkable how quickly this attitude changes when something goes wrong. It takes just one serious kitchen accident, one small fire or a few guests trapped in a lift to get everyone's attention. At this point they all turn to you, the Manager, for direction, and it will be useful if you have some plan in mind to deal with these emergencies. Afterwards, there will inevitably be a full and frank discussion with your General Manager, in which you will be given an opportunity to explain how the accident occurred, what precautions were in place to prevent it, and how those precautions will be upgraded to prevent another accident. The general trend in hospitality law towards the 'duty of care' owed to your employees and guests is now well established. If any public liability or worker's compensation claims arise out of a serious accident, you may be expected to explain why you should not be regarded as negligent in this duty.

The restaurant kitchen is, statistically, one of the most dangerous places in the building, which is not surprising when one considers the combination of hot surfaces, sharp blades, slippery floors and people in a hurry. What *is* surprising is that most accidents that occur in commercial kitchens are preventable. They are usually caused by someone making an already dangerous environment more dangerous by bending the rules. Blocked doors, missing safety guards, untrained staff operating machinery and poor traffic planning are all preventable risks which are the express responsibility of management.

Accidents in other parts of the hotel, restaurant or club can occur because of poor maintenance, inadequate training or dangerous practice, all of which are also preventable. The cost to your operation, if a worker is injured, is high: down time, increased training costs for a replacement, increased worker's compensation premiums, and the possibility of an expensive liability claim.

Guest safety is every bit as important as employee safety, and the risks involved are higher, since you do not have much opportunity to train your guests in the safest way to use your facilities. Compensation claims, in the event of even moderate injury, have skyrocketed over the past decade. A single serious injury claim can be enough to bankrupt a small business, and may make a large business uninsurable.

You have a moral, legal and financial duty to ensure that you minimise the risks to safety in all parts of the Food and Beverage department. One way to begin taking this seriously is to conduct a safety audit. You may call in an outside consultant to inspect your facilities and operations, or simply do a thorough walk-around with your supervisors and staff, identifying those areas or practices that need attention. If your restaurant staff tell you that a particular corner is frequently slippery, and that 'someone's going to get hurt there one day', you may take this as gospel truth: someone *will* get hurt unless you take preventive action now. If this seems to be low down on your list of priorities for today, take five minutes to run through, in your mind, exactly what would happen if a serious injury did occur. How long would it be before your telephone rang?

Security

It is also part of the manager's responsibility to see that all goods and services sold are paid for, that neither the staff nor the guests are walking off with the furnishings, and that the premises are reasonably secure from burglary, theft and vandalism. The effects of poor design on these areas should be obvious. If the back of the restaurant is dimly lit, covered by shrubbery and provided with numerous full-length french doors, then you are asking for a break-in. If there are six or seven different ways of entering and leaving the restaurant, then you must be prepared to accept guests wandering off without paying their bills. If you refuse to lock refrigerators or restrict access to stores at night, then you must expect loss of stock, even if you are not aware of it when it happens. In this area, the services of a security consultant might be called upon, to conduct a security audit and suggest useful alterations. Do not ignore electronic billing and cash handling systems when you conduct such a security check: electronic fraud is fast becoming the most common sort of white-collar theft, and the hotel environment is particularly vulnerable. You may encounter staff resistance to changes in security procedures. This may be entirely legitimate, and you cannot afford to ignore it; but be aware, too, that there may be people in your organisation who have something to gain from the way the present system works.

Impression and appearance

A piece of poor design in a restaurant operation tends to spread ripples outward like a stone thrown into a still pond. Because a door opens the wrong way, a service bottleneck is created. Because staff have to pause to cope with the 'wrong-way' door, guests are forced to walk around the bottleneck. Because guests are forced to make a detour, they block the natural entrance to the restaurant, and a vague impression of disorganisation is created in the mind of the guest who has just arrived for dinner. Guests like things to proceed smoothly and seamlessly, without apparent effort. They will report that such an operation is 'efficient', 'very well organised' and that 'they look after you well'. In another operation, guests are allowed to notice just a few snags. They go away reporting that 'they're very disorganised', that 'they don't seem to know what they're doing' and that 'it's a bit of a shambles'. The quality of food, service and décor may be equal in both restaurants, but guests will unhesitatingly recommend one over the other.

You must examine your operation from the point of view of the customer, which is much more difficult than it might seem. After all, you know where the toilets are; the guest may not. Because you are the Food and Beverage Manager, you will probably not have to wait at the door to be seated in the restaurant, but will your guests? If they may have to wait, is there any provision for elderly or infirm guests, such as bench seats or chairs? If there are several areas guests may wish to find, such as the cocktail bar, coffee shop or grill room, are there adequate and clear signs to direct them?

Good design and layout create smooth service and guest satisfaction. It is difficult enough to maintain quality standards for food, beverages and attention to guests—don't put yourself at a disadvantage by designing problems into your operation.

Efficiency of operation

It follows naturally that a smooth design will lead to smooth function. If you think it is desirable that guests be met quickly and greeted at the entrance to your restaurant, then you must make sure that your staff can see the guests when they arrive, and that it is easy for the supervisor to 'detour' to provide the first greeting. If the waiting area is comfortable and attractive, and is provided with some visual interest (such as a copy of the menu framed on the wall, historical photographs of the region, or a tropical fish tank) then you will have used good design to produce the desired result: customers who are in a good mood and receptive to good service.

A manager who fumes and stamps his foot because 'I keep telling those table servers not to use this counter to store their bags' is a sorry sight. The staff are no doubt aware of what the manager thinks; but they choose to ignore him because, for one thing, there is nowhere else suitable to keep their bags, and for another, that counter is in the logical place for bag storage. This is an example of bad design undermining the authority of the manager. Another way of looking at it is that we have a bad manager, who thinks that poor design can be overcome by stamping his foot or writing interminable memos to the staff.

It is the manager's job to look at, and understand, whole systems. Generally, people will do a given job in the most sensible and convenient way available to them. If your staff habitually take short-cuts, use equipment for something other than what it was designed for, or complain about the way a system works, then it is time to review that system and see where it can be improved.

A case in point

David G., the manager of the University College Tavern, was ready to tear his hair out. He had issued numerous instructions that after-hours entry to the main food stores should be for emergencies only. Already this month there had been sixteen entries late at night, and problems had followed. Twice the keys had been misplaced, causing chaos the next morning. Once, the locks had been left open, and the Stores Manager reported that she suspected stock losses. The Chef said that while kitchen staff tried to requisition sufficient stock during the day, it just wasn't possible to predict the highly variable level of business in the three night-time restaurant outlets. The duty managers complained of being repeatedly called away from their rounds to open the stores. David looked at the overall system, and realised that the kitchen was not able to store enough supplies to cope with evening demand. He arranged for a small lock-up storage area to be built in the kitchen, and keys issued to the chef on duty. After-hours entry to the main stores became a rarity, and kitchen staff were able to keep sufficient supplies on hand.

Flow patterns

If you accept that good design is a desirable thing, then it is in your interest to understand how whole systems work in the hotel and restaurant industry. Minor changes to the way we locate equipment, organise traffic flow or lay out the furniture can have significant effects on the smooth operation of the business. There are three 'flows' that will interest us: the goods flow, the staff flow and the customer flow. In order to discuss them, let us take a look at the layout of a small (82-seat) licensed restaurant with a self-contained kitchen (see Figure 5.1, next page).

Note that the layout is a traditional one. The kitchen is out of sight of the dining room; the bar is in the restaurant and serves as a meeting area for guests waiting for a table. There is a mix of banquette and round table seating, and the kitchen is set up to receive deliveries and store goods. Modern restaurant design has many variations on this rather plain setup; we might have an open kitchen, multiple-level seating, a self-service salad bar or a small stage for entertainment. However, for the purpose of this exercise, all the basic elements are there.

The goods flow

The cycle of goods in and out of a restaurant operation can be simply stated: the Chef prepares a list of what is required, orders are placed with suppliers, deliveries are made and checked; the goods are stored, then requisitioned, prepared and served to the guests. A small portion of the goods will be returned as table waste and must be collected and disposed of. With this pattern in mind, we can examine the restaurant plan to see if the physical design suits our requirements.

A small office is provided near the delivery area. This will serve the Chef to gather the orders, get telephone quotes and track orders as they are placed and received. At the delivery point, a set of accurate scales is provided to check incoming goods. There is a small area for unloading trolleys and so on, and it is a short run to the stores (dry, refrigerated and frozen) without crossing any other major traffic flows. The same entrance may be used for staff arriving and leaving work, and the office will provide a measure of security to check on the movements of visitors, delivery people and the like.

The next step, from storage to preparation, is straightforward. Kitchen staff have direct access to the stores, and may be required to fill out a requisition sheet hanging on the wall as goods are opened or taken out for preparation. In a larger operation, requisitions and issues would be the duty of a storeperson, to give better control and accuracy. Again, the movement of goods from storage to preparation does not cross any other major traffic flow.

When preparation is complete, the food must be collected by the service staff. Hot and cold dishes are brought to the passe, where the table servers can pick them up

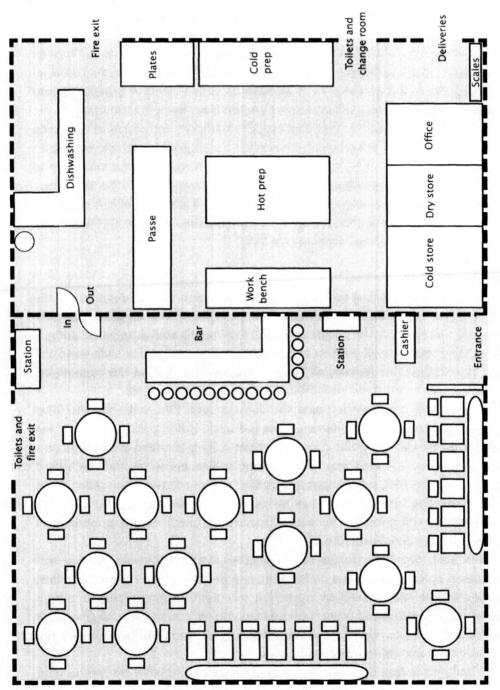

Figure 5.1　A workable layout for a small licensed restaurant

and deliver them to the tables. Again, this movement does not cross any other major flow, and the service and preparation areas are physically separated by a counter.

Waste food returning to the kitchen is handled immediately inside the kitchen door, with bins and waste disposal close at hand and a place provided to drop and sort dirty crockery. Dry waste will be taken out later, after service, for final disposal in the rubbish bins outside the back door.

For comparison, let us look at a kitchen plan that would not be quite so easy to operate (Figure 5.2, next page). In this case, we have all the same elements, and they are exactly the same size as in the restaurant plan in Figure 5.1. Yet, clearly, this kitchen would be a disaster to work in. Receiving is not too bad; we still have a set of scales in the right place, and a clear run to the stores. However, the dishwasher will have to cross that line of traffic to store clean plates and crockery.

Kitchen staff have a slightly longer walk to pick up supplies, but this is nothing serious—until we notice that they will have to cross paths with table service staff heading for the dishwashing area. Service staff carrying full, hot dishes in their hands have to reverse against the flow of staff carrying dirty crockery, to get back into the restaurant. The food preparation area is more cramped, and the fire exit is now fairly inaccessible for anyone but the cooks. Staff going to use the toilets or changing rooms will have to cross two lines of traffic, and the Chef's office does not have nearly so good a view of what is going on.

It would be would be an unfortunate chef who was presented with a kitchen layout quite as bad as this, but the majority of working kitchens will fall somewhere in between the two examples given.

The staff flow

When designing how a restaurant, bar or banqueting space will be laid out and operated, it is important to remember all the people who will be working in it. There are cooks and table waiting staff of course, but the bar staff will also need a space to work, as well as the dishwasher, the cleaners, the storepeople and the cashiers. Each one of these people will arrive at work, use a changing room, get supplies, prepare for service, perform their duties, clean up and go home. If you are to understand and adjust whole systems, you must be able to think your way through every one of these duties.

If the bartender needs more ice during the evening, where will he get it and what will he carry it in? Can he leave the bar unattended to fetch it? If the cashier needs to use the toilet, how far does she have to walk? If a guest spills a glass of wine and a fresh tablecloth is required, where are they kept? Imagine the complete process of greeting guests, seating them, preparing mise-en-place for their meal, placing the order, collecting drinks or a bottle of wine, collecting the food order and serving it. Consider what happens when it is time to clear the table and reset for dessert, and how that will be ordered and served. Walk through this process

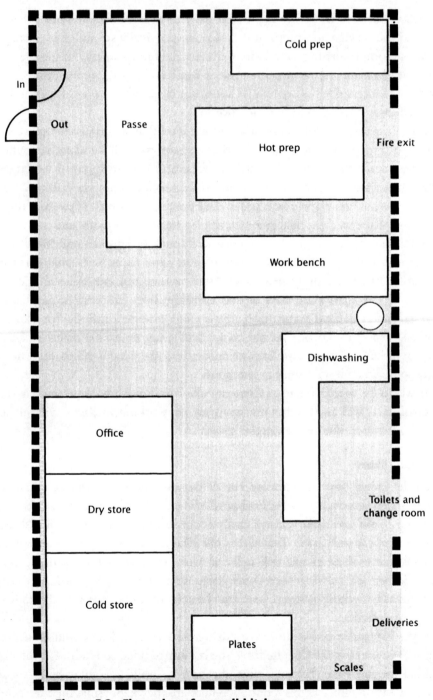

Figure 5.2 Floor plan of a small kitchen

alone, or with your staff, to see where possible bottlenecks will occur and how they could be prevented. Spend plenty of time in the restaurant and kitchen during service to see how your design works. Ask yourself: is there an easier or more sensible way of moving people around to do these jobs?

In the restaurant, provide an adequate number of servers' stations, where spare mise-en-place is kept and service trays may be put down in a hurry. Do not make it necessary for a table server to go all the way to the kitchen every time she needs a teaspoon.

The guest flow

If you have dined out in restaurants, you have already seen the numerous design flaws that stick in the mind long after the bill has been paid. You may remember sitting at a table near the kitchen door, where the noise level was unbearable, or queuing to use the washroom in a restaurant under-supplied with these essential facilities. Consider the last time you stood uncomfortably in the centre of a busy restaurant, while a panicky table server attempted to find you a table, or waited at the bar for ten minutes before anyone noticed you had not been served. These are the seeds of guest complaints, and no restaurant or hotel can long continue to make these mistakes and expect to remain in business.

A foyer, or standing area, is always useful at the entrance to a restaurant. This allows guests to take off their outer clothes, wait for friends to join them, inspect a menu or simply say goodbye to each other before leaving. When the guests are ready, they should be able to approach a desk to confirm a reservation or request a table. The same desk will serve for the preparation of bills and payment of accounts when the meal is over. It is sensible design to have just one entry and exit for guests (though you will almost certainly be required to have other emergency fire exits), so that your cashier, receptionist or maître d' can keep an eye on who is entering and leaving the restaurant. The desk should be large enough to cope with the busiest periods (breakfast time in a business hotel, for instance) when many guests will be in a hurry to get in, be served, settle an account, and get out again.

If the bar is inside the restaurant, separated by a low divider or brass rail, guests who wish to wait for others, or socialise before sitting down to a meal, may do so. The bar should be easy to reach from the entrance, and guests should not have to compete with service staff for the attention of the bartender. Provide comfortable bar seating if you want to increase your average beverage check. If space allows, provide bar tables and seating, for the same reason.

Your guests may be seated, but that does not necessarily mean that they have stopped moving around. If you offer a self-service salad or buffet, consider carefully where people are going to stand, in which direction they are going to move, and how they will get back to their tables. Be particularly careful to avoid clashes between guests who want to go in one direction, and staff who need to go in another, opposite direction. Even with full table service, guests will be getting up to use the toilets, so make sure that signs directing them are clearly visible, and do not run staff 'highways' across the path the guests must use.

Equipment and layout

Part of the design of your operating areas is the provision of adequate equipment, and it is necessary to familiarise yourself with the cost, type and standard quantity of this equipment. Every restaurant is a unique case, and there may be special reasons why you will need more or less equipment, but you will still need some sort of industry average to begin with, especially when you are planning capital expenditure for a new restaurant.

Restaurant and banquet layout

The first thoughts usually given to designing a restaurant are furnishings, décor and colour schemes. It is, however, more important to consider the location and arrangement of the working areas before becoming deeply involved in choosing the colour of the table napkins. Study the layout of the restaurant space, and experiment by sketching staff, goods and guest flows as described above. Start with the immovable (fire exits, toilets, lifts, walls and stairs), then add the semi-permanent (cashier's desk, entrance and exit, bar, kitchen, walkways) and finally sketch in the movable equipment (tables and chairs, signs, servers' stations, salad bar). If you are taking over management of an existing operation, you may feel that you are obliged to accept things as they are until you have settled in. On the other hand, it is much easier to convince senior management that substantial changes are needed during this 'honeymoon' period, when you are newly appointed and at least some of your requests may be granted.

Restaurants are often described by their seating capacity, so that we talk about a 120-seater coffee shop or a banquet room with a 450/250 capacity (that is, a room that will accommodate 450 people for a stand-up cocktail party and 250 people for a sit-down dinner). This figure is vital when estimating how many covers you are likely to serve in a given month, how much your overhead costs are per seat and how much equipment you will need. If there were a single formula for calculating the number of people who can be seated in a given area, hoteliers would use it all the time. Unfortunately, there is no single formula, because the number of people varies according to what kinds of tables and chairs you use, whether there is an allowance for a buffet or salad bar, what style of service you have in mind and even the type of menu you offer.

Guests in a busy, trendy supper and jazz club will almost expect to be squeezed in like sardines, since this adds to the atmosphere, but if you try the same thing in an expensive, luxurious hotel restaurant, you will find your patrons walking to the competition to find more comfortable surroundings. The seating capacity of a restaurant is not something that happens accidentally—it is a design decision that will have a profound effect on the whole operation.

Having decided what purpose you want the room to serve, and laid out on paper a workable plan for the traffic flows, you can begin to look for appropriate equipment. Whether you use wooden or metal tables; whether the chairs are to be cane, bentwood or steel; or whether you have full linen tablecloths or plastic table-mats, are decisions more likely to come from the interior designer than from the Food and Beverage Manager, especially in a large hotel property. It is your job to see that the practical aspects of the design are workable and intelligent. If the interior decorator has a passion for intricate cane furniture, you might point out that cane furniture has a much higher maintenance cost and a much shorter working life than, say, stainless steel. This may not be an issue if you are planning to redecorate every two years, but be aware that these costs will be coming out of your operating budget, and will affect your profitability.

The table plan*

There is one decision to be made, which will severely limit your seating capacity if it goes the wrong way. Here it will pay to present your case early, before the purchase orders are placed. This decision relates to the use of round or rectangular tables, and it is more important than you might think. Whatever happens in the future, you can be certain that at some time you will be asked to make your dining room hold the maximum possible number of people, and it will never be quite enough. If you decide to use round tables (even with changeable tops) you will never achieve more than about 85 per cent of the room capacity that you could achieve with rectangular tables. This has nothing to do with squashing people into small spaces; it has to do with the fact that you can join up square or rectangular tables to make larger ones, but you cannot join up two round tables.

First, you will need to know the standard size of a place setting on a banquet or restaurant table. Allowing for a 24 cm mains plate, with a basic setting of entrée knife and fork, main knife and fork, two wine glasses and a side plate, we can estimate that a place setting will occupy a space 55 × 35 cm on the table. This does not take into account room for flower vases, table numbers, condiments and so on, because the individual setting is not symmetrical; there is some space left over for these extras, and you will not need six sets of condiments for six diners. 55 cm is

---

* The definitive argument on the subject of restaurant and banquet seating plans was given by Harry Sebel, in a paper delivered to the Australian Catering Trade Fair in 1968. Copies of this invaluable leaflet are widely circulated in the industry. This section is largely a paraphrase of Mr Sebel's convincing logic.

also approximately the width the average person takes up in a chair, allowing a reasonable amount of room for elbows and movement. This standard place setting might need to be increased to 57, or even 60, cm if the setting is more elaborate, or if there is a show plate; but as a general rule of thumb, 55 cm will suffice (Figure 5.3).

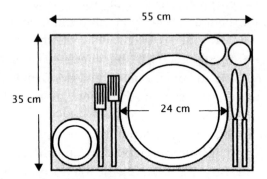

Figure 5.3   Standard table setting

On a round table set for six people, then, we will need 330 cm of circumference (six people at 55 cm each), which means that the table would have to be at least 1 m in diameter. (This works out to slightly less than 330 cm, but there are small savings to be made with place settings on round tables, and a slight increase in elbow room, compared to square tables.) However, the story does not end here. We have chairs and people to put at the table, and now we must allow for another standard measurement: 50 cm from the edge of the table to the back of the chair with a person sitting in it. Now, we can calculate that the table will actually occupy a circle 2 m across on the floor (Figure 5.4).

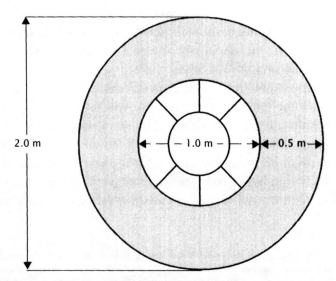

Figure 5.4   Banquet setting for 6, round table

Next, look at a rectangular table seating six people. The width required for each person is 55 cm; therefore the table must be at least 1.65 m long. The table must be at least 70 cm across, for two settings opposite each other. Then we allow for the guest and the chair: another 50 cm on each side of the table (Figure 5.5).

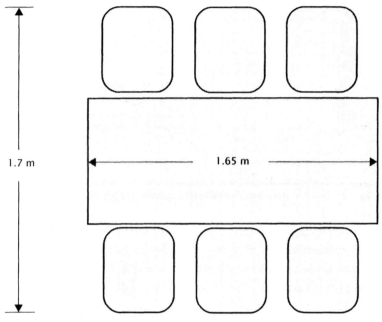

1.7 m   1.65 m

Figure 5.5   Banquet setting for 6, rectangular table

Of course, not all tables are for six people. For banquet rooms, you might consider tables for six, eight, ten or twelve people. Using round tables for any more than twelve people results in a very wide table, making it difficult for guests to talk to each other, or reach for condiments and wine (see Table 5.1).

Table 5.1   Floor space needed for round tables

No. of guests	Minimum table size (rounds) cm	Floor space (diameter) m
6	100	2.00
8	140	2.40
10	175	2.75
12	210	3.10

It may be useful to cut out templates for the table size you have in mind, and see how many you can get to fit in a scale plan of the banquet room. A setup with round tables of eight in a ballroom might look like Figure 5.6 (see next page).

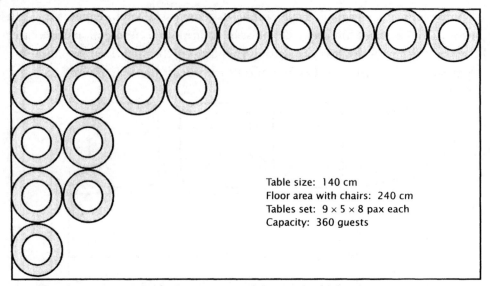

Table size: 140 cm
Floor area with chairs: 240 cm
Tables set: 9 × 5 × 8 pax each
Capacity: 360 guests

Figure 5.6   22 × 12 m banquet room with round tables (A)

This is obviously not very practical, since there is no allowance for aisles, or for a buffet, entertainment or anything else. Clearly, we will have to allow at least two aisles to provide access for guests and service staff. A one-metre aisle is about the minimum; so we can shade that in, and try the table fit again (Figure 5.7).

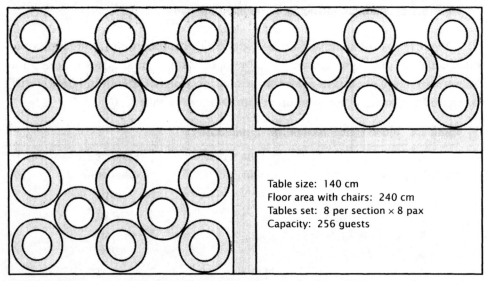

Table size: 140 cm
Floor area with chairs: 240 cm
Tables set: 8 per section × 8 pax
Capacity: 256 guests

Figure 5.7   22 × 12 m banquet room with round tables (B)

You will notice that we have lost more than 100 seats, and there is still no allowance for a buffet or a stage. Even with staggered tables, our capacity is down to 256 guests. Now examine the arrangement with rectangular tables of eight (Figure 5.8).

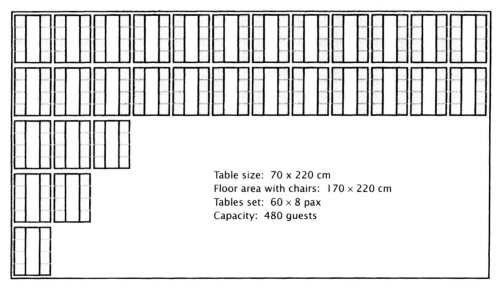

Table size: 70 x 220 cm
Floor area with chairs: 170 × 220 cm
Tables set: 60 × 8 pax
Capacity: 480 guests

Figure 5.8   22 × 12 m banquet room with rectangular tables (A)

The seating capacity looks good; but once again, there is no allowance for aisles. If we shade in the same dimensions as those we used in Figure 5.7, we will have a more realistic picture of how this banquet setup will work (Figure 5.9).

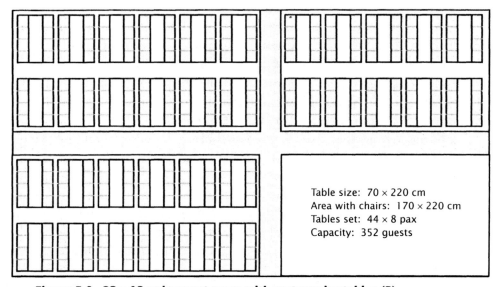

Table size: 70 × 220 cm
Area with chairs: 170 × 220 cm
Tables set: 44 × 8 pax
Capacity: 352 guests

Figure 5.9   22 × 12 m banquet room with rectangular tables (B)

By using rectangular tables, we are able to seat more people (96 more people, to be exact) and we can also provide narrow aisles between the tables, so that guests can more easily move about, visit other tables and so on. If banquet seating capacity will ever be at a premium, there is no question but that rectangular tables will provide a better result. Incidentally, there is nothing to be gained by seating guests at the ends of rectangular tables. This greatly increases the space occupied by the table, without significantly changing the capacity of the room. Try this with cut-out templates and you will be convinced: it becomes necessary to allow a minimum of 1 m (2 × 50 cm) between the ends of the tables. If you are going to take another metre of floor space, it would be better to lengthen both tables by 55 cm and gain *four* seats, not two.

What suits banquets does not necessarily suit the restaurant, but even here it is difficult to go past the flexibility provided by rectangular tables, particularly if they are combined with banquette seating. It may be desirable to have some round tables, if that is the look you prefer, but any sensible Food and Beverage Manager will understand that seating means turnover, and turnover means profit. We can use the same template-and-floor-plan method to experiment with restaurant layout.

The most common table shape seen in restaurants is the square table, intended to seat two, three or four people. Many experienced restaurateurs will swear by the square table, certain that it gives the best flexibility. Unfortunately, it is also the most costly in terms of floor space, and a restaurant set with a mixture of square and round tables will often have less than 70 per cent of the capacity of the same room set with rectangular tables. Some managers will argue that this is a good thing, since it does not do to overcrowd a restaurant, and it is important that every guest have a comfortable amount of space to relax and enjoy the meal. But if you spend some time experimenting with table plans, you will discover that rectangular tables actually provide the customer with *more* table space than the alternatives.

The smallest square table normally used is 75 cm on a side—just barely big enough for four people. If we compare this with the smallest rectangular table that will seat four people, we can measure the table space available for each person and the floor space used to accommodate them (Figure 5.10).

With rectangular tables, guests enjoy more room to eat their meal, and yet the table and chairs take up less than two-thirds the floor space of a square table. The extra floor space taken up by a square table is really of no benefit to the guest; the space is wasted. The tables shown here are the smallest that any full service restaurant could realistically use. Larger tables will simply widen the gap and waste more space. The comparison with round tables is similar. Setting square tables on the diagonal can save a little, but the best arrangement of all uses banquette seating (Figure 5.11).

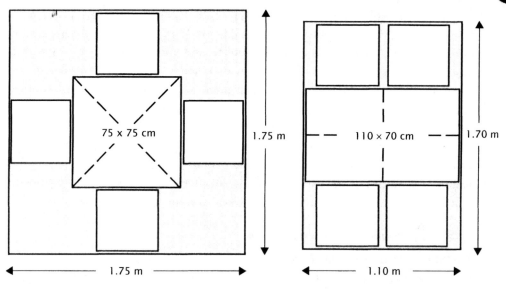

Table space: 0.14 m² per person
Total floor space: 3.06 m²

Table space: 0.19 m² per person
Total floor space: 1.87 m²

Figure 5.10 Comparison of square and rectangular tables

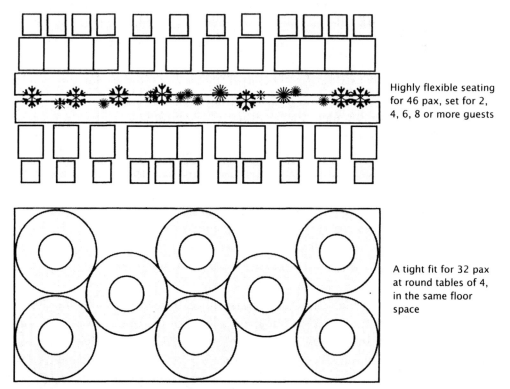

Highly flexible seating for 46 pax, set for 2, 4, 6, 8 or more guests

A tight fit for 32 pax at round tables of 4, in the same floor space

Figure 5.11 Comparison of round and banquette table layouts

In this case, tables can be joined or separated according to need. There is no fuss involved in preparing an unexpected table for 22 guests—the tables are simply joined up. You may even gain enough room to add another two seats, since each join gains floor space. The gap of 40 cm between tables is enough to afford moderate privacy, and yet make access to the banquette seats easy. A half-banquette may be built against one wall (preferably with a mirror behind), or the full banquette can be divided with plants or a decorative screen.

No one seating plan will answer all needs, and it is up to the Food and Beverage Manager to decide how the available space may best be used. You may have good reasons to use round or square tables, but be aware that these are the least efficient layouts, and they will cost you seating capacity and turnover.

Restaurant décor and furnishings

Talented restaurant designers have emerged in Australia and New Zealand over the past few years, who offer a combination of architectural and interior design services to hoteliers and restaurateurs. Consultants will, for a substantial fee, recommend a layout, a choice of furnishings, floor and wall coverings, colour scheme and lighting. They may even make suggestions for choice of crockery and cutlery, menu covers, tablecloths and the like. While some excellent restaurant designs have been produced, it is vitally important that the design works. The Food and Beverage Manager should be closely involved during the design process to advise on practical considerations, and to describe exactly what market and what type of customer the bar or restaurant is aimed at.

Floor coverings include vinyl, wood, carpet and tile. Impermeable surfaces such as vinyl are relatively easy to clean, and may be suitable for a snack bar, a cafeteria or a fast food restaurant. Wooden floors can set off the look of a modern restaurant beautifully, and soften the appearance of steel and glass. Carpets provide a luxurious feel but require constant, time-consuming cleaning. The modern fashion for bare, uncluttered surfaces and wooden floors has resulted in a clamorous noise level in some restaurants, as the racket of service and the din of conversation bounce back and forth off hard surfaces. Tile floors are attractive, but must be chosen carefully to avoid a surface that is dangerously slippery when wet or greasy. It is extremely difficult to judge the overall effect of a floor covering from a small sample. Before choosing a surface for your bar or restaurant, visit as many other establishments as you can, paying particular attention to the flooring.

The choice of lighting is another design decision that will affect the mood and appearance of the room. Micro-lighting, using low-voltage lamps, gives an attractive atmosphere, but maintenance costs are high. Use natural light whenever possible, but be prepared to boost it on a dull day. Keep in mind that restaurants have to be cleaned and reset when there are no customers present, so an auxiliary lighting system of bright fluorescents may come in handy.

Sound is an important part of the atmosphere in a public area, and the smaller the area, the more important it becomes. Be aware of background noise, street noise and the noise produced by operating equipment (a glass washer, for instance, or a coffee grinder). Reflected sound can be a problem in some settings, and it is important to allow for the noise generated by the customers in a full restaurant. It is a good idea to call in an acoustics consultant before expensive decisions are made. This should not be the same person who is supplying the sound equipment. The choice of background music is the last step in this process, but it is an important one, and a lot of expensive design can be rendered useless if the choice of music is left to the 19-year-old bartender.

Customer comfort will have a noticeable influence on the length of time spent in the restaurant, and this can be managed in more than one way. For an elegant fine dining room, where guests are expected to spend a full evening, it would be appropriate to choose wide, comfortable chairs, preferably with arm rests and upholstered seats. A longer stay, in this case, means a better average check and a more satisfied customer. On the other hand, a busy coffee-and-snack bar in a city location will probably want to encourage fast table turnover; so simple, functional chairs or stools, bright lighting and small tables will be preferred.

Do not ignore the appearance and dress of the staff when considering the overall design of the establishment. If the customer is expecting to find creative food in an informal, trendy café, then white T-shirts, short aprons and jeans may be appropriate attire for young, personable table servers. However, the business client entertaining guests at an important formal dinner in the hotel restaurant would not find that style acceptable, and would expect to find professionally dressed table servers in long aprons or jackets. It is false economy to ask service staff to provide their own uniforms (for example, 'black and whites'), since the variety of results you will get will defeat the purpose of having uniforms in the first place.

External advertising (media, signs, posted menus) will also help to set the style of a restaurant operation. The choice of typeface, photographs, models and settings will give customers an early indication of what to expect when they arrive at the establishment. If your target market is families with children, then you should include children in advertising photographs, or feature the children's menu as part of a news-paper advertisement.

Salad bars, buffets and self-service bars

The addition of self-service areas to a restaurant floor plan requires careful think-ing. There will be much more traffic as guests get up, walk around, queue and return to their tables. Staff will have to cope with lines of customers, which may make access to the buffet or salad bar difficult. The design of the salad bar or buffet itself will have to match the existing restaurant décor and satisfy stringent health regula-tions concerning food holding temperatures, sneeze guards, utensils and so on.

When estimating how many people will be standing up at one time, plan for the very busiest period, when queues will form. In which direction should they queue, and is this obvious to the guest? Will people standing be unacceptably close to people sitting? (Few guests can enjoy a meal while others stare over their shoulders.) Will guests be standing, like Oliver Twist, with an empty plate in their hand, or will the crockery be on the buffet itself? If guests help themselves to condiments, sauces, garnishes or bread rolls, are these located separately from the main buffet? If so, this will ease the crush and decrease the time each guest spends at the buffet.

When the salad bar or buffet inevitably needs replenishing, from which side will the staff have access? Will they have to cross a line of guests while carrying a stack of plates, or a container of hot soup? What about an accident or a spill? Should a guest knock over a vase or a glass of wine, is there provision for a quick clean-up and replacement? It is preferable to have staff access from behind the buffet, but this may not be possible if you have used an 'island' design to improve guest access.

A messy, stained or depleted buffet can produce such strong negative reactions from your guests that you might have saved yourself the trouble of installing it in the first place. You must make provision for frequent replenishment or replacement of hot and cold foods, utensils, napkins, crockery, glassware and cutlery. A buffet or a salad bar can be an attractive and efficient means of serving people, but do not imagine that it requires any less staff time or attention than plate service.

Table linen

The first impression of a restaurant is a combination of many things, but there is no denying that the sight of a room laid with crisp linen tablecloths and napkins, ready for service, conveys an atmosphere of luxury and grace. Unfortunately, fine table linen is extremely expensive, both to purchase and to maintain. Because it is very much a part of the visual design of the restaurant, it is vital that you make a decision early in the planning stages about how you will handle the linen question, and then allow for the appropriate costs in your budget.

There are several alternatives. In the traditional large hotel property, an in-house laundry will be responsible for the washing, pressing and folding of the hotel's own table linen, and also for mending and replacing it as required. You will want to discuss requirements with the Executive Housekeeper or the Laundry Manager, to be sure that you are agreed on how the system will work, what is considered adequate stock, and who will make the decision about when to replace damaged linen.

Some properties will choose to hire all their table linen from an outside laundry. Capital expense is saved, but this will be offset by higher maintenance costs. The hotel or restaurant is at some advantage, in that it may refuse any linen which is not up to standard, but at the same time will have limited control over delivery, turnaround times, weekend service and so on. Some restaurants use overlays to control linen costs. Here the table is covered with a standard cloth, with a fall of 30 to 40 cm on each side. This is then overlaid with a smaller cloth, slightly larger than the table top. In most cases, it will only be necessary to change the overlay after a meal has been served, thus reducing laundry costs.

Other restaurants will leave the table surface (of wood, tile or plastic) bare, and set it with placemats. These may be of fabric, disposable paper or laminated card, and may be printed with all or part of the menu. Napkins may be of cloth or of high-quality paper. In this case, the table surface is carefully cleaned after each service, the tablemats relaid and the cutlery set on top. This system is suitable for quick-service cafés, coffee shops and moderately-priced family restaurants. In some cases, a hotel restaurant will use this system for breakfast or lunch service, and go to full table linen for dinner service.

Avoid tablecloths made of cheaper polyester or nylon materials, even though the range of colours and initial cost may be attractive. High-quality, restaurant-grade cotton damask is expensive, but provides unrivalled wear and washing characteristics and takes pressing like no other fabric (except real linen, which has almost priced itself out of the market). If the expense of high-grade cotton tablecloths is out of the question, it is preferable to use an attractive bare table surface, and set it with good-quality cloth napkins and placemats.

A basic operating stock for an average restaurant would be four tablecloths for each table (one on the table, two for reset and one in the laundry) and four napkins per cover. If the restaurant does more than one meal service (say, lunch and dinner) with table linen set, this stock should be increased to six cloths per table and six napkins per cover. Table napkins should not be used as cloths for the service of wine, for lining plates or bread baskets or for handling hot plates. A separate stock of service cloths should be kept for these purposes. Table napkins have no place whatever in the kitchen.

Cutlery, flatware and hollow ware

The bewildering choice of different styles, patterns, materials and sizes of table cutlery is often a headache for the F&B. Unfortunately, the final decision is often made by leafing through a manufacturer's catalogue until 'we see something we like'. This is not the most sensible way of going about things. It is better to determine exactly what you want the cutlery to do, then determine how much you are willing to spend, and compare quotes from suppliers before deciding on which types of cutlery to order.

Strictly speaking, cutlery refers only to knives, but it has come to mean all the utensils normally set on the table. Flatware is the proper name given to spoons and forks, and hollow ware means other table utensils made of metal, such as sugar bowls, milk jugs, teapots and so on. Hollow ware is rapidly disappearing in quality restaurants and being replaced by earthenware or china. Part of the reason for this is that real silver, which looks very attractive on the table, has become extremely expensive, and stainless steel is a poor substitute.

The choice of metal is limited. While silver plate is still used in some very luxurious restaurants it is very costly, requires difficult and time-consuming maintenance, and tends to discolour on contact with certain foods. When buying silver plate, it is important to compare the thickness of the silver layer deposited (measured in microns) between one manufacturer and another. Purchasing domestic-quality silver plate is a false economy, since it will require replating after only a short time in restaurant service.

Stainless steel has almost completely replaced silver as the metal of choice in restaurant tableware because it is virtually indestructible, polishes well, handles automatic dishwashing with ease and comes in a wide range of different finishes and weights. Stainless steel tableware can range from the very cheap, stamped cutlery used in institutional canteens to superb silver-look tableware that costs nearly as much as silver itself.

Generally speaking, heavier and larger tableware is perceived to be higher quality, and you will pay accordingly for the metal content in each piece. It is best to avoid ornate or complicated designs, since they are harder to polish and may be discontinued, leaving the establishment with no way of topping up lost or damaged stock. Ask your supplier which standard lines have been in production for several years, and look likely to remain in production for the foreseeable future. It is one of the enduring mysteries of the trade where all the cutlery goes to; but this must, unfortunately, be accepted as a fact of life, and you should make allowance for frequent replacement. One hotel company in the United States announced significant savings when they installed a metal detector on a rubbish-handling conveyor belt and paid a cash bounty to staff for recovery of teaspoons, knives and forks. With prices for top-quality imported French and German cutlery passing the $10-a-piece mark, this does not sound so outlandish an idea.

Minimum quantities per cover in a typical restaurant would be three of each standard piece of tableware (bread-and-butter knife, entrée knife and fork, main knife and fork, dessert spoon and fork, soup spoon, teaspoon). This allows for one set on the table, one in the wash and one ready for reset. A 50-seat café will require 150 entrée knives, 150 entrée forks and so on. This does not make any allowance for replacements, and most larger establishments will purchase four pieces per cover if the budget allows. For occasional pieces, such as oyster forks, butter knives, cake slices, shell crackers, parfait spoons and the like, your par stock should reflect your menu. If oysters are a feature, then obviously you will need an adequate supply of oyster forks. (Entrée forks are simply too large to get inside an oyster shell.) If they are an occasional item on the à la carte menu, then a few dozen may suffice. Note that if the restaurant does a large proportion of table d'hôte meals, tour meals or banquets the tableware requirements will be greater, since these meals are usually preset with all cutlery on the table before the guests are seated. In general, avoid getting carried away with grape scissors, asparagus tongs, lobster picks and so on, as these are expensive items, easily lost and seldom called for. Steak knives, which were once a feature of every Australian bistro, are now well out of fashion, and their presence on a table would raise some questions about the quality of the beef being served. Fish knives are similarly falling out of use. These blunt, flat knives were originally invented to assist with removing fish from the bone. The modern trend is to serve almost all fish boneless, so the practical reason for using a fish knife has all but disappeared. To reset a cover with a fish knife, in order to serve a main course of garlic prawns, is pretentious and silly.

China and earthenware

The manufacturers of ceramic plates, bowls, cups and other table pieces are constantly improving the hardness, strength-to-weight ratio and chip resistance of their hotel and restaurant ware. Look for these qualities first; size is the next most important decision and pattern last. Once again, it is in your interest to compare various products carefully, and choose those which will suit your operation and continue in production. If you are unable to obtain replacements, you will be faced with the expensive proposition of replacing your entire inventory of crockery, once breakages and loss have accounted for about 15 to 20 per cent of your par stock.

The very best china is the hard, thin, semi-translucent material known as bone china. It was originally made in Europe as a substitute for high-quality Chinese porcelain. It is extremely fine and very expensive, and its applications in the commercial food service industry are limited to such occasions as afternoon teas in five-star hotels and special occasion dinners in private dining rooms. Most hotels and restaurants will use some form of earthenware, which goes under a variety of trade names. Vitrified china is earthenware which has been further hardened by the addition of silica or other minerals to the clay, to improve strength and chip resistance. Another possibility is Arcoroc, a type of toughened glass which has been manufactured to look very much like fine china. This is relatively inexpensive, durable and heat resistant. There is a wide gap between domestic china and restaurant ware and, once again, false economies can be made by purchasing an unsuitable grade for restaurant service.

Badged plates, which were once fashionable, have now given way to simple stripes or patterns. A brief fashion for octagonal or ludicrously large show plates has also subsided, and the more practical considerations of clean style and ease of handling have driven most restaurateurs back to classic round, white plates. The minimum size for main course service in a restaurant is about 22 cm, and it is now more common to see a 24 or 25 cm plate as standard. Many establishments use larger plates, but there are factors of table size, handling, storage and portion size to be considered before settling on an oversize plate for a particular restaurant.

The par stock is more difficult to set for china than for tableware or linen. The number of main plates required will depend on whether the restaurant serves one, two or three meals a day. The dishwashing facilities, and the number of staff available to 'turn around' crockery, will also have an influence. As a rule of thumb, it would be unusual to have fewer than two main plates per cover on hand, and more would be required for a busy banqueting operation. Keep in mind that staff will normally reset a room as it is cleared, and cannot wait for every piece of crockery from the previous service to be cleared, washed and dried before beginning the task. Items such as soup bowls or dessert bowls are not usually preset, so a stock closer to one per cover may be enough (without allowance for replacements). Entrée plates and side plates, on the other hand, are used for many purposes other than their primary one: as underliners or chocolate plates, for cocktail parties and for coffee stations. A simple restaurant might get along with one-and-a-half times the number of seats, but in a hotel with multiple food service outlets, three times the maximum seating would not be excessive. Standard stock for normal service will include main plates, entrée plates (these may double as dessert plates), side plates, soup bowls, salad bowls, cereal and dessert bowls, teacups, coffee cups and saucers. Par stock for these is based on the number of seats, or covers, in the restaurant. You will also require sugar bowls, milk jugs, salt-and-pepper sets, teapots, coffee pots, butter dishes, ashtrays, table numbers, flower vases and service platters. Par stock for these is based on the number of tables in the restaurant.

Some Food and Beverage Managers, particularly in larger properties, choose to have different patterns of tableware and crockery in different food service outlets. While there may be good reasons for this (fine bone china in the private dining room, unbreakable crockery at the pool snack bar), it limits the ability to move equipment around in emergencies. A compromise is to have one or more restaurants share the same pattern as banquets, so that controlled 'borrowing' can help to cope with unusual demands.

CHAPTER SUMMARY

The success of a food and beverage operation is not simply a result of good luck, hard work and staff training. The smooth operation, public success and ultimate profitability of a restaurant, club or bar depends, in large part, on a series of design decisions. How will the restaurant be laid out, and what sort of clientele do you expect to attract? Where will the bar go, and what size should the tables be? Where will the staff work, and where will deliveries be made?

These decisions are not made just once, before the restaurant opens for business, but in a continual process that requires the Food and Beverage Manager to be conversant with everything from fire safety systems to the standard width of a table setting. Rather than choose a style of furniture or the colour of the chair cushions as the result of a hunch or a salesperson's recommendation, it is important to understand the principles of good design and put them into practice.

Sound financial planning is very much a part of the Food and Beverage Manager's job. If your budgets are sketchy about exactly what equipment will be needed, and how much of it, then it will be difficult to project returns on investment with any confidence or accuracy.

REVIEW QUESTIONS

1 What is 'duty of care'?

2 Name the three principal 'flows' to consider in restaurant and kitchen design.

3 What is the width in centimetres of a standard place setting?

4 Give some arguments for and against using a linen hire service for restaurant tablecloths and napkins.

5 What considerations would affect the choice of cutlery for a restaurant?

6 What is vitrified china?

CHAPTER SIX

BEVERAGES

Responsible service of alcohol and licensing regulations

Beverage selection and pricing

Bar design, operation and equipment

Stock control and standards

The relationship between stock, turnover and profit margin in beverage sales

Cash registers, docket control and security

Beverage service

The management of all bars and beverage service within the hotel, club or restaurant is, of course, the responsibility of the Food and Beverage Manager. Beverage service provides an attractive source of profits—and a number of pitfalls that can lead to considerable loss. The general principles of beverage service are the same as for food service, but there are specific problems to be considered in design, operation, stock control and security.

Licensing regulations

There is probably no area of hotel or restaurant operation so tightly controlled by regulation and law as the service of alcoholic beverages. As well as satisfying the normal requirements of occupational safety legislation, public health regulations, weights and measures and building codes, you will also have to deal with numerous stringent rules laid down by the State or Territory Licensing Commission. These rules have the force of law and, since no hotelier or restaurateur may legally serve alcoholic beverages without a licence, it is up to the operator to prove that the requirements are met. A licence may be withdrawn for a variety of reasons, and Licensing Commission rules are open to a range of interpretations by individual inspectors. The local Police Department will also be involved, since enforcement of licensing laws falls within their realm. To further complicate matters, licensing regulations vary considerably between States. There are specific licences for different types of establishment, and the rules change frequently. It is vital to keep yourself informed of the latest developments in your own locality.

Generally, regulations control the types of beverage that may be served and to whom, the location and size of the bar and seating area, and what other facilities are required (toilets, exits, number of seats and so on). Regulations govern what other services the establishment offers (such as entertainment, gaming or food), what hours and days of the week it may operate, and even the décor and appearance of the public areas. The Licensing Commission collects licence fees, refers disputes to the Licensing Court and usually publishes a simple guide to the requirements of the local Licensing Act. This guide, and a copy of the Act itself, are essential items on the Food and Beverage Manager's bookshelf.

Changes to the law in recent years have generally tended to increase the responsibility licensees carry for the care and behaviour of their guests. There are penalties for minors who use false identification to obtain alcohol, but these penalties are trifling compared to the larger fines, and possible loss of licence, that hoteliers face should they be found guilty of supplying it. Intentional deceit by the customer is, unfortunately, no defence: the hotelier is still guilty. It is also an offence, under most jurisdictions, to supply liquor to someone who is already intoxicated, though the condition may or may not be apparent. In the United States, similar laws have been interpreted to mean that the restaurateur or hotelier may actually have a 'follow-on' responsibility. This means that if a guest is already intoxicated, and is served with another drink by the hotel, then goes on to injure himself or another in an accident, the hotel may be found liable for damages claimed by the guest or the third party. This precedent has yet to be set in Australia or New Zealand, but it cannot be far away, so any prudent hotelier will make provision for it now. In addition, though licensees can be prosecuted for serving a person who has already had enough to drink, they can also be prosecuted for refusing to serve someone on the grounds of sex, race, ethnic origin or appearance.

Responsible service of alcohol

The general direction of licensing law in Australia and New Zealand is toward 'responsible service of alcohol'. This recognises that, while alcohol is an accepted and quite legal drug available for sale to the public, it does carry numerous risks to the health and safety of those who consume it. The law requires that licensees, hoteliers, restaurateurs and their staff take precautions:

- to avoid serving alcohol to those under the legal drinking age
- to encourage consumption within safe limits for all patrons
- to discourage drinking and driving
- to refuse service to those already intoxicated
- to train staff in the responsible service of alcohol.

Education programs, public safety campaigns and changes to the law have been promoted to change the average patron's drinking habits. Extended licensing hours (to discourage rapid drinking), the service of food in licensed premises (to encourage moderate consumption) and consumer education (to make patrons aware of the law) have all been put forward as ways of achieving a 'European' model, in which alcohol is consumed as an adjunct to food and social gatherings and not as an aim in itself.

The licensee is faced, however, with several difficulties. First, cultural habits in Australia are well established, and the consumption of hazardous levels of alcohol is still associated with 'a big night out', with some sporting events and with the (mostly male) 'session' in the public bar. Nightclubs, in particular, are extremely attractive to teenagers, and licensees may face determined attempts by under-age patrons to gain entry and service. Intoxicated persons are notoriously difficult to deal with, and may object strenuously to being refused further service of alcohol. To complicate matters further, licensing laws in Australia are not uniform between the States and Territories and, in some cases, are difficult to interpret:

> A person shall be taken as drunken if, at the time, the person is visibly affected by liquor to the extent that any further consumption of liquor is likely to produce drunkenness.
>
> *Section 115(3) WA Liquor Licensing Act 1988*

Licensees and their staff may be prosecuted for a number of offences, and the penalties can be severe. In Western Australia, to sell, supply, permit or allow consumption, to obtain or aid to obtain liquor for a person who is drunken carries a $5000 penalty for the licensee and a $2000 penalty for an employee. Yet the definition of 'drunken' is, as we have seen, somewhat difficult to grasp. While a measurable blood alcohol level (0.05 grams per 100 millilitres of blood in most States) is set as the legal limit for drivers, there is no such limit in law to determine when a person is intoxicated. Different people handle liquor in different ways, and in any case it would hardly be feasible to ask guests to take a breath test before serving them another drink.

In practice, the courts have taken a sensible approach and have rarely imposed maximum penalties, except in cases of repeated offences or wilful disregard of the law. While the threat of civil liability exists, however, any sensible manager will take precautions to observe the regulations, and be seen to do so. There are several ways to go about this.

Under-age drinking

The best way to avoid problems with under-age drinkers is to prevent access in the first place. Many States and Territories now issue some form of identity card for those over the age of 18. Licensees and their staff can reasonably refuse to serve alcohol to anyone who cannot produce one of these, or some other form of photographic identification with a birth date, such as a driver's licence. In certain cases it is illegal for those under the age of 18 to be on licensed premises, so service staff should be trained to gently and politely insist that identification be produced if there is any doubt about a patron's age. Nightclubs and other entertainment venues must establish control at the door to prevent illegal access.

Intoxicated guests

When a guest is visibly affected by alcohol (for example, displaying aggressive or inappropriate behaviour, lack of physical co-ordination or slurred speech), bar staff should politely refuse further service of alcohol, and offer instead to serve a non-alcoholic drink or call a taxi to take the guest home. When the patron insists (as is often the case) that he or she is not intoxicated, service staff should gently insist that the law requires the licensee or server to make that judgement, and that the penalties for breaking the law are severe. Staff must be trained to handle this difficult situation, and to remain firm and polite at all times. If necessary, the manager should be called to back up the server's decision. To reverse a staff member's decision and permit a patron to have 'one for the road' is to destroy the server's confidence in her training and to invite liability.

Designated drivers

Many hotels and clubs have found it successful to offer a designated driver (one person in a group who will not drink alcohol, in order to drive the group safely home) free soft drinks or some other complimentary item. Staff can be trained to ask whether there is a designated driver in a group and, if so, to present that person with a badge or pin which will identify him for the rest of the evening.

Alcohol awareness

Since beverage staff will be called upon to make judgements on a patron's level of intoxication, it is necessary to provide training on general guidelines. A standard drink may be defined as one which contains about 10 grams of pure alcohol. The volume of the standard drink will vary according to the alcoholic strength of the beverage. In general, it is easiest to remember that the following drinks are roughly equal:

- two 285 mL glasses of light beer (2 to 3% alcohol)
- one 285 mL glass of heavy or full-strength beer (4 to 5% alcohol)
- one 120 mL glass of table wine (11 to 13% alcohol)
- one 60 mL glass of port, sherry or other fortified wine (18 to 20% alcohol)
- one 30 mL nip of standard spirit (35 to 40% alcohol).

Whether a standard drink is mixed, served with ice, combined with other drinks or served in a cocktail makes no difference: it is the amount of pure alcohol in it that produces the intoxicating effect. Intoxication varies considerably according to a person's age, weight, sex and metabolism. As a rough rule of thumb, an average male would be likely to fail a '.05' driving breath test if he had consumed more than three or four standard drinks in one hour without food. A female would prob-ably reach the same level after two or three standard drinks. (Note that cocktails usually contain more than one standard drink—sometimes as many as three.) It may take considerably more than this to produce visible signs of intoxication, depend-ing on the consumer's regular level of consumption, age, personality and so on. The consumption of food slows the absorption of alcohol into the blood, but does not decrease the total amount that will eventually find its way into the bloodstream. The average male metabolises about 10 grams of alcohol per hour, so if a male patron consumes one standard drink in 60 minutes, his blood alcohol level will stay roughly constant. Any more than that will increase it.

In general the licensee, restaurateur or Food and Beverage Manager is expected to put in place a visible program to prevent irresponsible consumption of alcohol. This should include security measures to prevent entry by under-age patrons, to remove patrons who have become aggressive or intoxicated, and to ensure that the surrounding community is not unduly disturbed. Other steps might be to offer a designated driver benefits or provide a courtesy bus for patrons. Full food service should be available whenever alcohol is served, and staff must be well trained in their legal responsibilities when dealing with patrons who may be intoxicated or under age. Notices may be posted to inform or remind customers of the licensing laws. With such a program in place, the weight of evidence is in favour of the licensee. If a court is asked to determine whether a breach has been committed (where an under-age drinker, for instance, has managed to obtain alcohol), consideration will usually be given to the licensee's *intent* to prevent such a breach.

On the other hand a club, hotel or tavern that promotes drinking competi-tions, 'two-for-one' offers, free alcohol or heavily discounted drinks will be seen as encouraging excessive consumption. If the licensee does little to prevent drunken-ness, or turns a blind eye to under-age drinking, then little sympathy can be expected in the Licensing Court or in a civil liability suit.

Identifying the market

In the same way as a menu should be designed to suit the customers who are expected to use it, so the choice of beverages offered for sale should be tailored to suit your clientele. To the professional Food and Beverage Manager, dispensing draught beer to a thirsty crowd in the public bar is really no different from maintaining a superb cellar of vintage wines for a discerning restaurant clientele. The point is not which product is sold, but that it is sold professionally, responsibly and profitably. To this end, you will need to be as familiar with beer reticulation systems as you are with the finer vintages of Grange Hermitage, or the exact ingredients of a Singapore Sling.

There is no point in offering a complete cocktail bar, with all the stock, equipment and specially trained staff that implies, if your customers are more interested in purchasing jugs of draught beer. So the first step is to understand exactly what market you are trying to service, then fit the stock and equipment to suit.

Beverage outlets

The public bar

The public bar, in a traditional tavern or hotel, is an area offering casual seating and minimum dress requirements, draught beer on tap and an informal atmosphere. It may be a principal profit centre for the establishment, or something tacked on as an afterthought. The attraction may be music (weekend jazz, bands, solo acts, dance music), food (business lunches, counter meals, simple buffets), or location (a riverside or seafront setting, a lobby or station bar). Some managers establish successful connections with sporting clubs, associations or a TAB office. In the public bar, the quality and range of beers served will be important, and there may be potential for simple cocktails, quality wines by the glass or non-alcoholic drinks. Some city bars have found good coffee to be at least as popular as, and often more profitable than, beer. There is a temptation, in larger properties with multiple outlets, to overlook the public bar. This is a mistake, since it can be a significant contributor to overall profitability.

The restaurant bar

A licence to serve alcohol with meals is the most popular and widely adopted licence in Australia and New Zealand, partly because it is the easiest one to obtain. Some restaurants actually derive more profit from liquor sales than they do from food; however, as long as the requirements of a restaurant licence are adhered to, the Licensing Commission is unlikely to object. These rules may specify the type of meals served, the opening hours and even the number of tables occupied by diners at any given time. It is vital that you be familiar with these details, since violating the rules may result in a court hearing at which you will be asked to show cause why the licence should not be suspended or revoked.

Aside from the legal considerations, there are many decisions to make about the types and range of beverages served. In short, the range of drinks should match the style of food and the type of customer served. In a smart city bistro serving

THE FOOD AND BEVERAGE MANAGER

modern cuisine, it will be essential to offer quality wines by the glass. In a fast-service family restaurant, a limited range of bottled beers and inexpensive wines would suffice. Installing a draught beer system would be of questionable value in a small, ethnic restaurant, but it would be a necessity in a large, open-air café in a holiday area. Since a modern beer reticulation system might easily cost $10 000 or more to install, this is a decision best taken early in the planning stages.

The cocktail bar or nightclub

Décor and atmosphere play an important part in the success of a cocktail bar or nightclub, whether it be an intimate, romantic piano bar or a large and very busy discothèque. Entertainment is also important, and the sensible manager will allow a substantial budget for this and the advertising that goes with it. Bar staff will obviously need to be skilled in cocktail making, and may be chosen for their speed, stamina and skill at dealing with guests. Particular attention must be paid to security and the danger of having under-age persons on the premises. The nightclub business is perhaps more fickle than any other, and the Food and Beverage Manager or Club Manager will need to stay well in touch with the clientele to anticipate changes in fashion.

The service bar

The service bar supplies wines, beers, spirits and mixed drinks to table staff, who then serve them to guests. The requirements are slightly different from those of a customer-service bar, since speed, accuracy and strict stock control are the primary objectives. A service bar may be a permanent facility, or a temporary setup for a banquet or special function. It may be elaborate enough to prepare cocktails, or simply dispense bottled wines and beers for a wedding or a party. Even a temporary service bar will need lighting, refrigeration, a cash register, a glass washer and glass racks, if it is to function smoothly. Note that if one bar is expected to perform two roles, for instance a cocktail bar that also dispenses bottled wine and mixed drinks for the restaurant, it is important to consider both functions when you are planning layout and equipment.

The bottle shop or takeaway

Facilities for customers to purchase alcoholic beverages for consumption off the premises may vary from part of a counter in the public bar to a 2000 square metre drive-in liquor barn. What is appropriate for your establishment is a retail marketing decision that will depend on the location, demographics, existing competition and best use of available space. Specialist planning advice from liquor retailing experts will be needed to determine layout, equipment, advertising and stock selection. Many independent hotels and taverns choose to join national liquor marketing schemes to take advantage of improved buying power, specialist advice and joint advertising.

Room service and the mini-bar

It is customary in larger hotels to provide 24-hour room service for guests, with a limited menu of snacks and beverages that can be prepared and served by a single room service attendant. The preferred system for liquor control is to provide room service with its own secured stock of wines, beers and spirits for use when all other bars in the hotel are closed. This stock should be kept small, and replenished daily against recorded sales. The mini-bar is a selection of alcoholic beverages, soft drinks and snack foods placed in a guest's room. The guests help themselves to what they want, and then (at least in theory) record their consumption on a mini-bar docket. The high rate of pilferage, substitution, unrecorded consumption and straight theft means that the mini-bar is rarely a profitable operation in a hotel. Losses can be controlled by the use of vending machines or electronic key systems, but then the capital cost of outfitting the rooms rises sharply. The best method of controlling losses is to make sure that consumption is promptly recorded and charged for. To this end, you will need sufficient staff to check and replenish all room mini-bars as early as possible in the morning. Particular attention should, of course, be given to check-outs, and undocumented shortages should be called down to the front desk immediately.

The wine cellar

Choosing a wine list that is appropriate and successful for a food and beverage operation is no easy task, since the Food and Beverage Manager must balance a complicated set of variables. First, she must determine what the customers actually want to buy, which is not always the same thing they wish to see on the wine list. She must carefully weigh up the cost of keeping operating capital tied up in the wine cellar against the need to have an adequate range of wines on hand to suit a variety of palates. It will certainly be necessary to spend time and money training specialist beverage staff in the correct selling and service of wine. To keep a $20 000 wine cellar, and then rely on an untrained and ill-equipped table server to sell that wine, is foolish in the extreme. There are few subjects in the realm of food and beverage service more wrapped up in snobbery, pretentiousness and the concealment of ignorance than the consumption of quality wines. This creates, in many customers, a disinclination to go anywhere near the subject for fear of embarrassment. A good Food and Beverage Manager will understand that the most important step in achieving profitable wine sales is to make it easy for the customer to buy it.

In the golden age of the grand hotels in Europe—roughly from the 1890s to the Second World War—it was a matter of some pride, and no small measure of showmanship, that a great hotel should have a great wine cellar. Wine lists with several hundred different vintages were by no means uncommon, and many grand hotels were able to offer superb Bordeaux and Burgundy wines that had been aging gracefully in the hotel cellars for twenty years or more. The hotels made a practice of buying up the finest château wines as soon as they were released and laying them down for aging, with no intention of selling them for at least ten years—as in the case of a premier grand cru from a famous vineyard such as Château Lafite-Rothschild or Château Latour. In the post-war years there were severe changes to the economic climate in which hotels operated, notably a dramatic rise in the cost of labour, increased competition, and greater pressure to show a speedy return on investment. Many of the great hotel cellars were broken up and sold off, and only a handful of the oldest and most prestigious hotels were able to retain their expensive, and by now irreplaceable, wine cellars.

Many in the industry would argue that we are now in a modern 'golden age', with increasingly luxurious and expensive hotels being built all around the world. The wine list has once again become a point of showmanship and prestige, but some things have changed for good, and there is no longer any justification for keeping very large and costly cellars. First, the demand for high return on investment does not allow a purchase that will have to be kept for ten or fifteen years before it is sold, however high the eventual mark-up may be. Second, the range of high-quality wines has widened to include hundreds of excellent New World producers, so that keeping a comprehensive cellar is now a much more difficult proposition than it was in 1921. Third, the market has changed, as more people of relatively modest income have begun to travel and use hotels. These customers will buy and enjoy a bottle of good wine at a reasonable price, but they will absolutely refuse to pay the $200 or $300 per bottle for a first-growth Bordeaux that would represent an adequate return for the hotelier. Finally, the wines themselves have changed, with vignerons and blenders deliberately seeking to make wines that are ready for drinking as soon as they are released. Wines do not always improve in storage, especially if storage conditions are less than ideal. Stock deterioration is less of a risk if the turnover is brisk.

Several strategies may be used by the Food and Beverage Manager to offer a good range of quality wines, and at the same time be able to rely on lively sales and a reasonable return. In nearly all successful hotels and restaurants, there is a tendency to specialise in a particular type of wine. In an Italian restaurant, obviously, it will be a good idea to offer several Italian wines, ranging from the inexpensive to the premium. Customers may be encouraged to order a bottle by a menu description that emphasises the great match between these wines and the style of food served. In a busy, medium-priced family restaurant, it would be wise to specialise in a selection of wines within a certain price range, say from $12 to $19 a bottle, and encourage customers to try something they have not tasted before, confident that they will not pay a lot of money for something they may not enjoy. A restaurant specialising in creative Australian cuisine would carry a selection of boutique Australian wines from small growers, and would probably offer several of them by the glass, to encourage diners to match individual flavours with the food. A seafood restaurant on the waterside would sensibly concentrate on a good range of semillons, chardonnays and sauvignon blancs, to complement the food.

Wines produced in Australia and New Zealand have achieved such high quality at comparatively reasonable prices, that there would have to be a very specific reason for carrying expensive French vintages on the wine list. If they are stocked, it is wise to keep a careful eye on sales results and drop them if they are not showing a reasonable turnover. One or two bottles of Dom Perignon in the cellar may add to the tone of the wine list, but any more than that must be justified by sales to keep a place on the list.

Sale of wine by the glass is resisted, somewhat unreasonably, by many restaurateurs who fear losses from spoiled stock. The modern method of gassing bottles with inert nitrogen and resealing them means that opened wine may be kept for several days without appreciable loss of quality, and the equipment is cheap and simple to use. The advantage of sales by the glass, of course, is that customers will readily pay $3 or $4 to taste an interesting wine, where they would resist paying $24 to open the bottle. Especially if the bottle is brought to the table for pouring, the customer perceives a greater value in the $4 glass of bottled wine than in the $4 half litre of generic riesling. Tastes are changing in the restaurant-going public, and it is no longer acceptable to most patrons to be served a carafe of poor-quality cask wine as the house standard.

A requirement for accuracy

It will come as no surprise that there is strict government regulation of the standard measures used for the dispensing and sale of alcoholic beverages. While the local names for glass sizes may vary (a middy, a pony, a schooner or a pot, for instance), the law takes no notice and specifies the volume in millilitres (mL). Metric measure is the Australian standard and, though there are minor variations between the States and Territories, legislation is fairly uniform across the country. For the dispensing of draught beer, most regulations require that the glass be 'badged' or indelibly marked with the volume in millilitres. The standard measure for spirits is 30 mL, which neatly divides a standard bottle (750 mL) into 25 portions. This measure can be halved (15 mL) or doubled (60 mL). Whole bottles of beer, wine, cider and so on may be served without further measuring, as long as the label specifies the metric volume clearly. Wine is a notable exception to most of these rules, and may be dispensed in a variety of glasses. This does not, however, remove the requirement to specify the amount dispensed for a given price, if asked by the customer to do so. 120 mL is the usual measure for table wine, and 60 mL for fortified wines such as vermouth, port, sherry or ginger wine. If table wine is sold by the carafe, the hotelier must specify the volume of that carafe (500 mL, 750 mL or 1 L). The local Department of Consumer Affairs, or Weights and Measures, will often provide written guidelines for the hotelier. It is not wise to presume that you know all you need to know, since regulations vary slightly from one State to another and change from time to time.

Permissible measures for dispensing drinks may include the nip measure (a standard 15, 30 or 60 mL metal cup, stamped with the volume), badged glasses, bottle-top nip pourers (only those marked, sealed and approved by Weights and Measures), optic measures (both manual and electronic) or bottles, tins and cartons clearly marked with the volume in litres or millilitres. It is not permissible to dispense spirits by the glassful, carafe, cup or pour, unless this measure is standardised by metric volume and the customer is aware of what that measure is.

In practice, this is in the interest of the hotelier as well as the consumer, since we need to know exactly how much liquor is being served for a given price. If the drink being served has more than one ingredient, as in a cocktail, then you will need to specify exactly what quantities are used, in what order they are poured, and the correct glass and garnish for the drink. Every one of these 'compound' beverages should have a standard recipe card, prepared with the assistance of the bar manager or head bar attendant. The cards should be stored in waterproof sleeves, preferably in a simple ring binder, so that additions and deletions can be made easily, and a copy of the full set must be available in each bar.

HARVEY WALLBANGER		Date checked: 7/8/97
GLASS: 225 mL Tulip Cocktail	**Qty**	**Price**
GARNISH: Orange wheel, cocktail straws (2)	ea.	0.40
INGREDIENTS:		
Ice		
Vodka	30mL	0.82
Fresh Orange Juice	120 mL	0.35
Galliano Liqueur	30 mL	1.54
METHOD: Fill glass with ice. Add 30 mL vodka, fill with orange juice 1 cm below rim. Float 30 mL Galliano on top, garnish with orange wheel and cocktail straws.	**Total cost** 3.11 **Sales price** 7.50 **Bev. cost** 41.5%	

Figure 6.1 Standard beverage recipe card

In addition to the drinks poured and paid for, there will inevitably be some mispours, spills, breakages or returned drinks. It should be made clear to all the bar staff that these variances will make a difference to their results at the end of the week, and so must be recorded. If a draught beer system is in place, it is vital that overpours and spills, including the contents of the drip trays, are not discarded until they have been measured and written down. A stainless steel bucket of a marked capacity (such as 10 litres) may be useful for this purpose. If one particularly careless bartender regularly pours away 16 glasses of beer per shift, the revenue for that shift will be down 16 times the price of a glass, against the revenue you would expect for that amount of stock consumed. If you explain to the bartender that recording the quantity discarded will help explain why his takings are down, you may convince him that it is a good idea to do so. If you notice unusually high wastage on a particular shift, it may indicate that more training is required, or a technical fault needs fixing. If you believe that monitoring wastage is too much trouble, then your profit-and-loss figures will have a wide margin of error built into them, and you will never be precisely sure what is going on in the bar.

Computerised point-of-sale terminals, with automatic stock control features, have been touted by some in the industry as the answer to all problems. Because a point-of-sale terminal can record every drink paid for, and automatically calculate the standard ingredients of that drink, it is presumed that tight inventory control and accurate beverage costing will naturally result. The experienced Food and Beverage Manager regards these claims with scepticism. No computer is more accurate than the information typed into it by fallible humans. Computers are remarkably dim when it comes to detecting dishonesty. Computerised point-of-sale tills may slow down customer service badly, while staff struggle to fix errors, perform unfamiliar procedures or understand why the computer refuses to do what is asked of it. Sales data recorded by a good point-of-sale system are valuable and useful, but simply recording a thing is not the same as managing it.

It is more important to select and train good staff, and make sure they understand the need for accurate, professional service of standardised drinks. If you can then devise a method of measuring this accuracy, and reward those who achieve it, you will be managing the people in your bar service operation rather than the machines. In the end result this is far more effective than any computer system, however sophisticated.

Once standards have been accurately set and clearly explained, you can monitor the value of the beverages requisitioned into a particular bar and compare expected returns with actual figures. To illustrate the idea, let us imagine that the pool bar in a resort hotel carries only four beverages. (In a real bar, of course, there would be several dozen.) Usage and anticipated revenue for one week are shown in Table 6.1 (see next page).

Table 6.1   Usage and anticipated revenue for a pool bar for one week

Item	Scotch	Beer, bottled	House wine	Crème de menthe
Usage last week (bottles)	4	72	11	1
Bottle size	750 mL	375 mL	750 mL	700 mL
Portions per bottle	25	1	6	23
Price per portion	$3.50	$4.00	$3.00	$3.75
Anticipated revenue	$350.00	$288.00	$198.00	$86.25

Total anticipated revenue	$922.25
Recorded wastage	$10.50
Adjusted total	$911.75
Actual revenue	$899.10
Variance	2.5%

In this example, usage has been determined by the number of bottles requisitioned in one week. To be really accurate, we would need to do a stocktake in the bar to measure the actual consumption, since a bottle of Scotch on the shelf can be nearly empty or almost full. Allowance should be made for inter-bar transfers and special price promotions, but for this exercise we are interested in the pattern, rather than an absolute number. To arrive at the variance percentage, we take the anticipated revenue ($922.25) and subtract the actual revenue ($899.10). This leaves us with a variance ($23.15), which includes the cost of spills and waste. Using the familiar method for calculating a percentage cost, we arrive at a useful figure:

$$\text{Variance cost} \div \text{total revenue} \times 100 = \text{percentage variance}$$
$$\$23.15 \div \$922.25 = 0.025 \times 100 = 2.5\%$$

This calculation can be done quickly, on a daily or weekly basis, to provide a running report on the performance of each bar outlet. If the percentage variance were to rise suddenly, closer monitoring of that outlet would be called for. A high variance can be caused by one or more factors: inaccurate requisitions, unrecorded transfers, dishonesty, excessive waste, sloppy portion control or theft of stock. In any case, you would want to investigate further.

Something to watch for

One of the more unusual scams recorded in the hotel industry is the practice of bringing extra stock into an operation without recording it. The dishonest bartender, knowing that a 300 per cent profit is not unusual on a bottle of spirits, will bring several bottles of his or her own liquor into the bar, then skim off that amount of revenue from the sales. There will be no stock missing, and the hotel's beverage cost figures will look normal, but bar takings will be inexplicably down.

Beverage pricing

Setting the sales price of a bottle of wine, a cocktail or a glass of beer is an exercise in judging the market, calculating overheads and knowing the real cost of stock purchased. In some cases (draught beer served in the public bar, for instance), there may be recommended prices set by your local Hotels Association. These are not compulsory, but customers will expect to see some added value if they are asked to pay higher prices. Though the general principles are the same as those applied to setting menu prices, there are some particular differences in beverage service that you will need to allow for.

With very few exceptions, every licensed premises will pay a licensing fee to the Government, based on the amount of total purchases during the financial year. This may be payable in instalments, or at the end of the reporting period. The licence fee varies between States and Territories, and between specific types of licensed premises. In general, the fee is seldom less than 10 per cent of total purchases, and there may be special provisions for the type or strength of alcohol purchased. It is essential that the Food and Beverage Manager be familiar with the exact provisions of the applicable Liquor Act, since these fees will be part of the real cost of beverages as purchased.

Unlike food, which is purchased in bulk, then portioned and further prepared before serving it to guests, beverages are often sold directly to guests in the same package in which they were purchased. These bottles or cans are the same ones the customer can buy from a retail shop, so it is not uncommon that your customers will know the retail price. It comes as a surprise to many customers to learn that hotels and restaurants often pay as much, if not more, for their liquor supplies as does the public. By the time the licence fees are calculated, there is seldom any advantage for the hotelier, even when buying in bulk.

When a restaurant charges $23 for a piece of grilled fish served with vegetables or a salad, the restaurant-going public does not object, as long as the product is fresh and well-prepared, the service good and the surroundings comfortable. Customers are willing to accept that price, even if they are well aware that 200 grams of fish, some butter and a few vegetables are unlikely to cost more than $6 or $7. However, if the restaurateur stocks a bottle of wine that commonly sells for $7 in a retail liquor barn, customers may regard a price of $23 on the wine list as unacceptable. Even when it is pointed out that the sales price has to cover numerous overheads, labour, glassware and so on, they remain unconvinced: a 225 per cent mark-up is too much to bear. Curiously, these same patrons are ready to accept as much as a 300 per cent mark-up on a can of beer or 500 per cent on a glass of post-mix lemonade without complaint; it is wine, for some reason, that arouses the deepest feelings. There is no point in fighting this perception; you simply allow for it when pricing your wine list. One way of doing this is to avoid the top-selling, instantly recognisable products from leading winemakers. Choose, instead, less-known but high-quality wines from smaller vineyards. You may also take advantage of the fact that a glass of premium wine for $4.50 is often seen as better value than a bottle of the same wine for $27.

In the chapter on menu pricing, we saw that it was important to correctly measure labour cost, overheads and desired profit and build these calculations into menu prices. The same principle applies to beverage pricing, but in this case a 'per cover' cost will not serve. Customers may consume only one meal per visit, but you are hoping that they will consume more than one drink. How many drinks are sold is easy to record on electronic cash registers, so we have all the figures we will need to apply overhead costs on a 'per drink' basis, as in Table 6.2.

Table 6.2   Trading figures (beverage)—Central City Hotel

	$	%
Beverage sales last year	854 000	(100)
Beverage purchases (including licence fee)	264 750	(31)
Labour cost	281 800	(33)
Overheads	102 500	(12)
TOTAL COSTS	$649 050	(76)
PROFIT BEFORE TAX	$204 950	(24)
No. of drinks served	305 200	
Average price	$2.80	
Average labour cost	$0.92	
Average overhead cost	$0.34	
Average profit per drink	$0.67	

If we calculate for a carton of Australian beer purchased at $23.50 per carton and subject to a 10% licence fee, we get a price of $23.50 + $2.35 = $25.85. This yields a per-bottle price of $1.08 (rounded up to the nearest cent). If we than add an averaged amount for labour ($0.92), overheads ($0.34) and profit ($0.67), we reach a break-even sales price of $3.01. From this point we can make adjustments up or down according to anticipated volume of sales, competition, recommended price and so on. These figures give us an average minimum mark-up for each drink sold:

$$\text{Cost} + 0.92 + 0.34 + 0.67 = \$1.93$$

Sales below the minimum must be compensated for by sales above it, in order to reach budget. Note that if volume were to drop (new competition next door, changes in the market), this minimum mark-up would have to be increased, or labour and overheads cut, to retain profitability.

To calculate the price of a bottle of wine, we multiply the minimum mark-up by the number of drinks in a bottle (6) to reach an acceptable per-bottle mark-up.

$$6 \times \$1.93 = \$11.58$$

If the cost of a bottle is $10.00, then the wine list price must be close to $21.58. Many restaurateurs still use a percentage mark-up for their wine list (for example, cost + 200%) even though this creates much too wide a price spread on the list. Compare an expensive wine with an inexpensive wine, using both methods (Table 6.3).

Table 6.3 Comparison of mark-up method and contribution method

	Cost $	Mark-up $	Sales price $
Premium wine:			
200% mark-up	27.50	55.00	82.50
contribution method	27.50	11.58	39.50
Inexpensive wine:			
200% mark-up	5.40	10.80	16.50
contribution method	5.40	11.58	17.00

At the top of the range, the percentage mark-up puts the wine out of reach of most customers, severely restricting the number of bottles you are likely to sell. At the bottom of the list, where most of the sales will occur, the sales price determined by the percentage method actually ensures a 50 cent loss on each bottle sold.

Using a minimum mark-up method, we are reasonably certain, looking at past performance, that our overhead cost, labour cost and an acceptable level of profit will be maintained with an average mark-up of $1.93 per drink. This translates to $11.58 per bottle of wine. At the top end of the list, we have a much more attractive price for the premium bottle, which will stimulate more sales. At the bottom end, we are confident that all sales will still result in a profit. This method can easily be used in the other direction: if you wish to list a bottle of wine at $19.50, because you believe that is a critical price level and customer demand will be high, then you simply calculate (sales price – contribution = cost as purchased) and seek out an attractive wine at that price, for example:

$$\$19.50 - \$11.58 = \$7.92$$

Setting the price of spirits is a similar exercise. If a bottle of premium top shelf Scotch whisky is purchased at $36.50 per 750 mL bottle, subject to a 10% licence fee, the cost as purchased is $40.15 ($36.50 + $3.65). The portion cost is then calculated:

$$750 \text{ mL} \div 30 \text{ mL portion} = 25 \text{ portions per bottle}$$
$$\$40.15 \div 25 = \$1.60$$
$$\$1.60 + \$1.93 \text{ (minimum mark-up)} = \$3.53$$

You believe the market will bear a sales price of $4.50 for this whisky, and set the price accordingly. Sales at this level will provide a 'cushion' which allows for a certain amount of waste, reduced price promotions, less profitable sales on other drinks and so on.

Draught beer is a special case, since the cost price is often negotiable according to the quantity regularly purchased from the brewery. It is not unusual for brewing companies to offer a range of incentives to the hotelier, to encourage purchasing of the company's product. These may include the cost of installing reticulation systems, painting and signage on the building, or even 'free' kegs of beer. Draught beer is traditionally a source of healthy profits for the hotelier, as long as an attractive price is negotiated with the supplier and care is taken to minimise waste. Because the product is served from a reticulation system (a network of kegs, pipes, refrigeration and taps), volume is more difficult to measure than for beverages purchased in discrete packages (cans or bottles). Though beer is dispensed in measured quantities (200 mL, 285 mL, 425 mL), a considerable quantity can be lost in service.

Inaccurate settings of gas pressure can result in excessively 'heady' beer, which causes waste as the beer is drawn from the tap. Low volume of sales (for a specialty beer, for instance) can result in over-gassing, which also produces waste. Beer pipes must be flushed and cleaned daily to maintain sanitary conditions and a 'bright' appearance; this also involves some inevitable waste. Unskilled bar staff may pour beer in such a way as to waste it, and finally, a small amount of beer will always be left in a keg after it has been disconnected. The best way to account for these various losses is to pay attention to the actual consumption, measured at the keg.

If sales records for a week indicate that 4207 285-mL glasses (or equivalent) have been sold, then it easy to calculate the total volume:

$$285 \text{ mL} \times 4207 = 1199 \text{ L}$$

A standard keg contains 50 litres, so we would expect to have used 24 kegs. A quick stocktake is done, and we find that 24.5 kegs have actually been used. (A partial keg is measured by weight; a full keg weighs 63 kg, of which 13 kg is the weight of the keg and 50 kg is the weight of the product.) The half keg, or 25 litres of beer, has been lost in mispours, cleaning waste or unrecorded sales. In the same way that food cost is measured by the actual cost of the ingredients ready to serve, so the beverage cost must allow for this margin of loss in draught beer systems. This variance between volume sold and volume consumed will also help the manager to determine how effectively waste is being controlled.

Bar layout and work flow

Other than a kitchen in the middle of service, there is no area in a hotel more physically and mentally demanding than a very busy bar. With customers standing four deep waiting for service and table staff from the restaurant clamouring for attention, the bar attendant has to move very quickly, keep several orders in mind, handle cash, pour drinks and prepare cocktails all at the same time. There is no place in a busy bar for poor design, thoughtless layout or equipment that does not work. It is squarely the responsibility of the Food and Beverage Manager to see that the bar is well designed, well equipped and well maintained. If you take over management of an existing operation it may be difficult, if not impossible, to have the cold-rooms moved or the ceiling raised, but simple rearrangement of storage, small equipment and patterns of work can overcome a number of problems. The requirements are straightforward.

Location, décor and access

Many of the same principles discussed in the chapter on restaurant design (Chapter 5) apply here. Considerable thought must be given to traffic flow of guests and staff, ease of re-supply during service and sufficient equipment to do the job.

Guests will often accept crowded conditions in a bar as part of the 'atmosphere', but they will not for long tolerate real discomfort or lack of adequate service. Décor and lighting play a great part in creating a comfortable environment, and professional interior designers can achieve some astounding 'makeovers' when given the opportunity. However stunning the design from the customer's point of view, however, a bar is also a working environment, and here the Food and Beverage Manager must ensure that the setup is practical and workable.

Safety

Any working area with very busy people, confined spaces, wet surfaces and electrical appliances calls for a thorough safety audit at frequent intervals. It is important to check floor surfaces, in particular, to prevent slips and falls. Electrical equipment such as blenders, juicers, cash registers and ice machines must be in good condition and adequately grounded. Glass breakage is almost inevitable, so allow for it when siting ice bins, glass storage racks and food preparation areas. Food hygiene precautions (discussed in Chapter 10) will also come into play when handling perishable ingredients such as milk and cream. Many problems can be avoided by paying attention to the correct placement of equipment, adequate walkways, sufficient working surfaces, safe storage and so on.

Security

There are several aspects of security in bar operations. Relatively large amounts of cash will be handled, and you will need to make provision for avoiding losses by removing cash from tills to a safe at regular intervals and by guarding against employee dishonesty. Under-ringing, short-changing and simple theft are, unfortunately, still with us in the industry and a tiny minority of dishonest bar staff make it necessary to take precautions such as unscheduled till readings, spot stocktakes and even surveillance cameras. An unusual number of till errors, banknotes or coins kept loose near the cash register, or notations made regularly on scrap paper are all possible signs of dishonest practice.

Storage and work surfaces

Operating even a simple bar requires refrigerated storage, an adequate supply of ice and water, a glass washer and racks, secure storage for back-up stock and display shelves in sight of the customer. Just as important as the volume of available storage space is the question of how things will get into it and come out of it. A large cupboard for storage of red wines, for instance, will be of little use if the bar staff have to climb a step-ladder to reach it. A high-capacity ice machine will be very welcome, unless staff have to fight their way through a crush of people to reach it. Adequate work surfaces must be provided for racks of clean glasses, glass drainage and washing, and cocktail preparation, for the maximum number of staff who will be working behind the bar.

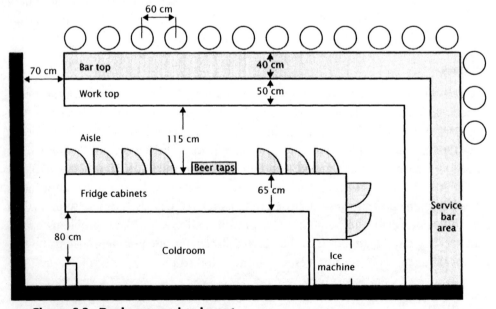

Figure 6.2 Dual-purpose bar layout

Figure 6.2 illustrates some standard minimum measurements for a typical dual-purpose bar, which serves customers sitting or standing at the bar as well as table staff supplying one or more restaurants. The service bar is a dedicated area, so there is no interference from table staff and bar customers. Refrigerated cabinets store white wines, beers and soft drinks for the restaurant, and the ice machine is conveniently located for filling ice buckets. The cold-room is of the double-sided type, so that kegs and cartons can be stored at serving temperature and cabinet shelves can be re-stocked from the rear. Access to this cold-room is along a clear corridor which does not interfere with customer service.

The walkway for staff is a serviceable 115 cm, which allows for two people to pass each other easily. The work bench is 50 cm deep to allow for bottle setup, ice bins, glass racks, cash register, cutting boards and so on. The bar top (approximately 110 cm high) is higher than the work surface (approximately 85 cm) and is 40 cm wide—about the average forearm reach for an adult and a comfortable width for patrons sitting at the bar. Bar stools, which may be fixed or movable, are set at least 60 cm from centre to centre, or may be absent altogether in a very busy bar such as a theatre lobby bar or a nightclub. Refrigerated cabinet doors are no more than 40 cm wide, so that they may be opened without blocking another staff member who wants to pass. The cabinets themselves are no more than 65 cm deep, a comfortable full-arm reach for the average person.

All of these measurements are conservative, and there would be few complaints from bar staff who had more room to move around and work. The volume of business done by the bar may affect some critical measurements. In an extremely busy operation, a wider walkway may be needed if five, six or more staff are expected to work behind the bar at once.

Stock control

Because alcohol is expensive, portable and almost universally popular, it is necessary to take reasonable steps to ensure that it gets where it is going to and that it is correctly recorded, sold and paid for. Designing a system that works is a matter of balancing efficiency with accuracy and practicality with security. An air-tight system that requires four signatures at every step will soon break down because it is impractical to work with. On the other hand, an overly casual attitude to beverage storage and requisition will inevitably lead to abuse, loss of profits and stock.

To begin, we might concentrate on what the system has to do. You will need to know how many drinks have been sold, and how much money has been taken for them. You will need to know how much stock has been taken from the stores, and how much is left in the bar. It will certainly be useful to know which products are the most popular, and it might be useful to know how much each customer spent on average. These are basic bits of information that will help you to manage your beverage operation and make sensible decisions about what to do in future.

Some managers lose track of what is important and what is not: though it may be of some conceivable interest to know how many cocktail straws were consumed last week, it is not a vital piece of information. A clever requisition form which has a box for every possible detail, and six copies for distribution, will do little good if staff are too busy to fill it out. Worse, they may actually take the time to fill it out— a job much less demanding than serving customers or moving stock to where it is needed.

The basic means of control are the requisition, the standard measure and the cash register.

The requisition

The simplest form of requisition control is the 'par stock' system, or 'one full for one empty' system. This means that a standard level of stock is calculated for each bar, taking into account the amount of expected business, average consumption in the past and the particular beverages that are most popular. Once this is established, bar staff are trained to keep all empty wine and spirit bottles and to complete a requisition at the end of the shift, or end of the day, to replace what has been used. The advantages of this system are that it makes requisition writing easy, accurate and quick, it is simple to understand, and the value of the stock in a given bar is unlikely to vary much over the long term. It is a good system for small bars and for bars that use only casual, part-time staff. The weaknesses of this system are that a missing bottle (taken away by a customer to her room, for instance) creates problems, bottle rubbish may accumulate in busy times, and an unexpected run on a particular beverage may necessitate an emergency after-hours entry to stores or an inter-bar transfer. It does not work well for control of canned beer or soft drinks, and control of draught beer is, at best, approximate.

Another method is to set a given value for the stock kept in a bar, based on the anticipated revenue for each item. If the par stock is valued at $8000, then any further requisitions will be added to that value (for example, one 750 mL bottle of house Scotch = 25 portions @ $3.00 per portion = $75.00) and daily revenues subtracted from it. The advantages are that all stock in the bar, including soft drinks, draught beer and so on are taken into account, and there is no need to keep empty bottles in the bar for checking. Beverage cost is easily monitored by comparing the value of stock put into the bar to the sales revenue received over the same period. The disadvantages are that inexperienced staff may requisition too much or too little, there may be more than one sales value for a given drink (for example, happy hour prices or mixers with spirits) and standard recipes must be recalculated whenever there is a price change for any ingredient.

Computerised point-of-sale systems, in theory, provide highly accurate control of inventory. Every drink that is sold is recorded by the machine with a wealth of detail about the ingredients, the cost, the time of the sale and the staff member. The advantages are clear: plenty of data on the nature of your sales, a precise record of which particular drink is sold, rapid one-step recalculation of prices, timed shift to happy hour prices, and even computer-generated requisitions. The disadvantages are that the real world does not always agree with the electronic one: small keying errors can become major problems, and the machine may not understand wastage or mispours, or customers who ask for non-standard drinks. Any discrepancy between what is on the shelf and what the computer thinks ought to be on the shelf can quickly create a time-consuming tangle.

In practice most hotels, clubs and restaurants use some combination of these three methods. In the normal run of events, bottle-for-bottle requisitions are used for spirits and table wines unless a special function, or an explainable loss of a bottle, requires more. A close track is kept of the value of stock going into each bar, by costing out daily requisitions and applying the figure to a month-to-date beverage cost percentage. Electronic recording of transfers is compared against physical stocktakes to determine where problem areas may lie.

The standard measure

As discussed above, both the law of the land and sensible management practice require that the dispensing of beverages be measured accurately and fairly. Staff training is the start, since people cannot be expected to serve correctly unless they have been shown what is required. Spot checks for accuracy, correct recipe and garnish may be conducted at irregular intervals. If an electronic record of sales is available, a spot stocktake can be done to determine how accurate the system is. The Food and Beverage Manager checks the last time a bottle of Chivas Regal was requisitioned by the cocktail bar. On that day, the bottle would have been full. The number of recorded sales of Chivas Regal since that date is looked up. In the bar, he measures how many servings remain in the bottle. A quick check should cover a handful of randomly selected beverages. If there is no electronic record available, a full bar stocktake should be scheduled four or five times a year on irregular dates. Waste and mispours should be carefully recorded and priced weekly.

The cash register

This machine, whether linked to a larger system or free-standing, is the most effective means of beverage control other than the stocktake. All sales should be recorded, including complimentary drinks, management drinks, replacement drinks and the like, so that there is no excuse for a beverage being served without a sale being rung up. Occasional discreet checks should be made for evidence of under-ringing (say, serving drinks worth $10, but only ringing up $7 and pocketing the difference), over-charging, substitution of one drink for another, passing out drinks to friends or employees without charge, or personal consumption.

There are more sophisticated systems, so bar staff should not be given access to X or Z readings on a till (X readings print out a summary of all charges and department readings; Z readings reset all totals to zero), nor to the journal tape (an internal printed record of every transaction made during a given period). When 'cashing up' a till, the duty manager or bar manager should do the X reading, then ask the bartender for the cash amount indicated on the summary tape, along with any records of charges. Only then should the remaining float be counted and any discrepancy noted.

Charge accounts, either to room numbers or to credit cards, are another source of fraud in a hotel bar. An employee who retains a room number or credit card number may later process an additional charge to that account and substitute this docket for cash from the till. Unsigned charge dockets, notes of numbers near the till and unusually frequent guest queries of bar charges are danger signals.

It must be reiterated that the overwhelming majority of bar staff are honest and hard-working, and enjoy providing professional service to their customers. The industry could hardly function if this were not the case. However, because bar service provides a mixture of opportunity, temptation and easily portable items of value, it is only responsible for the Food and Beverage Manager to take sensible precautions without creating an atmosphere of distrust or fear of accusation. For the honest employee, the best system is one that is plain, open, accurate and fair.

CHAPTER SUMMARY

The responsibility of controlling an effective and profitable beverage operation requires many skills in a Food and Beverage Manager. He or she must be familiar with—even expert on—a wide range of products, from mineral waters to single-malt Scotch whiskies. It is necessary to understand how marketing decisions are made to selectively sell products to particular groups of people, and to realise that it makes no difference whether a $100 000 profit is made by selling cartons of beer or imported French wines: the professional Food and Beverage Manager must be able to do either.

The hotel industry is tightly controlled by a net of laws and regulations which apply to building standards, weights and measures, customer care, health and safety. In particular, the direction of current licensing regulations is to encourage responsible service of alcohol and prevent abuse. The Food and Beverage Manager is expected not only to understand these regulations, but to put effective systems in place that will guarantee compliance.

Standardisation and stock control are just as important in beverage service as they are in food service. Standard recipe cards, careful recording of correct measures and accurate control of requisitions are essential tools in the battle to maintain the optimum selling price and ensure a profitable result.

Understanding the principles of bar design will allow the professional manager to identify problems that can slow down service, make work more difficult for staff or inconvenience customers.

Because of its very nature, the beverage service industry is open to occasional security problems and to a number of careless or dishonest practices. The Food and Beverage Manager is responsible for planning sensible precautions to offset these problems, and should have a good understanding of the tools and systems at his or her disposal.

REVIEW QUESTIONS

1 What aspects of beverage service are controlled by licensing laws?

2 Describe the key principles of responsible service of alcohol, and how they might be implemented in a bar or restaurant operation.

3 Give some arguments for and against the introduction of a computerised point-of-sale system in a public bar.

4 What factors should be considered when choosing a restaurant wine list?

5 If a case of wine (12 × 750 mL) is purchased wholesale at $93.10, subject to a 10% licensing fee, and you wish to sell it by the 120 mL glass, what price should be set if you wish to achieve a 29% beverage cost? What would the price be if you used the minimum mark-up method (labour cost + overhead cost + profit) and last year's records indicate an average of $1.93 per drink?

6 What are the disadvantages of the 200% mark-up system for bottled wines?

CHAPTER SEVEN

BANQUETS AND BUFFETS

Understanding banquet service and planning for a successful result

Banquet sales and customer service

Equipment and par stocks

Banquet operations, staffing levels and layout

The function sheet and the confirmation letter

A significant source of profit

'Banqueting' is a somewhat outdated term that includes many different kinds of food and beverage service. Banquet arrangements may be as simple as a boardroom lunch served for 10, or as elaborate as a theme buffet with entertainment for 600 guests. What all banquets have in common is that they are designed to meet the specific needs of a particular client, rather than the general requirements of the dining public.

The banqueting department is often an important source of profit for hotels, clubs and restaurants, and may serve to promote the image and prestige of the hotel in the wider community. A hotel chosen to cater the Lord Mayor's Gala Dinner can expect to gain valuable mention in the local media and cultivate a reputation for quality and service. The guest list at such a function may include many people who make decisions about where other dinners, conferences and seminars will be held. It pays, therefore, to do such events well, and encourage a steady stream of business in the future.

One of the attractions of banqueting, for the professional, is that the costs of the event can be measured and predicted. Knowing in advance the income for a given dinner, it is possible to predict menu cost, labour cost and overhead cost, so that a reasonable profit is assured. Compare this with the rather more risky business of staffing and purchasing for a public restaurant, with no guarantee that anyone will use it. No sensible restaurateur will turn down a group booking, even if the menu price has to be negotiated, because a modest guaranteed profit is better than a higher, but less certain, return. A banquet is, essentially, a group booking, and you have the advantage of talking to your clients in advance to determine exactly what they require.

Principal types of banquets

Small parties

After-work parties, small celebrations for a birthday or a promotion, an informal meeting, a family gathering or a private dinner party may be handled by the restaurant staff and use a part of the restaurant or a private dining room, if this is available. The only difference from normal restaurant service would be a prearranged menu and a set time for the group's arrival. This sort of small function is usually easy to arrange at short notice and can generate a useful profit for the restaurant. Care must be taken, however, that clients are treated as special guests, rather than as an obstruction in the way of normal operations. One staff member may be assigned to look after a group of up to 20 people, if he or she can call on assistance from time to time. Larger groups will require more staff, according to the menu and beverage arrangements.

Dining clubs and service organisations

Regular custom for a bar or restaurant may be encouraged by the formation of a dining club, whose members are offered special discounts or benefits when using the facility. The club may be formed of patrons with a common interest (such as doctors, golfers, businesswomen or lawyers) or regular customers (such as business travellers, tour leaders or airline crew members) who may take advantage of regularly scheduled events (a chef's table on the first Monday of every month, for instance). Service clubs such as Rotary, Lions, Apex or Zonta may be encouraged to hold regular luncheons or dinners with a simple menu and a competitive price. Arrangements for these events may be handled by the banquet office, or directly with the restaurant manager.

Cocktail parties

A cocktail party is the service of drinks to a group of people, usually for a set time, often accompanied by a selection of finger foods. It is one of the most commonly requested functions. An elaborate cocktail party may cost more than a sit-down dinner. The important considerations are the size of the area allocated, adequate food, enough staff to make sure that the guests are served promptly and frequently, and a specific set of instructions regarding what will be served and how much of it.

Beverages may be limited to beers, wines and soft drinks, or extended to include standard spirits or cocktails. The latter may prove expensive for the client, since guests offered an open tab at a well-equipped cocktail bar are inclined to indulge themselves. It is good business practice to ensure that the customer is given a close estimate of what the function is likely to cost, so that limits can be agreed on without embarrassment.

The Banquet Manager, or the Food and Beverage Manager, should explain clearly to the client what consumption can be expected, and how the choice of beverages will affect the final bill. As a rule of thumb, guests at a cocktail party can be expected to consume two drinks in the first half hour, and then another drink every half hour. A party that extends beyond two hours will record increasing consumption, as the 'serious drinkers' remain and get into full swing. Food is an important factor, and the client should be encouraged to offer substantial hors d'oeuvres, especially for a long cocktail party. This helps to control beverage consumption and promotes responsible behaviour.

On the operational side, it is important that the bar is well-stocked and well-staffed. Guests forced to wait for a drink actually increase their consumption, rather than the reverse. Food should be attractively presented and supplemented by tray service, to ensure that all guests are regularly served. A struggle to reach a central buffet through a crowd only increases consumption and is a common source of complaint. Though a cocktail party is usually a stand-up affair, limited seating should be provided for the elderly and the infirm.

Two skilled banquet bar staff can be expected to deal with a group of up to 160 without cocktails, and floor staff should be assigned at the rate of one for every 40 guests. Tray service from the bar is the most efficient method of distributing drinks. If guests go directly to the bar, or cocktails are offered, bar staffing must be increased. While floor staff may be able to handle food as well as drinks, it is useful to have one staff member per 80 guests assigned solely to food: serving it, collecting empty plates and debris, tidying the buffet and so on.

By these guidelines, a standard two-hour cocktail party for 160 guests, offering beers, wines, soft drinks and standard spirits, with a selection of hot and cold finger foods, would require eight staff: two behind the bar, four on beverage tray service and two on food service. If the beverages were very simple (pre-poured wines, orange juice and draught beer) and the food served was basic (finger sandwiches, crisps and nuts), staffing might be reduced to four (one bar, three tray service) but this would require skilled, quick and well-organised individuals.

Product launches

Companies often hire a function room to present a new range of products or promote a sales campaign. This could be an elaborate and expensive launch of a new automobile, or a low-key sales presentation for a line of cosmetics. Food and beverage service will be tailored to suit. A lavish affair will be treated like any other large banquet; a low-key event may be handled by keeping an account open at the bar and sending a beverage server into the room every 20 minutes or so. Requirements for staging, displays, wall fixings, lighting and directional signs should be discussed well in advance, and checked when the client arrives.

Meetings, forums and seminars

These events may run for one day or more. Organisers may require classroom seating (tables set in rows, in an open square or in a U-shape) or theatre-style seating. Further requirements may include slide, video or overhead projectors, sound systems, recording facilities, television monitors, whiteboards and the like. Depending on the number of people attending, meal service may be in the restaurant or in a separate function room. Coffee may be served mid-morning and mid-afternoon, and a cocktail party may be requested at the end of the business session. Water, pens, writing pads and mints are usually provided at the workplace setting.

This sort of function is often expensive for the client to arrange, so there will be little tolerance for microphones that do not work, rooms incorrectly set or lunches that run late. Long before the arrival of the meeting organiser, you will have confirmed an exact running schedule with the client's office, so that there are no misunderstandings about what is expected. It is vital to keep in close contact with the client to see that all requirements are met promptly and efficiently. For a larger meeting, one or more staff may be assigned to the room for the duration. It is important that all hotel staff are aware of the function, so that they may avoid disturbing a meeting with loud noises, cleaning machines and goods delivery during the sessions.

Shows and special events

The hotel, club or restaurant may promote a popular entertainer, a Christmas dinner, a Mother's Day brunch or a Melbourne Cup Day luncheon. These events put the banqueting facilities of the property to good use, and can provide a welcome boost in a period of low occupancy or quiet trading. In this case, the whole project is the responsibility of the Food and Beverage department, from the initial concept through menu design, advertising, ticket-selling, table layout and service. Decisions will be needed on a budget for entertainment, whether a buffet or sit-down meal is appropriate, what market you expect to reach, and the ticket price. If results are recorded promptly after the event, the figures will provide an invaluable reference for when you plan next year's event.

Conferences and incentive tours

Conferences and incentive tours form a growing sector of the market for larger hotels and resort properties. They usually run for more than one day, and call on every facility the hotel has to offer. Guests generally stay in-house and take most of their meals there. Large incentive groups may exceed 1000 pax, and these demanding projects will require meticulous planning, numerous checklists and dry runs, several layers of fall-backs, well-trained and well-briefed staff and regular planning sessions with the client. There may be requirements for spin-off functions, meetings at short notice, hospitality suites, communications equipment, secretarial services or entertainment. There is no more rigorous test of a hotel's professionalism and efficiency under pressure than a major conference or incentive group with a three- or four-day program of events.

The Food and Beverage Manager plays a major role in this. Obviously, the co-ordination of all food and beverage service is your business, but you may also be called upon to find a lighting crew, supply a crane to move displays, set up dressing rooms for performers, arrange printing of programs or locate an inflatable kangaroo. You will be responsible for the smooth functioning and timeliness of dozens of separate operations. You must, of course, be involved with every stage of the planning from the very earliest approaches to the last airport transfer.

A major event of this kind tests the training and staff development you have practised over many months. It will require an organised mind, an ability to plan things in fine detail many weeks before they happen, and steady nerves. Knowing the precise limits of what your staff, your equipment and your facilities can handle is a prerequisite for successful planning.

Tour meals

In a hotel or resort with a high proportion of tour bookings, the Food and Beverage department may find it easier to make banqueting arrangements for large tour groups, rather than rely on the restaurant facilities to cope with the strain. This is a matter that requires delicate handling, since some tour companies are sensitive to suggest-ions that their tour members be treated any differently from full-tariff, independ-ent travellers. However, if the arrangements for a tour meal are put forward as better, more creative or more efficient than standard à la carte service, the tour leader may accept readily. Examples are a barbecue meal with entertainment, a 'theme' buffet, or exclusive use of a particular area. When a tour group meal is handled as a banquet, staffing can be scheduled as required, table resets will be minimised, service can be more personal, and deadlines for group transfers, tours and so on will not be affected by other hotel guests using the restaurants. Another option is to offer exclusive use of a restaurant (the grill room, for instance) at a time when it would not otherwise be open for service (say breakfast or lunch).

Theme buffets

The fashion for 'theme' buffets has been with us since Roman times, but in the modern era hoteliers like César Ritz (who is said to have once flooded the ball-room of the Savoy hotel for a performance of *Swan Lake*) understood how show-manship, combined with food and beverage service, could prove irresistible to the public. A theme buffet may offer foods native to a particular country (Spain, Japan, Hungary or England, for instance) or in a particular style (such as seafoods, bush foods or carvery). The function room may be decorated with elaborate props or sets, or perhaps provided with entertainment. At the most ambitious end of the spectrum, the sky is the limit. A Chinese banquet might be accompanied by dragon dancing and fireworks; a Fantasy Island dinner might involve professional actors, dancers and a Hawaiian luau; a Christmas in June theme could include a panto-mime performance and a visit from Santa Claus. Particularly in the incentive market, this kind of food-as-entertainment event is very popular. Even in a smaller prop-erty, a reputation gained for staging creative and unusual events will practically guarantee more business down the line.

Weddings

A traditional market for hotels and clubs is the wedding reception, a formal affair at which the family may rely heavily on the hotel for the correct order of events, suitable table settings, floral decorations, the wedding cake, limousine hire and pho-tography. Planning begins some months before the event, with an approach (usually by the prospective bride and her mother) for an estimate of costs and suggestions for a menu. The sale is often made at this point, if the prospective client's enquiry is handled courteously and professionally. Each wedding reception is a unique event. The client may have little experience of dealing with catering arrangements, and feel somewhat out of her depth. Planning a wedding involves dozens of choices for the bride, from the colour of the bridesmaids' gowns to the names on the invita-tion list. The salesperson should steer the client carefully through the decisions that affect the hotel, gently suggesting the most suitable choice of menu, room decora-tion, beverage arrangements and so on. Weddings are highly subject to fashion, so you will need to keep up with changes through the popular and trade press.

Outside catering

The most demanding jobs the Food and Beverage department can undertake are those at outside locations, where the equipment and facilities are limited to what can be transported to the site. A champagne breakfast at the local racecourse, a ground-breaking party at a new building site or a luncheon in the Botanical Gardens will require a great deal of careful planning. You may have to arrange supplies of power, water, lighting and seating, or a marquee or other temporary structure. If the event includes entertainment, you may be responsible for providing the stage, sound desk and PA system. It is not enough to presume that the Executive Chef will look after the food preparation, or that the entertainers will provide their own equipment. The Food and Beverage Manager must take an active managerial role to ensure that all arrangements are checked, working and double-checked before the event. You may (indeed, you should) employ a skilled sound technician to set up the PA system, but if the microphone fails during the keynote speech, all eyes will turn to you. Experience in this field is vital, since it goes well beyond the normal requirements of food and beverage service. You will need to understand how large and complex events can be broken down into a series of steps and checklists, and how delegation of responsibility can work to your advantage.

Banquet sales

It is not enough to run a banqueting department passively, waiting for customers to approach the restaurant, club or hotel with a request for a quote. An active marketing plan will include a complete calendar of local events, a list of individuals and companies regularly involved in planning functions, and a schedule of holidays and special events for which the establishment will promote its own functions. In larger properties, it will be necessary for the hotel to be represented when national or international promotions are planned. Good relations with the Visitors' Bureau are important, as are contacts within the Chamber of Commerce, the local Council, the State Government tourism department, service clubs, sporting organisations, professional associations and so on.

Banquet sales staff will be asked hard questions about room capacities, menus, turnaround times, equipment and layout. It is vital that they know what they are talking about, and have accurate information to hand. A complete set of room dimensions with access points, door widths and ceiling heights should be part of your banquet sales kit, along with menus, wine list, lists of equipment available (in-house and for hire), seating capacity of each room (whether it is a theatre-style or classroom-style setup, or set up for a cocktail party, buffet dinner or sit-down dinner) and any other services available (such as airport transfers, tour arrivals desk, fax or computer facilities or projection equipment).

Banqueting staff

A capable Banquet Manager is a boon to any hotel, and experience in this position is often a prerequisite for promotion to Food and Beverage Manager. The Banquet Manager must have exceptional skill at handling customers, since the clients may be under considerable stress themselves. A client who has forgotten to book a slide projector needs quick and quiet help, not an argument about what was requested and what was not. Good staff management skills are also important, since the banquet crew are regularly asked to work long shifts, deal with large crowds of people, and do fast room turnarounds in the early hours of the morning. A smooth working relationship with the kitchen will prove invaluable.

Banquet sales staff should be carefully chosen, since they are on the front line and will guide the client through all the arrangements for a successful function.

They must have a sound understanding of technical detail, and it is a good idea to involve them in the operation of every event they have booked, so that there is a clear connection in their minds between what is written on the function sheet and what happens on the floor. A good salesperson will be able to gently steer a client towards the best choice of menu, function room and running order, without ever seeming to limit the client's choices.

Banquet service staff are a breed of their own in the hotel industry, usually employed on a casual basis, and often working for more than one property. Irregular hours, irregular income and very demanding work must be balanced by a sense of excitement and a well-cultivated *esprit de corps* which looks upon each new event as a challenge to their professionalism. Speed and skill are important; so is the ability to adapt quickly to late changes, client requests or special instructions. It is a mistake to think that 'anyone will do to carry a tray' in banqueting. Four skilled staff can often do the work of seven unskilled people, while delivering a better standard of service to the guest.

Banquet equipment

In a smaller property, it may be feasible to run a limited number of functions using the restaurant equipment, especially if the function is outside the normal operating hours of the restaurant. This quickly becomes impossible in a larger property, and it will be necessary to purchase and maintain separate banqueting stocks. Efficient banquet operation relies on the ability to preset for the next function, so higher stock levels will apply to tableware, linen and crockery than you might allow for the restaurant.

Linen

Begin with a par stock of table linen based on the normal configuration of the room; for example, if you plan to set maximum seating at 300 pax on tables of 10, you will need a minimum of 60 tablecloths (300 pax ÷ 10 = 30 tables @ 2 changes each = 60 tablecloths). For table napkins, a par stock of 450 should be sufficient to begin with, since some luncheons and cocktail parties will be set with paper napkins, and it is unlikely that the ballroom will be set for full-capacity dinner service every night. Note that every function will require tablecloths, even when no food is served.

It will be necessary to adjust these figures according to whether linen is cleaned in-house or sent out to a commercial laundry. Outside laundry will require more stock, to allow for linen in transit. If all banquet linen is to be hired, a minimum stock level may be agreed on with the linen company so that supplies are replenished as they are used. Discuss these requirements with the Executive Housekeeper so that the most cost-effective solution can be reached. It is a false economy to purchase cheap linen, since the replacement rate will be much higher if you choose lightweight cotton or polyester blends. Polyester in particular is subject to stains, and cannot be bleached in the same way as cotton or linen. The industry standard is heavyweight white cotton damask, and it is difficult to improve upon this for durability and suitability in a variety of settings. When calculating tablecloth sizes, allow for a 30 cm drop, or overhang, in each dimension.

Table skirting and clips will be required for buffets, side tables and top tables, so experiment with several typical room sets (classroom style, U-shaped conference table, large buffet, wedding reception) to see how many tables you are likely to skirt, and how many lengths will be needed. This is one application in which permanently-pressed or pleated synthetic fabrics may be suitable. Make allowance for regular dry cleaning or laundering of the table skirting.

Simple breakfasts, luncheons or light meals may be set with good-quality paper napkins, but these are really only suitable for informal meals. Paper napkins have the advantage of being ready for emergencies, and of course they are disposable, but high-quality 8-ply paper dinner napkins are themselves expensive, so a comparison should be made with the cost of laundering a cloth napkin. The industry standard table napkin is a heavyweight cotton square, which will bear repeated bleaching and washing and will retain a good crease and body when ironed. Table napkins should never be used for any other purpose but that for which they are intended—bar cloths, service cloths, glass cloths and so on should be provided accordingly.

Flatware, cutlery, hollow ware and crockery

Banquet flatware should be chosen for durability and appearance, applying the same criteria discussed in Chapter 5 for restaurant cutlery. Allowances must be made for circumstances specific to banqueting. In a restaurant, three dozen oyster forks may suffice, since it is unlikely that more than 36 guests will order oysters at the same time. In banqueting, however, that is exactly what they will do, so par stocks of flatware and hollow ware must allow for this. It will be useful to discuss the banquet menus with the Executive Chef, to determine what type of equipment will be required. In the interests of economy, consider multiple uses for each item. An entrée knife may double as a bread-and-butter knife; a cereal bowl may serve for desserts. The following par stocks may be used as a starting point:

		Per seat
Flatware	Dinner knives	1.5
	Entrée/side knives	3
	Dinner forks	1.5
	Entrée forks	1.5
	Soup spoons	1.5

	Dessert forks	1.5
	Dessert spoons	1.5
	Teaspoons	3
Crockery	Main plate	2
	Entrée/dessert plate	3
	Tea/coffee cup	3
	Saucer	3
	Soup bowl	1.5
	Cereal/dessert bowl	2
	Side plate	2

Some establishments choose plate service, hand-carried from the kitchen, for banquets; others prefer tray service (that is, a large service tray with six to eight plates carried from the kitchen into the function room). If you choose the latter system, you will need jackstands (portable folding stands used to put the tray down in the room). Allow one jackstand per four tables.

Buffets

Buffets require a specialised set of equipment. It is important that the Food and Beverage Manager be familiar with all of these items:

chafing dishes These consist of a frame, a heat source, a deep water pan, a food insert pan and a cover. They are designed to keep hot foods hot, and to look presentable on the buffet. The finish may be copper or stainless steel, and the sizes are based on the international Gastronorm system. The standard full chafing dish measures 530 × 325 mm and is referred to as a 1/1. Smaller sizes are designated 1/2, 1/3 and so on. The stainless steel inserts used in chafing dishes will generally fit the bains-marie, warming cabinets and ovens in a modern kitchen.

burners Metal cups set in the frame allow a low flame to maintain the temperature of the water, and therefore the food, in a chafing dish. The old-fashioned combination of rock salt and methylated spirit has largely been replaced by safer, cleaner proprietary fuels that come in a block or gel form. Burners should be adjustable so that scrambled eggs, for instance, can be kept at a lower temperature than a braised chicken dish. Note that these heat sources are designed to *keep* food hot: they will not heat food or water efficiently.

carving station This is an arrangement with a heat source (usually an infra-red lamp), a carving board and some method of containing scraps and juices, for portioning large joints of meat on the buffet. A chef will provide the expertise and the carving tools.

display stands These are special stands that add height and colour to buffets by displaying sliced meats, cut fruits, shellfish, flowers and so on. Tiered cake stands, giant clam shells, punch bowls and the like fall into this category.

platters These may include mirrors (for display of hors d'oeuvres or canapés), silver or stainless steel flats, ovals and trays. A good stock of varied sizes and styles will add visual interest to a buffet. It is best to avoid rows of identical steel ovals, which can look institutional.

lighting Lighting is often ignored in buffet design, but it can have a stunning impact when it is skilfully used. Twelve-volt track lighting is excellent for permanent buffets, but a stock of free-standing or clip-on lights will help to improve any buffet presentation. For elaborate theme buffets and special events, stage lighting provided by an outside contractor may be appropriate. Power boards and extensions will also be required.

plants These are the second most important detail (after lighting) to add life and colour to a buffet. Plant hire companies may be used or, in a larger property, a stock of suitable plants can be maintained by the grounds keeper or gardener.

props Creative chefs and Banquet Managers keep a store of appropriate props for particular buffets. Chinese lanterns, wine bottles, statuary, dried flower arrangements, decorative urns, paintings, draperies or ropework are all possibilities.

serving tools Good-quality, presentable serving implements are important, and should be kept solely for use on buffets. These will include ladles, tongs, serving spoons and cake knives.

Chairs

Banquet table sizes have already been discussed (see Chapter 5), but it is worth noting some practical considerations for banquet chairs. It is essential, for fast room changes, that banquet chairs be stackable and transportable with a trolley. Plastic 'feet' should be firmly attached and spares should be kept in stock. Light-coloured upholstery will show stains more quickly than a dark colour or a pattern, and a protective coating such as Scotchgard™ should be applied before the chairs are put into use. Avoid any design with rear legs that extend further backward than the edge of the seat back; staff and guests will trip over them in tight settings. Folding chairs are not suitable, except for the most informal settings.

Other considerations

In addition to furniture and buffet equipment, the banquet department may be called upon to provide staging, catwalks, lecterns or podium, audio-visual equipment, microphones (cordless or fixed), laser pointers, whiteboards, easels, registration desks, cash registers and so on. These requirements should be discussed with the client, and the various charges agreed to before the function sheet is written. It is a good idea to cultivate a working relationship with a number of hire companies in your area who can supply audio and video equipment, staging and marquees, extra crockery and cutlery, portable generators and other necessities for special events. It is normal practice to pass on all hire charges to the client, with a margin to allow for the hotel's work in planning, transport and storage. A professional attitude to special events means that no client request is too much trouble: virtually anything can be provided, if the client is willing to undertake the cost.

A case in point

The client was a multinational computer company, hosting an incentive sales group at a major resort hotel in Hawaii. Believing that extraordinary achievements deserve extraordinary rewards, the client requested an unusual breakfast for a small group of their very top achievers. The idea was to serve a formal breakfast for 20 people, at dawn, in the crater of an extinct volcano, 3000 metres above sea level. The special functions team at the hotel were called upon to plan and co-ordinate the whole event. Using a pair of chartered helicopters, banquet staff and support crew were airlifted to the site to begin setting up in the middle of the night. Just as dawn was breaking, the coffee was brewing, omelettes were being prepared and the helicopters returned to deliver the lucky guests. The event was a complete, if somewhat expensive, success.

Banquet planning

Banquet planning is not just a matter of choosing a menu and assembling the right staff and the right equipment. A good manager makes a study of guest behaviour at the various types of banquet, and plans accordingly. A working knowledge of psychology is an important professional skill. A guest attending a banquet is remarkably sensitive to small details in the seating arrangements, order of service, perceived status and protocol. There is a certain amount of social tension at any banquet, which can be eased by skilful service or made worse by clumsy planning.

At the beginning of every banquet, a briefing should be given to all the banquet staff, together with the banquet chef if possible. The order of service should be outlined and an explanation of the menu given. Staff should be informed of the beverage arrangements and sections assigned. An order of service and section plan should be posted on the wall, so that there is no confusion about what comes next.

The formal dinner

At any sit-down dinner there will be a 'top table' which must be identified early in the event. This table will seat the most important guests, the leaders of the organisation and often the person who made the booking. Even if the top table is not called the top table, a good Banquet Manager will be able to identify it, and make sure that service of each course begins with that table. The top table should receive attentive, but discreet, service throughout the meal. Assign an experienced staff member to look after it.

The first step in good service is to put something in front of the guest immediately he or she is seated. After the napkin is removed and placed in the guest's lap, water or wine should be served promptly, before food orders are taken. It is traditional to serve the ladies at the table first, then the gentlemen. You will normally assign some of your banquet staff to food service, and others to beverage service, but make it clear that they must co-operate when service demands it. When a course is ready to come out of the kitchen, or is to be cleared, all hands should work together to get the job done in a timely fashion.

The number of staff required will vary with the complexity of the menu, but as a guide, allow one food server per 24 guests for a menu of four courses (entrée, main course, dessert and coffee) with one or two choices. A more complicated menu with more choices means that ordering will take longer, and you may wish to increase staffing to one food server per 16 to 20 guests. An experienced beverage server should cope with 30 guests if service consists of bottled wine and soft drinks, but if service includes mixed drinks, or involves cash handling, you may increase staffing to one server per 20 to 24 guests. Since most banquet staff are employed on a casual basis, you may send some of the crew off duty as the evening progresses, but never before the coffee has been served.

Taking the guests' orders must be accomplished quickly, to give the kitchen time to adjust the amount of each dish they have prepared. Each food server should have a separate docket (Figure 7.1) for each table on his section. The server approaches each guest in turn, clockwise around the table, beginning with someone of distinctive appearance (say, the lady in the red dress) and makes a note on the docket to indicate which person this is. This simple precaution allows other staff to help with food service without having to ask which guest is having which dish.

Once the order is completed for each table on the section, the server will return it immediately to the Banquet Manager or expediter in the kitchen. When the Banquet Manager has received all the orders, a simple chart (Figure 7.2, page 128) is completed to co-ordinate service, and the numbers are passed to the kitchen. When the kitchen is ready, the Banquet Manager should pass word that the first course is about to be served, and all service staff then assemble at the passe, ready to pick up. As each table is despatched, the manager or expediter will tick off that table as completed, and call the next table 'away'.

Table No. 12		Server: David	
1	(lady in red) soup fish crepes	2	avocado fish crepes
10	avocado beef gateaux	3	avocado beef crepes
9	soup beef crepes	4	avocado beef gateaux
8	(no entree) fish gateaux	5	soup beef gateaux
7	avocado fish gateaux	6	soup beef crepes

Figure 7.1 Banquet table order

Some Banquet Managers are hesitant to leave the function room, believing that it is important to keep a watchful eye on service from the floor. In fact, better control will be achieved from the passe, at least during the actual service of each course. Ten minutes spent in the kitchen, assisting with an orderly dispatch of meals, is better spent than half an hour in the function room wondering why things are not moving more quickly.

For any function it will be wise to set a few extra places, which can be unobtrusively removed later on, when all the guests are seated. It is much easier to remove a place setting than it is to add another one, and three or four unexpected guests can throw a seating plan into disarray.

Beverage service

Beverage service may take several forms. In the simplest arrangement, table wines are preselected by the guest and agreement is reached with the client on what other drinks guests may order. These may include beers, mineral waters or soft drinks. Once the wine is poured, beverage staff will take orders for other drinks and obtain them from the banquet bar. These drinks are rung up at banquet prices on a 'dry

Sandhurst Wedding				8/7/97			
Table	Soup	Avo.	Fish	Beef	Crêpe	Gâtx	Server
1	9	1	7	3	4	6	Susan
2	2	8	4	6	5	4	Susan
3	5	4	8	2	5	5	Susan
4	3	7	4	6	5	5	Jim
5	6	3	8	2	4	6	Jim
6	3	7	9	1	4	4	Dean
7	3	7	5	5	2	8	Dean
8	2	8	4	6	4	6	Anna
9	7	3	7	3	4	4	Anna
10	4	6	5	5	5	5	David
11	3	7	5	5	4	6	David
12	4	5	4	6	5	5	David
13	3	7	4	6	3	7	Carol
14	6	4	7	3	8	2	Carol
Totals	60	77	81	59	62	73	

Figure 7.2 Banquet service chart

till' (a cash register with no money in it). Every bottle of wine is rung up as it is opened. Even though no money is handled, table staff must still complete dockets with the server's name and table number and hand them to the bar, where they are retained for checking. This provides a written record of what was ordered, should the client wish to see it. Bar staff should keep an accurate running total, so that the Banquet Manager can inform the client how the account stands at any time.

A limited bar means that some drinks are put to the client's account, and others are available for cash. Cocktails, spirits and premium wines, for example, may be served to guests on request, but may not be charged to the client's account. If a guest requests a premium Scotch, for instance, the beverage server will say, 'Certainly, sir. That is available from the cash bar. The charge is four dollars.' At this point, the server accepts payment, goes to the banquet bar and buys the drink for the guest. A second cash register is in place to ring up the sale and make change. The beverage server may be issued with a small float, so that she can make change at the table.

An open bar means that guests may order anything they like. Drinks are obtained from the banquet bar and the sale is rung up to the client's account. In this case, it is important to agree in advance with the client whether there are any exclusions (premium spirits, for instance, or wines from the restaurant list). The Banquet Manager must carefully monitor the running account and discreetly keep the client informed of the total.

A straight cash bar means that there is no beverage account to the client, and all drinks must be paid for in cash as they are ordered. The Banquet Manager will make a decision on whether cash will be asked for in advance, or whether a guest may run an account (usually with a credit card imprint) until the end of the function. If cash floats will be required, they should be issued and signed for, then returned as beverage staff go off duty.

The buffet dinner

It was not unusual, in the 17th century, for a banquet menu to list 144 courses for a royal dinner, including such curiosities as larks' tongues and dolphin meat. The truth is, no one ate all that, because the menus actually describe what we would call a buffet. If we were to list every item on a modern luncheon buffet (including the garnishes, the sauces, the seasonings and the ingredients of the fruit display), we would also have a very long list.

The buffet is a good choice for the client who wishes to make the most impressive display for a certain price. When the guests walk into the room they will see an elaborate assortment of delicious foods, artistically presented, and will be suitably impressed. The buffet is also a good choice for a group with a divergence of tastes. If you wish to accommodate adults and children, carnivores and vegetarians, trenchermen and the diet-conscious, all with the same menu, the buffet is an obvious choice.

The buffet, however, presents some particular problems for the hotelier or restaurateur. It is not just a matter of putting all the food on a table and hoping for the best. People behave in certain predictable patterns when they are serving themselves, and it is important that you understand what they are likely to do. At any buffet, there is a certain amount of tension: Will there be enough food? Will I have to wait hours to get some? Will all the best things be gone by the time I get there? However unfounded these concerns may be, the hotelier who ignores them makes a serious error.

If we were to place all the grilled fish or meat at the beginning of the buffet, guests would likely fill their plates with it, leaving no room for the vegetables, the garnishes or the salads. Since the fish and meats are the most expensive ingredients on the buffet, it will help to put them at the end of the line rather than at the beginning. People are inclined to fill their plates with food at a buffet in excess of their capacity to eat it, however much you may reassure them that they can come back a second or a third time. The best plan, then, would be to follow the arrangement in Figure 7.3.

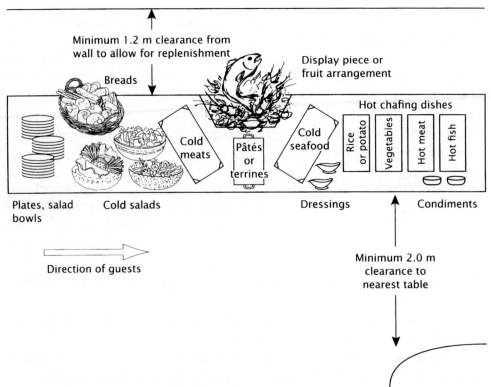

Figure 7.3 Buffet layout for 50 guests. Note: desserts may be brought out after the cold food has been cleared

Consider how long it will take your guests to pass through a buffet. Make things easy to serve, so that the guests still queuing with an empty plate do not become impatient. Plenty of serving spoons, tongs and ladles should be provided. Salads should be ready-dressed, meats already sauced. By placing four choices of dressing next to the green salad, you will slow down a buffet line significantly while guests ponder over which one they would like. If a dish does need a separate dressing, place the two next to each other, so that the connection is obvious. Use large displays (carved ice, butter, fresh fruit) and small serving bowls (these are more quickly replaceable and easier to keep looking fresh). If more than 100 guests are to move through a buffet, consider making two buffets, or a double-sided buffet, for quicker service. 120 guests is about the upper limit to be served on a single buffet line without crowding, long waits and certain complaints.

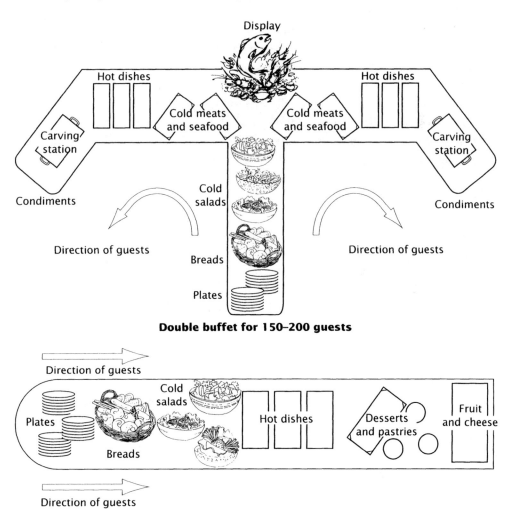

Double buffet for 150–200 guests

Fast service luncheon buffet for 150–200 guests

Figure 7.4 Alternative buffet layouts

There must be sufficient room for guests to queue, to serve themselves and to walk back to their tables. Allow for this in your table plan, and do not place tables too close to the buffet. Thirty people standing in a queue take up nearly 15 square metres of floor space, and seated guests will not thank you if guests still queuing are close enough to be looking over their shoulders. Traffic lanes must be wide enough to allow for staff and guests using them at the same time.

In general, it is not wise to put all the food out on the buffet at once. However beautifully arranged, it will always look considerably battered by the time the last guest makes her way through the line. It is better to put out two-thirds of what you have allowed, then replenish smaller bowls promptly as they are exhausted. This makes for a fresher appearance on the buffet and allows for some consolidation in the kitchen. For large functions, it will be wise to assign one or two staff to look after and replenish the buffet. Do not make the mistake of being less than generous with food on a buffet. Waste is part and parcel of this method of service, so it should be costed into the menu in advance. If 40 guests are to be served tournedos with mushrooms, allow at least 45 portions, and be more generous still with the salads, vegetables and garnishes. The whole point of a buffet is an appearance of abundance and plenty. There is nothing so lonely-looking as a single custard tart on a large, empty dessert platter, and the guest who feels short-changed will make the bitterest complaint.

Weddings

Special arrangements apply to wedding receptions. It is usually thought inelegant for the bride and groom to queue up to serve themselves from a buffet. In this case, meals may be plated in the kitchen for service to the top table. The menu will roughly match what is served on the buffet. Wedding receptions have their own complex and rather lengthy protocols, which can vary greatly according to the religion, nationality or ethnic origin of the families involved. It is important to discuss all of these details with the bride's family in advance, and agree upon a clear order of speeches, the grace, the cutting of the cake, arrangements for wedding presents and the seating plan. Often the bride will seek advice from the Banquet Manager or banquet salesperson about the 'correct' way of doing things, and if this happens, help should be offered. In other cases, the bridal couple may have strong opinions on how they wish their wedding reception to be organised, and the sensible hotelier will bow to their wishes.

The function sheet

Any function will affect every other department of a hotel, so the function sheet listing the details of the event will become an important document. The function sheet may be issued by the banquet sales office, but always over the signature of the Food and Beverage Manager. It is unwise to issue a function sheet if details are still sketchy, but it is also imperative that every department be given as much notice as possible. One week should be regarded as the minimum.

The circulation list for function sheets should include the General Manager, Front Office, the Concierge or head porter, telephone switchboard, Maintenance/

THE LANCASTER HOTEL
Function Sheet

Name of function Basedow Pharmaceuticals Dinner	
Day Sunday	Type of function 4-course dinner
Date November 12, 1997	No. of guests 120
Time start 7:00 pm	Organiser's name Andrew Horton
Time finish 12:00 midnight	Company CAD Public Relations
Booked by D. Brenner ext. 4343	Contact 02 3434 5555

ROOM SET-UP

Tables: 12 of 10 pax	Stage no
Top table no	Lectern yes, with microphone
Linen white cloth, grey napkins	Catwalk no
Extra tables registration table	Sound house system
Buffet no	Lighting spot on lectern
Dance floor no	AV equipment slide projector & screen
	Whiteboard no

MENU
Smoked salmon tartlet with sun-dried tomatoes
Fillet of beef with oyster mushrooms
OR
Chicken ballottine with saffron rice
Selection of vegetables
Fresh fruit sabayon
Tasmanian cheeses with dried fruits
Coffee or tea

Price per person: $45.00

BEVERAGES
Limited bar, charge on consumption to account
Bottled wines, beers, soft drinks, port. Spirits are cash bar.
Wines: St Phillip's Chardonnay @ $21.00 per bottle
Tea Tree Shiraz @ $26.50 per bottle
Old Winery Port @ $24.00 per bottle
Beverage account limit $2000. Advise Mr Andrew Horton if reached.

SPECIAL INSTRUCTIONS

Check sound system and projector before function starts.
Client will make 30 minute presentation between main course and dessert.
No service in room during presentation.

Account to: CAD Public Relations, GPO Box 0000, Sydney NSW 2000	
Account number: DB45-8943	Authorised by: (signature)
Attention: Andrew Horton	Date issued: 24/10/97

Figure 7.5 Function sheet

Engineering, Housekeeping, Accounts, the Executive Chef, the Food and Beverage Manager, the Banquet Manager, the Bar Manager and Security. When a substantial change is made to arrangements (such as a time change, or a change in the number of guests), written notice should be distributed to the same circulation list. If the change is significant (a cancellation, a change of venue or a doubling of numbers) then the notice should be followed up with a telephone call to each department, confirming the message.

The whole point of a well-written function sheet is to answer all questions at once, so it should carry every detail available. A seemingly minor point, such as the arrival time of the wedding party, may have a great deal of significance for the Concierge Desk, if they happen to be expecting four tour groups at the same time. It is better to put too much on a function sheet than too little.

The confirmation letter

The most important single document relating to any function is the confirmation letter sent to the client before the function. This should set out, in detail, every arrangement agreed upon, including the menu selected, the beverage arrangements, equipment requirements, timing, the function room selected, the agreed charges and the method of payment. It is customary to include a requirement that the client confirm guaranteed numbers at least 48 hours in advance. This is the number of guests for which the client will be charged, even if the actual number attending should be less. (If the number is more, the client will be charged accordingly.) This letter will allow the client to review everything he or she has agreed to, and to contact the hotel should any detail be unclear. It also serves as insurance for the hotel, so that no disputes arise later. The letter, signed by the Food and Beverage Manager, should reach the client no later than one week in advance—earlier if the function is particularly complex or important.

CHAPTER SUMMARY

Banqueting is an important profit centre for many hotels, restaurants and clubs. Because the requirements for menu, beverages, staffing and equipment are usually known in advance, the Food and Beverage department has the opportunity to plan a profitable function with a minimum of guesswork. A fast, flexible and experienced banquet crew is a major asset to any food service operation, and they may be called upon to handle anything from a small private dinner party to a major event held at a remote location.

A good Food and Beverage Manager has an excellent working knowledge of banquets, including the most suitable arrangements for cocktail parties, conferences, incentive groups, tour groups and weddings. He or she will be expected to provide accurate, detailed planning and to delegate various parts of a complex operation, while maintaining overall responsibility to see that things happen in their proper order and at the proper time. This role requires complete familiarity with banqueting equipment, order of service and banquet floor plans, as well as tight co-ordination with the kitchen for efficient service. The Food and Beverage Manager must be familiar with the various types of beverage service, and have a sound understanding of display, traffic flow and replenishment for successful buffets.

It is customary for the Food and Beverage Manager to sign the function sheet before it is distributed to the other operating departments, and to write the letter of confirmation to the client, specifying clearly what arrangements have been agreed upon.

REVIEW QUESTIONS

1 Why is banqueting a significant profit centre for most restaurants and hotels?

2 You receive a confirmed booking for a two-hour cocktail party from a local company. The client requests hot and cold finger food and a limited bar serving spirits, beers, wine and soft drinks for 150 guests. Approximately how many staff will you need?

3 What factors would you consider in setting the price for a Mother's Day luncheon at a city hotel?

4 Why would the par stock of cutlery and crockery for banquets differ from the par stock for a restaurant?

5 Give definitions for the following terms: dry till, limited bar, open bar, cash bar.

6 What details should be included in a banquet confirmation letter to a client?

CHAPTER EIGHT

PURCHASING AND STORAGE

The Purchasing department and the role of purchase specifications in an efficient Food and Beverage operation

Receiving control, weights and measures

Specifications for fresh meats, poultry, vegetables and fish

Safe storage and handling of dry goods and tinned goods, frozen foods and beverages

A comparison of requisition systems

Managing costs and profits

It is the first purpose of any business to make a profit, and the hotel and restaurant industry is no exception. Whatever systems we design, whatever training we do or marketing plans we make, the whole point of the exercise is to make a profit. A profit is the difference between what it costs to produce a thing and what the customer pays for it. In order to determine whether or not an operation is making a profit, it is necessary to measure accurately what is going on in that operation. If you have only a vague idea of how much today's luncheon special costs to produce, then it will be difficult to set a sales price that guarantees an acceptable profit. Measuring things in a food and beverage operation is more complex than it looks at first. It requires a working knowledge of weights and measures, contract law, storage procedures and bookkeeping. Without this knowledge, the Food and Beverage Manager is working in the dark and can neither explain a poor result, nor duplicate a good one.

Some restaurant managers have few, if any, control systems in place, believing that their 'feel for the business' will tell them if anything is going wrong. Some hotel operations grow so large that the Food and Beverage Manager may not be aware of what is going on in the loading dock on any particular day. In either of these situations, there is enough slack in the system to guarantee that dishonesty, waste and inaccuracy will flourish and do considerable damage to operating profit. The after-tax profit, even of a very successful restaurant, is often measured in single digits. There is just no room for complacency.

If profits are too low, there are only two possible cures: one can increase sales (as long as some profit is being made, this should increase the return to the owner or investor), or one can cut costs (which will give a better return for the same sales turnover). To increase sales, it may be necessary to spend more on marketing, defeat the competition, lower prices or change the product. All of these are accomplishable, but fairly difficult to do. On the other hand, we might control costs. If we can do that by tightening up slack in the operating system, without affecting the quality of the product, then it is by far the easier solution.

Consider the example in Table 8.1. Restaurant B is in a better position, because of slightly better controls on labour cost and overheads. Now imagine that both restaurant managers are given a target of $45 000 for next year's operating profit. The manager of Restaurant A believes that increasing sales is the way to increase profits, and so launches a campaign to draw more customers in by cutting prices, competing aggressively in the market and speeding up customer turnover. At the end of the year, Restaurant A succeeds in increasing sales by $40 000, and the manager expects a good result on the yearly report.

Table 8.1 The results of tightening operating costs (Restaurant B)

	Restaurant A		Restaurant B	
	$	%	$	%
Yearly sales	380 000		380 000	
Cost of sales	133 760	35.2	133 760	35.2
Labour cost	124 640	32.8	118 560	31.2
Overheads	90 820	23.9	81 320	21.4
OPERATING PROFIT	$ 30 780	8.1	$ 43 360	12.2

The manager of Restaurant B takes a slightly different tack, believing that there are still some areas in the operation that can be tightened up, and that with a modest increase in sales the target can be achieved. At the end of the year, the results are as shown in Table 8.2.

Table 8.2 Cutting prices (Restaurant A) as opposed to tightening costs (Restaurant B)

	Restaurant A		Restaurant B	
	$	%	$	%
Yearly sales	420 000		390 000	
Cost of sales	150 780	35.9	136 890	35.1
Labour cost	141 540	33.7	121 290	31.1
Overheads	99 960	23.8	81 510	20.9
OPERATING PROFIT	$ 27 720	6.6	$ 50 310	12.9

By cutting prices, Restaurant A has generated more sales but caused a slight increase in cost of sales. More customers necessitated more staff hours, leading to a slight increase in labour cost, and more business has probably placed a bit more

wear and tear on the restaurant equipment. Overheads, which include maintenance costs, have risen in dollar terms and will probably rise more next year. The
manager of Restaurant A is very pleased to record a $40 000 increase in sales, but
is devastated to hear that he has actually made *less* profit than he did last year. The
manager of Restaurant B has achieved only a modest increase in sales, but managed to shave a few tenths of a per cent off her costs and has easily reached and
exceeded the profit target for the year. The inevitable conclusion is that it is easier
to increase profits by controlling costs than by increasing sales.

Aside from producing better profits, sensible purchasing, receiving and requisition controls also promote good organisation and a sense of professionalism. This
is not to say that you ought to swamp your staff with a mass of forms to be completed in triplicate every time someone needs a ream of paper or a bottle of wine.
In fact, this kind of over-regulation is counter-productive; sensible people tend to
find ways around it. The goal is to set up some commonsense procedures to ensure
that things are done easily, efficiently and accurately.

Purchasing

Tradition has it in the hotel industry that a good purchasing officer is worth his or
her weight in gold. This is not hard to understand, when one considers that the
person buying all the food and beverages for a large hotel may spend several million
dollars a year. Good purchasing procedures, a thorough knowledge of the market
and a keen eye for the best product at the best price can make a great deal of difference to the operating profit at the end of the year. It is not enough to find a
good purchasing officer, though. The Food and Beverage Manager must take an
active role in the purchasing process.

Standard specifications

To begin, determine what it is you want to buy, then be specific about exactly what is
required. If a chef requests a bottle of vinegar, is she asking for malt or wine vinegar?
Does she want a 4 L container or a 500 mL bottle? Is it balsamic vinegar or rice
wine vinegar? Will the domestic product do the job, or is an imported brand necessary? Without specifications, it will be extremely difficult to get a supplier to quote
an accurate price. One might as well ask how much a piece of meat costs. Which
meat? Which cut? How much do you want to buy?

The first step, then, is to draw up a list of products that the hotel or restaurant
buys. Next, determine the exact qualities of these products, specifying the type, the
grade and the size of the package required. You may specify a country of origin, a
particular cut, or a frozen, chilled or fresh product. You may specify a particular
form of packaging, a certain delivery schedule or a standing order. The more speci-

fications that you can write down, the more accurate your pricing and purchasing will become.

A purchasing officer could sensibly ask a supplier to quote on supply of A10 tins of peeled Italian plum tomatoes, with a minimum net weight of 2.9 kg, packaged in cartons of 6 tins, and the tins to be clean, labelled and free of perforations, rust and dents. It may be helpful to estimate the monthly consumption and the frequency of delivery (daily, weekly or monthly).

If beef is the product, you might specify that the item is chilled Australian two-year-old lot-fed steer meat, *Handbook of Australian Meat* (HAM) cut number 2140, with 21 days age, with a maximum 12 mm fat cover, portion cut to 250 g with an acceptable 5% variance, layer packed in sealed meat cartons and delivered at no more than 3°C.

Industry specifications

There would be little sense in asking a supplier to deliver milk in 750 mL bottles, if the standard container sizes were 300 mL, 600 mL and 2 L. It will help to be familiar with standard industry specifications and package sizes for a wide range of products.

Meat

Meat is one of the most expensive items on the order sheet for any hotel, club or restaurant, so it is particularly important to be familiar with the cuts and qualities of Australian meats. The Australian Meat and Livestock Corporation (AMLC) has made this process easier by publishing numerous training manuals for chefs and purchasing officers, including the *Handbook of Australian Meat* (HAM), which provides a ready reference for meat processors and buyers. The HAM number allows the buyer to specify exactly which cut is wanted (such as a sirloin or rib eye of beef). It is then possible to stipulate the age, weight and sex of the animal, and how the animal has been fed. These will have a bearing on the fat content, tenderness and eating qualities of the meat. Further, you can specify the age of the carcass (counted in days from slaughter) and whether it is delivered chilled, chilled cryovac or frozen. These will also affect tenderness and keeping qualities. The meat may be delivered whole, sliced, diced, ground or portion cut. This will influence labour cost; a trimmed portion cut will obviously be convenient, but more expensive than a primal cut. You may specify bone-in or bone-out, or indicate a minimum acceptable 'chemical lean' percentage. This is used for diced and ground meat, to indicate the amount of fat in relation to lean muscle. If you are not familiar with these technicalities, you are working in the dark and must educate yourself by obtaining and using industry references.

Fish

Fish is another expensive commodity on the order sheet, and here the variables are more difficult. With the exception of some farmed products (notably shellfish, some prawns and Tasmanian salmonids), the supply of fresh seafood is dependent on season, weather and competition from foreign markets. It may be impossible, or very expensive, to obtain fresh coral trout at certain times of the year, but if you are familiar with alternatives such as John Dory or barramundi you will be able to make more sensible purchasing decisions. Prawns are available in at least six commercial species, with a size classification that indicates a U-12 as a much larger prawn than a 21–25. Prices may vary widely through the year according to season and available supply. Once again, self-education will make for better decisions, and the Department of Primary Industries (DPI), the Fish Marketing Board, the Department of Fisheries and the larger national wholesalers are helpful sources of information and seasonal charts.

Beverages

Purchasing for the restaurant wine list is a difficult calculation based on several factors: the reliable supply of a given wine, its perceived value to the customer, national advertising support, the wholesale price (less any discount), the past sales record, the balance of the wine list, and so on. If you do not understand the difference between a cool-climate Clare Valley riesling and a riesling produced in the Riverina, you will be at a considerable disadvantage when it comes to buying them. Fortunately, there are many books available that will remedy this problem, and you will want to study them, along with trade periodicals including *Winestate* and *The Australian Wine and Spirit Buyer* and general periodicals such as *Australian Gourmet Traveller*, *Wine Spectator* (US) and *Decanter* (UK).

Even more expensive are the spirits, liqueurs and aperitifs purchased for the bars. Bottle sizes are not uniform (spirits, for instance, may come in 375 mL, 500 mL, 700 mL, 750 mL, 1000 mL and 1125 mL bottles, or larger bulk containers); nor are all spirits created equal: alcoholic strength may vary from 28% by volume to 45% by volume, with a few notable oddities going as high as 60% or even 90% by volume. Here it is essential that you specify precisely what you want, noting brand names if appropriate, bottle size, country of origin, alcoholic strength and so on. A 700 mL bottle of Australian-bottled Scotch whisky at 37% alcohol is clearly not going to sell for the same price as a 750 mL bottle of single-malt, Highland-bottled Scotch whisky at 45% alcohol. You may specify a house or pouring brand, and one or two acceptable alternatives. These details should be noted on a written purchase specification card so that the supplier, the purchasing officer and the receiving clerk are all aware of precisely what the product should be.

Item:	GREEN PRAWNS, 21–25
Description:	Uncooked whole frozen Australian prawns, packed in random weight cartons (approx 10–13 kg), delivered at –18°C, clearly marked with name of wholesaler, variety and count class. Acceptable varieties are Endeavour, King, Tiger or Banana. Prawns should show no evidence of thawing, deterioration or black spot disease. Size class 21–25 count per 500 grams.
Inspection:	Check –18°C internal temperature with probe. Prawns must be hard frozen in undamaged cartons. Scale and verify marked gross weight, size class and Australian origin. Visually inspect contents, reject any product with unpleasant smell, evidence of thawing, freezer burn or black spot.
Storage:	Freezer, immediately. Maintain –18 to –20°C.
Price range:	$11.50 to $18.50, seasonal (review 15/12/—)
Suppliers:	ABC Seafood, Gamberi Bros, Sea-Set Wholesalers

Figure 8.1 Product specification card

In general

Study the industry standards, seasonal variations and historical price range for any product with which you are unfamiliar. Suppliers may be of assistance; government departments can also help. A visit to a primary producer, to a wholesale market, to a large retailer or even to the local TAFE library may prove valuable. In consultation with the Executive Chef, the bar or restaurant manager and the purchasing manager, draw up product specification cards so that ordering, price comparisons, receiving and subsequent stock checks are all carried out to the same plan.

In small restaurants, this may seem a luxury that only large organisations can enjoy. The head chef will often do all the ordering, the goods will be received by the apprentice cook, and suppliers will be chosen according to which one offers the most generous Christmas presents every year. In this situation, inevitably, some suppliers and staff take advantage of a slack and poorly controlled system, and a narrow margin of profit disappears out the back door.

Purchasing policy

Unfortunately, kickbacks, hidden commissions, false discounts and preferred suppliers are some of the oldest problems in the hotel industry. When one considers the amount of money involved, the temptation will always exist to favour one supplier over another, and inducements will be offered. Even the great chef Escoffier was eventually accused, in 1898, of accepting undeclared commissions from suppliers, and was asked to leave London's Savoy Hotel in disgrace.

These days, electronic record-keeping has made it easier to detect dishonest practices, as purchasing decisions can be compared against a database of past prices, and even slight discrepancies can be isolated and investigated. Clever as these methods are, however, human beings are cleverer, and the cornerstone of any effective cost control system should be a statement of the organisation's purchasing policy. This should outline the basic aim of good purchasing: to obtain the best possible product at the best possible price, to maintain adequate supply and timely replenishment, and to carefully check incoming goods for quality and conformity to specification.

It will also help to spell out house policy on the inevitable temptations: no staff member or manager should accept any kind of gratuity, cash payment, commission, or payment in kind from a supplier. If there are exceptions (such as attending a supplier's Christmas party, accepting free samples for bona fide testing or accepting a small gift of a specified maximum value, such as a pen or a cap of a promotional nature) these should be clearly explained, written down and rigorously controlled. Senior managers should be aware of the impression created when they accept a supplier's invitation to a lavish luncheon, or line up bottles of 'complimentary' liquor on their sideboards at Christmas time. It is difficult to convince the receiving clerk that honesty is the best policy if the General Manager is sporting a set of golf clubs with a supplier's logo on the bag. The receiving clerk, after all, has the opportunity to even the score every day.

Purchasing control

There is no worse time to buy an item than in an emergency. If supplies of blank menu cards are exhausted and the lead time for printing is normally ten weeks, then the purchasing officer will be forced to pay a much higher price for a rush service, or compromise the quality of the product used. This situation can apply to almost any product purchased and is to be avoided. A general lack of organisation, leading to recurring short-supply emergencies, will cost the restaurant or hotel dearly. There are four steps to avoid this:

- Standardise order quantities.
- Forecast consumption accurately.
- Set par levels for regular items.
- Do regular stocktakes.

As noted earlier, 'a bottle of vinegar' can mean more than one thing. The chefs and bar staff should be encouraged to specify exact brands and package sizes when ordering. They should also be provided with market lists or stocktake lists that prompt them to check all the items ordered on a daily, weekly or monthly basis.

Average consumption per month or per year can be forecasted from the previous year's purchasing records, and made more accurate by relating consumption to sales. If you are predicting $40 000 in beverage sales for a given period and beverage cost is hovering around 25 per cent, then you might reasonably expect to see purchases of around $10 000 for that period, presuming there were no other extraordinary circumstances. A figure markedly above that or below it would be cause for investigation.

The easiest way to avoid out-of-stock emergencies is to set a par level for all regularly-ordered supplies. Simply put, this means a minimum number of items to be kept on the shelf at all times. The par level will be influenced by the lead time required to obtain more, the value of the item, the average stock turn or usage of the item, and the amount of capital budgeted for inventory. It is the role of the Food and Beverage Manager to help set these levels, not just for food and beverages, but also for equipment, glassware and consumables.

Stocktakes are a fundamental cost control procedure, just as important as counting the cash in the restaurant till at the end of the night. The F&B should certainly take part in stocktakes often, and will be called upon to set policy on what is counted, how it is valued, and what adjustments are made to reach a usable inventory value.

Purchase quotations

In very large food service operations, particularly multiple hotel properties with co-operative buying schemes or chain restaurants with uniform menus, the contract bid process is often used to select suppliers. A contract to supply a certain item (for example, dairy products, bread rolls or cleaning chemicals) for a certain time is advertised and sealed bids are accepted from suppliers. Product specifications are very detailed. Bids are reviewed by the purchasing officer and senior management and the contract is awarded. As long as specifications are adhered to, the supplier will retain the contract for the agreed term, after which time bids are invited again.

In large-to-medium operations, a simpler method is used. Possible suppliers of a product are short-listed by the Purchasing department and put forward to the Food and Beverage Manager. Specifications are written down, then suppliers are invited to quote on a list of products or services. When quotes are received, they are compared for price, service level, terms of payment and quality record. A preferred supplier is chosen and the purchasing officer is directed to use that supplier under normal circumstances. No formal contract is entered into, though a letter accepting the supplier's quote may be written. One or two alternative suppliers may be nominated, in case of shortages or delivery problems.

In a small operation the process can be further simplified, but the principles of correct purchasing should still be applied. Written specifications are provided to suppliers, so that orders are accurate and clearly understood. Quotes from several suppliers should be sought, at regular intervals, to ensure that the best market price is obtained. Careful records should be kept of everything ordered and received. Except in the smallest owner–operator business, it is still good practice to have at least two people involved: one who places the order and another who receives and checks the goods.

The purchase order

Written purchase orders are essential if you wish to exercise any sort of control over the amount of money being spent. Even if the order is placed by telephone, a purchase order should be created for each delivery. Suppliers should be advised in writing that no invoice will be honoured unless it carries a purchase order number.

Once the purchase order has been written, it is passed to the receiving clerk who checks the goods when they arrive, notes any discrepancies in the order and attaches the delivery docket or invoice. The purchasing officer approves the invoice for payment, retains a copy and sends the original to the Accounts department. A daily order sheet, listing all orders placed on a given day, will provide a useful cross-reference. The system can be manual or electronic, but it should be universal; that is, nothing should be authorised for payment without a written purchase order. This is the cornerstone of an effective cost control system: first control what you buy.

Receiving

However detailed the purchase specifications, and however skilled the purchasing officer, all efforts are wasted if the goods are poorly received. The Chef may have ordered 120-day, export-grade, milk-fed veal, but if the storeperson who signs for it on the loading dock is unable to tell the difference between veal and pork, there will be a problem. While it is impractical to call the person who ordered the goods to the loading dock for each delivery, it is possible to train the receiving clerk, who will become your best insurance against sub-standard quality, short deliveries or mistaken orders.

A new receiving clerk should be briefed on the names and specifications of all the items ordered. It is wise to ask the Executive Chef, or the sous-chef, to spend time training the new person until he is confident that foodstuffs will be correctly identified and checked when delivered. When there is any doubt about whether a food product meets the specification, the receiving clerk should have instructions to call the kitchen for assistance. For beverages, the receiving clerk should be taught to identify correct labels, package sizes and brands.

Any hotel or restaurant that receives goods without an accurate scale to check weights is simply inviting trouble. The scale should be close to the loading dock and be capable of weighing cartons up to 100 kg. An electronic scale with a tare

THE LANCASTER HOTEL

22 Wyndham Street, Gennelong 2164

PURCHASE ORDER

To: Purchase Order No:

                             Date:

Please supply the following: Delivery required:

QTY	SIZE	DESCRIPTION

Deliveries accepted from 7.00 a.m.–5.00 p.m. Mon–Fri
and from 7.00 a.m.–1.00 p.m. Sat–Sun only.
If you are unable to supply the specified product or
quantity, or to meet the required delivery date, please
contact the Purchasing Office:

Tel: (033) 2342 9999   Fax: (033) 2342 1111

Figure 8.2 Purchase order

function (that is, one that can be set to ignore the weight of the container) is best.
A small electronic scale, weighing goods up to 5 kg to an accuracy of 1 g, will be
useful for checking portion control products and small items. All products sold by
weight, particularly fish, meat and cheese, should be weighed on arrival and the
actual weights recorded on the docket. When there are multiple cartons of the same
item (for example, 3 kg boxes of mushrooms), sample checking may be done at
random. Any supplier can make an error, but a pattern of repeated variations from
the invoiced weights would be grounds for suspicion.

A thermometer is useful for checking the internal temperature of chilled or frozen goods. Temperature has a significant effect on the shelf-life of many food products, so extra care should be taken, especially with dairy foods (including ice-cream), seafood and meat. A spike-type thermometer with a range of −20 to +20°C is convenient and reasonably accurate. An electronic thermometer, with a metal probe and a digital read-out, is more accurate still. Chilled meats should be within the range of 0 to 3°C on delivery, seafood should not exceed 2°C and dairy foods such as cheese and butter are acceptable in the range of 1 to 5°C. Frozen goods should not be accepted if partially thawed, or if the internal temperature is above −18°C. A close look at the delivery vehicle will give a clue to the conditions under which the goods have been kept. Unless the food is iced, and transported only for short distances, the vehicle must be equipped with a refrigeration unit or freezer. Vehicles used for delivering meat must be registered and regularly inspected.

In order to ensure that all goods are properly inspected and recorded on delivery, it is normal practice in the industry to specify delivery times (say, 7.00 a.m. to 4.00 p.m.), outside which goods will not be accepted.

Common receiving errors

Serious faults in receiving practice will lead inevitably to waste, higher costs and the possibility of fraud. Short weight, undetected, will result in dramatically increased food cost. Product substitution is another way of delivering rather less than what has been ordered. The driver reports that 'they were all out of the one you asked for' and that a substitution has been made. While two products look similar, the yield may be very different; which is why one product was specified in the first place.

A new receiving clerk should be encouraged to question practices that are already in place. If it has become the practice to allow vegetables to sit out unrefrigerated, or to receive some items without weight checks, or to accept 'freebies' from a supplier, then the F&B should be concerned. An interview with a new clerk four or five days after hiring can sometimes call attention to careless practices that have become entrenched in an organisation.

Delivery drivers are often under pressure to complete a round in the minimum time. They would like a quick signature, no questions asked and a rapid departure. This may be in their interest, but it is certainly not in yours. No delivery docket should be signed until a full inspection has been made and any variances have been noted on the docket. These are initialled by the driver and the receiving clerk. A reputation gained for being a 'hard stop', with accurate scales, careful inspections and efficient receiving practices, will do your operation absolutely no harm at all.

The goods received book

Questions about a delivery may come up long after the event, when a chef questions the grade of meat delivered, the Accounts department queries an invoice or

GOODS RECEIVED BOOK

Date	Time	Supplier	Invoice No.	Amount		P/O No.	Rec'd by
24/8	8.15 a.m.	Davidson's	154	122	55	595	P. Smith
24/8	8.30 a.m.	Manning Dry Goods	A22598	450	19	612	P. Smith
24/8	9.20 a.m.	North Coast Catering	4548	160	20	620	T. Wills
24/8	9.50 a.m.	Central Liquor	15–3641	1126	11	591	P. Smith

Figure 8.3 Goods received book

a storeperson cannot find a particular item. To answer these questions, a goods received book will prove useful. It is kept by the receiving clerk and lists, in order, all the goods delivered and signed for on a particular day.

The loading dock is the first place to begin an effective system of controlling costs. Experienced hoteliers regard deliveries on the loading dock as piles of cash, and understand the need to be careful about counting them, checking them and keeping them safe. We demonstrated earlier that shaving costs by a few tenths of a per cent can make a significant difference to operating profits at the end of the year. Tightening up receiving practice is one way of doing this without affecting product quality or customer service.

The food and beverage stores

Once goods have been purchased and received carefully, they must be stored correctly, to avoid waste by deterioration, damage or theft. The main objectives are to keep supplies secure and in good condition, to make them easy to find and count, and to ensure that you do not run out of them when they are needed. Balanced against these requirements is the need to keep the capital invested in stock at a reasonable level. There is always a temptation to overstock against shortages, or to buy in large quantities to obtain a better price. This can be a trap if storage space is limited and a timely return on investment is important. A well-organised Stores department provides just enough, just in time, to run the operation efficiently at a clean-burning profit.

Frozen stores

The need for frozen storage space has increased steadily as more products come on the market, particularly 'convenience' or partially prepared foods. Frozen storage space should be sufficient to prevent overcrowding, and properly equipped with racks and storage bins. It is best to keep carton goods separate from foods that have been prepared by the kitchen. Two freezers are best, but if only one is available it should be partitioned to prevent cross-contamination. Most freezers are designed to keep frozen foods frozen, and have difficulty freezing things down from room temperature. The time required to freeze an item of food has much to do with its storage life and its quality after defrosting. Faster is better, so a commercial system capable of maintaining −18 to −20°C at all times will be required. Frozen storage is not a long-term option for food; this simply slows down deterioration at different rates for different foods.

All frozen goods should be marked with the date received or processed, and a careful eye kept on use-by dates. First in, first out is the accepted practice, to ensure correct stock rotation. As a general rule, three months should be regarded as the safe limit for most foods, if adequate precautions are taken to prevent sublimation (the evaporation of moisture from frozen foods caused by fan-forced circulation of air). Failure to wrap and package foods carefully will result in premature deterioration, poor thawing qualities and freezer burn. Note that if accidental partial thawing occurs (due to a breakdown, for instance), the freezer life of any foods affected will be reduced by as much as half. This sort of damage is cumulative, and is not cured by re-freezing.

Take care to ensure that all freezer compartments are constructed in such a way as to be easy to clean and maintain. Though expensive, stainless steel wire shelving is really the only appropriate material for freezers. Floors, walls and ceiling should be of fibreglass or other washable material.

Chilled stores

Construction and ease-of-cleaning considerations apply equally to chilled storage, but here further precautions must be taken because of the higher ambient temperature. Cross-contamination is a significant danger when fresh meats, vegetables, dairy foods and cooked foods are stored in the same coldroom. In larger operations, it is good practice to have separate coldrooms for prepared foods, for meats and fish, and for fresh vegetables and dairy foods. If these are available, they should be set at different temperatures. Fresh meat and fish keep best at 0 to 1°C, cooked foods at 1 to 3°C, fresh vegetables, dairy products and most fruits at 4 to 7°C. If separate coldrooms are not available, a single coldroom should be run at 1 to 3°C, and strict separation maintained between raw and cooked foods. All raw meats and fish, in particular, should be kept in covered plastic bins. Fresh vegetables should be stored on the lowest level, and strictly quarantined from cooked foods. All items must be covered to prevent accidental spills, drips or splashes. Removable date tags are an important tool for the storekeeper. Any food nearing its use-by date should be brought to the attention of the Executive Chef, so that it may be used before it is lost.

Most local health authorities require that freezers and coldrooms have digital temperature read-outs, or at least a wall-mounted thermometer. Note that the ambient temperature affects the performance of coldrooms and freezers. In tropical climates, including most of northern Australia, heavy-duty compressors will be required to maintain correct temperatures, and any economies made on equipment will be lost many times over in food spoilage.

Dry storage

Temperature is also a factor in dry storage of packaged goods such as grains, flour, bakery mixes, spices and seasonings. The Australian climate is generally much warmer, for a longer part of the year, than that of Europe or North America. Use-by dates and estimated shelf-life of many products will be adversely affected when the ambient temperature is above 20°C. Humidity also plays an important role in the development of moulds, bacteria and insect damage. Dry storage should be just that; air-conditioning or dehumidifying equipment may be required to maintain the ideal 50–60% humidity required for safe storage. Even tinned and bottled goods (including wines) may deteriorate in hot, humid conditions.

The main defences against spoilage in dry stores are temperature and humidity control, good air circulation, insect-proofing and regular cleaning. All dry goods should be kept off the floor. Wooden pallets are not an adequate solution, since they provide a ready source of contamination and may harbour insects or other vermin. Heavy-duty metal wire shelving is the best answer, with the lowest shelf set at least 150 millimetres off the floor to allow for cleaning and air circulation. Layout of the shelving should allow for easy stocktaking, and consideration should be given to safe working practices: light goods are best stored high, heavier packages stored low. All goods should be marked clearly with the date received, and rotated on a first-in-first-out basis. Fixed bin cards, which indicate the movement of goods and the minimum reorder level, will make life easier for store-room staff and promote more efficient monitoring of stock levels.

Stock requisitions

The last step in the accurate control of goods bought into a hotel or restaurant is the requisition form, which records the end user of a product. The data obtained from the requisitions will allow you to close the loop and determine how successful your cost control systems have been.

Requisitions provide many other kinds of useful information, including expected compared with actual return, average consumption and best-selling products. Therefore, it is important that every item issued from stores is recorded. To do this, you will need a requisition system that is simple and straightforward. If a system is clumsy, slow or inefficient, staff will simply find their way around it, and the object of the exercise will be defeated.

Bar requisitions

Many hotel and restaurant bars use the 'one-for-one' system, meaning that bottles of spirits and wines will be issued only if the bar staff can produce an empty bottle with the requisition. The idea behind this system is to prevent overstocking and discourage theft (if a bottle were to disappear, an explanation would be necessary). The disadvantages of the system are several: it is not universal (beers and soft drinks are usually excluded), there are innocent reasons why a bottle may not be there (a guest takes a bottle of champagne to his room, for instance), and it will be necessary to retain several dozen empty bottles behind the bar, at least until the next day. This method can provide close control, but it is difficult to apply, and results are not entirely reliable. (It is not too difficult for a dishonest bartender to obtain an empty bottle.) On balance, there may be more effort involved in getting staff to adhere to this system than the information generated is worth. The 'one-for-one' system was invented in the days before modern electronic tills were introduced, and before managers gained the benefit of daily read-outs.

A 'straight' requisition system for bars means that staff need not keep empty bottles. A requisition is filled out every day by referring to a par stock list kept in the bar. The par stock of Benedictine, for example, might be five-tenths of a bottle. When the level of the bottle drops below half, the bartender orders a fresh bottle. Par stock for house brand vodka might be four 750 mL bottles in the cocktail bar. Bar staff check the shelves and wine bins at the end of the night and requisition accordingly. There may be occasional over-ordering (when stock is miscounted, for example), but this will tend to correct itself over several days. Control is exercised in two ways. First, the requisition must be signed by a bar supervisor, and the stock signed for as it is delivered to the bar or collected from the store. Second, records of the goods issued will be compared against PLU (price look-up) information recorded by the cash register or POS (point-of-sale) machine. If two 750 mL bottles of Glenfiddich are issued in a given period, we will expect to see approximately

50 drinks recorded sold over the same period. As we saw in Chapter 6, it will prove quite difficult to hide shortages or waste over a period of a week or two. If any question arises, a spot check of the bar inventory will reveal any discrepancies. The 'straight' requisition system, matched with modern cash registers, has the advantage of being easy to understand and implement, while providing a very effective check on results.

Food requisitions

Food requisitions can be treated in the same way: a requisition form is completed by the Executive Chef or the section chef, it is presented to the stores, and the supplies are issued. The requisition is then valued according to the latest price records, and that amount is charged out to the outlet that ordered it. No supplies can move without being recorded, and we gain useful information about the amount and type of goods consumed, and who is consuming them. The system is straightforward and easy to run. In some institutional food service operations, a tighter control system is preferred: a chef may call at the store-room with the intention of preparing 100 portions of Greek salad. Referring to a standard recipe card, the storeperson then weighs out and issues the appropriate amount of feta cheese, olives, oil and so on. While this system encourages accurate cost control in school or hospital catering, it would be extremely cumbersome in a restaurant or hotel, where demand for a particular dish is highly unpredictable.

Minor deviations

The gadflies of the requisition system are the inter-departmental transfer and the after-hours store entry. One bottle of Scotch whisky moved from the pool bar to the cocktail bar will distort figures for both outlets, unless the transfer is recorded and Stores are notified. An emergency requisition for more frozen chips from the main kitchen may require that the stores be opened after the storeperson has gone home. In neither case is any real damage done to the control system, as long as the movement is clearly recorded on a requisition. Usually, this responsibility is given to the senior manager on duty, who will have access to the stores keys for emergencies and will document inter-bar transfers.

CHAPTER SUMMARY

If the purpose of business is to make a profit, then the Food and Beverage Manager must have a clear understanding of how profit is made, and how it is measured. While every business seeks to compete for market share and increase sales, it is easy to demonstrate that good control of costs has a dramatic effect on the bottom-line operating profit in any food and beverage operation.

The effective control of costs within a hotel or restaurant can be thought of as a loop: it begins with accurate product specifications, moves through good purchasing and receiving practice, then to proper storage, on to good requisition control and back to the next order. At each stage efficient and practical controls are maintained to monitor how the operation is performing.

Product specifications are essential if we are to be clear about exactly what we want to buy, and suppliers will appreciate a working knowledge of industry terminology, package sizes, grades and measures. A written purchasing policy will help to keep everyone clear about what the goal is, and what is considered ethical practice in the organisation.

Receiving is every bit as important as purchasing, to guarantee that what was ordered is actually delivered and measures up to specification. Proper storage, with particular attention to climate control and cleanliness, will save money by reducing waste and deterioration.

Requisition control will keep track of how the products are used, and provide valuable raw data to enable the Food and Beverage Manager to analyse the efficiency of the cost control system.

REVIEW QUESTIONS

1 'The only way to make more profit is to sell more product.' True or false?

2 What specifications might be given to a prospective supplier of beef Scotch fillet?

3 How might the specifications of two bottles of Scotch whisky differ?

4 What steps can be taken to avoid emergency purchasing?

5 What are the recommended storage conditions for fresh meat? For frozen fish? For fresh vegetables?

6 Give some disadvantages of a 'one-for-one' bottle stock control system.

CHAPTER NINE

STOCKTAKES AND REPORTS

Cost controls, stocktake procedure and stock turn ratio

Understanding financial reports

Testing anticipated cost and anticipated revenue

Controlling labour cost

The role of computers in stock control, par stocks and automatic reordering

Measuring results

A well-designed control system provides an abundance of information; the trick is knowing which figures are important and which are not. Particularly with integrated electronic systems (where the POS machine is linked to Stores, the Front Desk and Accounts), it is possible to generate reams of reports every day. The experienced Food and Beverage Manager understands that figures are no more than a reflection of what has already happened. They may point to something that needs attention; they should not *be* the centre of attention. The role of the manager is one of constant guidance and adjustment. Understand your goals clearly (profitability, customer satisfaction, motivated staff, consistent quality) and seek to achieve them by gently pushing the operation along in the right direction. Reports are like the instrument gauges on a high-performance automobile; they are there to alert you to conditions that may need some correction or adjustment, but staring at the gauges is a dangerous way to drive a car.

Stocktaking

There is no electronic substitute for a physical count of what supplies are on the property at any given time, so the traditional stocktake is still very much part of an effective control system. End-of-month and end-of-year stocktakes may be supplemented by randomly scheduled stocktakes in particular areas (such as the cocktail bar, the banquet store or the butcher's cold-room). Consistency is the main qualification for useful results. If there are no written guidelines for how the stocktake will be conducted, the results will be of questionable value.

Equipment stocktake

To avoid equipment shortages and to plan capital expenditure for the next financial year, it is essential to count equipment at regular intervals. This means a physical inventory of all crockery, glassware, menus, linen, uniforms, chairs, tables, buffet and audio-visual equipment, flatware, utensils, restaurant, kitchen and bar equipment. This is a major job that will require planning and sufficient staff. An equipment stocktake is normally scheduled for overnight at or near the end of the financial year. Equipment may be dealt with *in situ*, with a list of locations written down and checked off as each one is counted. A 'grand stocktake' involves moving all equipment to a central location and counting it there. It may be unpractical to go through this time-consuming procedure every year, but it does have the advantage of retrieving all equipment from the many curious locations it may have moved to, and possibly redistributing surplus or under-used equipment from one department to another. This method is commonly used at the sale of a restaurant or hotel property, since it is by far the more accurate of the two methods.

Some items will inevitably have been lost, pilfered or damaged beyond repair, and a decision can be made on whether replacement is necessary. Other items, particularly glassware and cutlery, must be regarded as consumable supplies, since breakage and loss are frequent enough to require regular replenishment during the year.

Arriving at a result is a matter of confirming the opening inventory, adding any purchases made during the year and subtracting the closing inventory. Excessive losses may point to operating problems. High consumption of glassware, for instance, may be due to careless handling, unsuitable storage racks or poor-quality glassware (which is more prone to breakage). High uniform costs may cause the manager to reconsider how uniforms are issued and cared for. Translated into dollar values, the numbers will be useful to calculate the next year's equipment budget.

Food stocktake

In order to arrive at an accurate food cost, the food stocktake procedure must be well defined. The most workable system counts food in closed containers and unopened packages as purchased: that is, tins of tomatoes are counted; a bucket of cooked tomato sauce is not. Portion-controlled meats such as crumbed chicken breasts are counted in closed boxes as purchased, not by the individual piece. Other meats are counted by the piece: a tagged, sealed package of prime rib of known weight in the butcher's cold-room is counted at purchase price. A pot of beef and red wine casserole is not, since it has already been partially prepared.

This method will leave a certain amount of food in preparation unvalued on the final stocktake list. The presumption is that this value will not change dramatically from month to month, and can safely be considered a constant. The advantage is that stocktaking becomes much faster and more accurate if you are only counting items of known weight or value.

Notice of a stocktake should be given to each department well in advance, so that the actual movement of goods (requisitions, deliveries and returns) can be halted for a reasonable period. Stocktake sheets or hand-held tape recorders are issued, and teams of two people move through an agreed list of storage areas. One person counts; the other records. Since proper identification of foodstuffs is important, at least one person should be a trained chef or storeperson. The Food and Beverage Manager's role will be to check that all areas have been covered, to answer any questions that may arise and to see that proper procedures have been followed.

The raw data must then be processed. First, it is valued. The manager has a choice of using an average price (over three months, for instance), the actual price at which the goods were purchased (even though it may be old stock of questionable value), or the most recent price paid for that item (the 'replacement value'). Each method will give slightly different results. It is consistency that provides an accurate result, so pick a system and stick with it for at least 12 months.

Adjustments must be made for food which has been thrown away, or sold for less than the normal mark-up. (If these were included, our food cost as a percentage of sales would be inaccurate.) Spoilage or waste should be recorded, and the cost taken off the food purchases figure and added to a spoilage account. Food used for staff meals should be treated similarly. If meals or drinks are taken by management in the bars or restaurants and charged at full price, you will not have to adjust for this, since the food has been sold at the normal price.

Beverage stocktake

Counting beverages is easier than counting food, but the principles are the same. Spirits and liqueurs are of high value and are easily measured, so the usual practice is to count open containers in tenths. A bottle of gin may be measured with a cardboard template, or estimated by eye at six-tenths full and so recorded on the stocktake sheet. Open bottles of wine are generally ignored, but we do count full bottles of wine, soft drinks, beers, cider and the like. Kegs and barrels of beer are measured by weight, if a large scale is available. (A litre of beer weighs close enough to one kilogram for this purpose; an empty 50 litre barrel weighs 13 kilograms.) Modern integral beer kegs cannot be opened for inspection, so if no scale is available the contents may be estimated, or ignored. Whichever procedure is followed, make sure that it is written down so that the next stocktake is consistent with the last. Post mix syrups in open packages are generally ignored.

All bars are counted and, of course, the main liquor store. There is a temptation to adjust par stocks during a stocktake, when it is discovered that the pool bar has somehow accumulated seven bottles of cherry brandy, but the temptation should be resisted, since it will only create unnecessary confusion on paper. Make a note of the overstock and have it corrected by a return to stores the following day.

As for food, a policy must be set for valuation of the stock. The last price, price as purchased or average price method may be applied, as long as the same method is used each time. Adjustments are made for beverages issued to kitchen (such as cooking wines, sherry and brandy), for spills and mispours (which the bar staff have been encouraged to record), and for spoilage in stores (a leaking cask, for instance, or a wine damaged by a mouldy cork).

If the hotel authorises management or staff to consume beverages or entertain guests on the premises, these should be recorded at normal prices and charged to a management account or entertainment account.

Operating supplies stocktake

You may be surprised to learn just how much money is spent every month on consumable supplies such as matchboxes, napkins, straws, toothpicks, coffee filters, cleaning products, printed forms, menus, doilies and register supplies. These supplies represent a cost, just as food and beverages do. With operating profits often measured in single digits, they are just as important to control.

An oversupply of these items in the outlets can lead to waste and carelessness, so it is appropriate to set par levels and check them at stocktake. In this case, unopened cartons, boxes or packets will be sufficient for an accurate count. Adjustments are unlikely, unless there have been significant transfers between one department and another.

Interpreting reports

Food cost percentage

Food cost is calculated:

Opening stock + purchases this month – closing stock = food cost

Then the standard formula is applied:

Cost of goods sold ÷ value of sales × 100 = food cost percentage

The food cost percentage is more useful than the actual dollar cost, since it gives a useful result, whether sales are high or low. There is no 'correct' food cost percentage for a food and beverage operation; the range of possibilities is too wide. In outside catering, for instance, food cost may be as low as 20%, but this only reflects the high costs of labour, equipment and transportation as a percentage of the sales price. In a fine dining restaurant, food cost may run as high as 40%, reflecting the price paid for expensive ingredients. In a family restaurant or a hotel coffee shop, a food cost percentage above 32% may be cause for concern. The aim is to set a budget target for food cost percentage, based on industry experience and the past trading records of the establishment, then to watch deviations from this figure.

If the food cost percentage is too high, there may be several reasons. Bad purchasing decisions could be at fault—goods purchased at unnecessarily high prices, or in uneconomical quantities. Poor-quality ingredients often result in excessive trimming, low yield and customer rejection. Poor adherence to standard recipes or inaccurate portioning by kitchen staff may be the cause. Excessive waste or spoilage, either in stores or in the kitchen, could be investigated. Staff pilferage, uncontrolled consumption or outright theft may be problems. If all of these prove to be within acceptable limits, menu prices should be reviewed to ensure an adequate return.

A low food cost may be superficially welcome, but it provides its own message to an experienced manager. Quality of finished product should be checked, to ensure customer satisfaction. Menu prices should be reviewed to see if slightly lower prices, or a special offer, could stimulate more sales.

A 'flash' food cost is sometimes produced by the food and beverage controller, which compares a day's purchases against a day's sales. This rough estimate is of limited value (a large delivery of food may arrive on a slow day for sales), but if it is accompanied by a figure for the month to date, the manager may be able to take action before the end of the month to correct a problem.

Anticipated cost test

Another useful control is the anticipated cost test. The PLU information recorded on a cash register or POS machine gives the numbers of each dish sold in a month. If the records show sales of 1024 portions of garlic prawns in that period, you could check the standard recipe card and the yield test to see if the results make sense (Table 9.1).

Table 9.1 Anticipated cost test

Yield test—green prawns:	
Delivered weight of green tiger prawns	1000 g
Average price per kg	$18.50
Weight of shells, heads, trimmings	480 g
Clean weight of prawns	520 g
Portion size	200 g
Portion price as served	$7.12
Menu price	$21.00

Anticipated cost:
1024 portions @ 200 g = 204.8 kg
204.8 kg clean weight = 393.8 kg as purchased (204.8 ÷ 0.52 = 393.8)
393.8 kg @ $18.50 per kg = $7285.30

In this example, we would expect to see consumption of green prawns total-ling approximately $7285 for the month, if prawns were not used for any other dish on the menu. Several variables may affect this figure (seasonal price fluc-tuation, portion accuracy or other dishes containing prawns), but it does give the Food and Beverage Manager an indication of what results to expect. If records show $10 000 worth of prawns used during the month, for instance, this would merit investigation. The anticipated cost test is more accurate with portion-controlled products, which explains their popularity in fast food restaurants where margins are likely to be tight. Anticipated cost can be used to judge the accuracy of the yield tests and indicate how well standard recipes are adhered to.

Stock turn ratio

Another significant figure derived from the stocktake is the stock turn ratio. This indicates the amount of time goods spend in store before they are prepared and sold. The more quickly a product is cooked and served, the more quickly the operator sees a profit on the sale. In general, a rapid turnover of stock is desirable. To calcu-late the average value of stock held during the month, we use the formula:

Opening stock + closing stock ÷ 2 = average stock

Next, we calculate the number of times the stock turns over in a month:

Stock used this month ÷ average stock = monthly stock turn ratio

To illustrate, let us presume that the average food stock held by Glendowne Grill Restaurant is $64 000, and that food sales for the month are $155 750. The formula is applied:

$155 750 ÷ $64 000 = 2.43

That is to say, the whole stock can be expected to turn over 2.43 times per month. This figure is monitored every month, or every quarter, to determine how fast purchases are turned into sales. A rising stock turn ratio (goods selling faster) is generally welcome, as long as suppliers are delivering promptly and there are no shortages experienced. A falling stock turn ratio (goods selling more slowly) is a warning to the Food and Beverage Manager that excessive capital is tied up in stock, over-ordering may be a problem, or that some stock is becoming obsolete due to changes in the menu or public taste.

Beverage cost percentage

The beverage cost percentage is calculated in the same way as the food cost percen-tage. The adjusted beverage cost is divided by the beverage sales figure and multiplied by 100 to give a percentage cost. This calculation may be applied to individual bars, or to the operation as a whole. Again, there is no 'standard' beverage cost in the industry: the banquet bar may run as low as 20%, reflecting brisk sales of high-profit carafe wines, spirits and soft drinks. A restaurant with a fine wine list may show a beverage cost as high as 40%, reflecting the high cost of premium bottled wines as a percentage of sales. It is a *change* to the average beverage cost percentage that will alert the Food and Beverage Manager to possible problems.

A rising beverage cost in a particular outlet may point to careless dispensing by bar staff, excessive waste in draught beer systems, poor attention to standard recipes, pilfering or drinks dispensed without payment. Any of these would demand prompt investigation. A rising beverage cost across the board would call attention to purchasing practice (paying too much for supplies, or buying in uneconomical quantities), poor storage (losses due to theft, spoilage or careless handling), or poor receiving practice (short deliveries or wrong product). Careless supervision of ullage (the amount of beer left in a barrel when returned to the brewery) may also be a cause.

A falling beverage cost is usually a good thing, but it may also indicate a change in customer buying habits. Check which products are selling well, and how much contribution they make to your overall running costs. A restaurant that sells a lot of cask wine will have a low beverage cost, but will miss out on the higher contribution from sales of premium bottled wines.

Anticipated revenue test

As described in Chapter 6, the anticipated revenue test looks at whether the amount of stock consumed is matched by the amount of sales produced. This is a useful management tool, particularly in beverage operations, where portions are tightly controlled and remaining stock is easy to count. It is the most common method used to spot dishonesty or theft. If a bottle of Scotch whisky is purchased at $24.95 (inclusive of taxes and licence fee), it is easy to calculate the number of servings it contains. A 750 mL bottle dispensed in 30 mL servings yields 25 portions (750 mL ÷ 30 mL = 25). If the bar price for a serving of Scotch is $3.50, then you may expect sales revenue of $87.50 for each bottle of Scotch used. Next, calculate the anticipated revenue for each type of beverage. (Not all bottles yield the same number of servings, and prices vary from one beverage to another.) Then add up the total anticipated revenue for each bottle, keg and cask used in a particular bar in a month and compare it to the actual revenue for the same period. After allowances have been made for transfers, mispours and stock remaining in the bar, you arrive at a variance figure, expressed as a dollar amount or as a percentage of sales.

A high negative variance means that some product has disappeared without producing the expected income. The reasons may be carelessness, unauthorised consumption, excessive waste or dishonesty. A positive variance (more revenue than expected) can, in some circumstances, point to the more unusual ploy of bringing liquor into the hotel and selling it at bar prices. Neither of these should prompt the Food and Beverage Manager to make any premature conclusions, but either one may suggest a closer look at operations in that bar.

Labour cost percentage

The cost of employing staff is often the biggest cost the restaurateur or hotelier has to deal with. The hospitality industry is by nature labour-intensive, and profits may be severely eroded by an inability to control labour cost, even in a successful operation. Labour cost is a complex calculation which includes many 'on-costs', such as staff training, uniforms, sick pay, penalty rates, holiday pay and loading, superannuation, insurance and subsidised meals. A full-time table server earning an award wage of $10.50 per hour may actually be costing the establishment more than $12.50 per hour after 'on-costs' have been taken into account. This makes a casual server's rate of $13.20 per hour more understandable; the casual rate is meant to compensate the casual worker for benefits normally given to full-time staff, and the part-time nature of his work. It is the total cost of employing staff that is applied against the sales to calculate a labour cost percentage. The formula is the same as for any other cost:

$$\text{Total labour cost} \div \text{total sales} \times 100 = \text{percentage labour cost}$$

Part of the total labour cost will be fixed; that is, it will not vary appreciably with the amount of sales. Examples are the costs of employing cashiers, managers and supervisors, the full-time kitchen staff and full-time service and bar staff. Another part of the labour cost does vary with the amount of business: the cost of casual staff employed to cope with busy periods or a banquet, for instance. Because we are dealing with people, labour cost is inherently more difficult to control than food or beverage cost. The variables include rostering, staff efficiency, level of training, work practices, the type of equipment available to do the job, the design of the restaurant and the pattern of customer demand.

Labour cost percentage may rise dramatically if sales drop; you cannot dismiss trained full-time staff because of a slow night in the restaurant. Neither can you employ half a person. The key to controlling labour cost is the ability to forecast sales. In a banquet function you can use casual staff, roster them on during peak periods and then send some of them off duty when demand drops. In the restaurant or bar this is more difficult, since the venue must stay open for a certain number of hours, even if there are no customers at all. Business may be affected by the number of guests staying in a hotel, by the weather, by the night of the week, by other events happening in the locality, by holidays or sporting events or even by what television show is on that night.

To understand labour cost results, you will need to collect other statistics. For instance, in a large hotel there is usually a direct correlation between room occupancy and the number of covers served for breakfast. If you maintain records for several months and learn that, on average, 78 per cent of guests staying in-house eat breakfast in the hotel, then a forecast from the Front Office, predicting 220 rooms occupied next Thursday night, will give a reasonably good indication of how many breakfast covers to expect on Friday morning. The relationship between room occupancy and number of luncheon or dinner covers may be more tenuous, but there will still be a relationship, and it provides a starting-point for staff rostering.

In a free-standing restaurant or club, there will be an obvious difference between the number of customers on a Saturday night and on a Monday night. But if the restaurant manager records more detail in the restaurant diary (weather conditions, other events in town, special promotions, sporting events), then a useful record is created to help predict future demand. If tour business is a part of your organisation, an accurate forecast from reservations, with tour numbers, arrival times, meal arrangements and so on, will be useful when writing staff rosters for the restaurants and bars.

The actual labour cost percentage for a given period may be broken down into separate operating areas (say kitchen, cocktail bar, coffee shop), then compared with the projected revenue (was the roster written sensibly to fit the forecast?) and the actual revenue (was the forecast accurate?). While there is always some room for adjustment on the day, cost-efficient rostering is very much a product of accurate forecasting.

Staff factors

If labour cost percentage were entirely dependent on sales, and an accurate forecasting model could be devised, there would be little difficulty in controlling it. Unfortunately, it is more complicated than that. Two inexperienced staff may take four hours working together to complete a task, where one skilled person might do the job in three hours alone. Many job classifications in the Australian hotel and restaurant industry (such as table server, bartender and porter) do not recognise any difference in the wages payable to a skilled or an unskilled worker. There may be considerable resistance to differential pay rates, not only from staff and unions but from management as well. The principle of 'the same rate for the same job' is well entrenched in the Australian award system. The cost of getting a job done, then, can vary greatly according to who is doing it. In this case, staff recruitment and on-the-job training become very important factors in labour cost control, and a high labour cost may reflect poor hiring practice, or a failure to build productivity through training.

Since the rate for full-time and casual staff is little different after 'on-costs' are built in, it would not seem to make much difference whether one or the other were rostered on for a particular shift. The difference is, of course, that the full-time worker is guaranteed a 40-hour week (37.5 or 38 hours in some job classifications), whereas casual workers can be sent home if business does not justify keeping them on. This leads some managers to believe that all staff should be casual, but such a reaction ignores the increased costs of recruiting and training a group of people who inevitably have a higher rate of turnover. The answer is a well-considered mix of full-time staff in production, supervision and core hour service, supplemented by casual staff at peak periods. How well this mix is handled will be reflected in the labour cost figures.

Some managers are all too eager to blame a high labour cost percentage on poor staff productivity or high rates of pay, and yet will staunchly refuse to take responsibility for their own decisions on methods of work and organisation. The manager who carelessly tells an employee to 'get something done about that', while he carefully avoids giving exact instructions about what is to be done or how it is to be accomplished, opens himself to derision and practically guarantees a labour cost problem. Active management is the only solution to organisational problems; four hours spent helping staff cope with a heavy rush of business will tell you far more about workplace efficiency than four days of studying reports. This is not to say that a manager's role is to operate the dishwashing machine; the point is to see at first hand where changes to method, equipment or practice could achieve better productivity, and therefore a lower labour cost.

Too low a labour cost can also indicate some problems. If employees are seriously overworked, they are likely to leave (although a well-motivated employee's capacity for work should not be underestimated). If staff are forced to cut corners anywhere, it is often customer service that suffers first, which inevitably leads to dissatisfaction and falling sales. Inefficient methods of work or poor equipment will not only place severe strains on the staff, but will also shorten the service life of what equipment there is, causing higher repair and maintenance costs.

Average check

There is a danger in concentrating exclusively on the control of costs and ignoring the benefit of increased sales. Electronic cash registers and POS machines can generate very detailed information on the average check achieved for each meal service and outlet. This information should be closely monitored by the Food and Beverage Manager. In Chapter 4, we discussed the rules of 'menu engineering' and how changes can be made to improve results. However, you cannot wait until a new menu is introduced to do something about a poor average check. If the current average check at breakfast is $5.50, you may conclude that most customers are choosing to have a croissant and a cup of coffee and are ignoring the cooked breakfast selections and the fresh orange juice. There are three ways to deal with this, before deciding to make any changes to the menu:

- Make the product more attractive to the customer.
- Include the product with another product.
- Promote suggestive selling.

If you are not satisfied with an average breakfast check of $5.50, you may consider redesigning the breakfast buffet, putting a chef in the restaurant to make omelettes to order, or improving advertising to attract a greater market share. A better average check would result if all customers had a small glass of fresh orange juice with their breakfast. If the standard glass is $3.00, consider offering a 'breakfast upgrade' at a slightly reduced price (coffee plus croissant plus orange juice for $7.50) or use a smaller glass and offer an 'eye-opener special' for $1.50.

As discussed in Chapter 3, suggestive selling is used to great effect by skilled restaurateurs, from those in fast food outlets to those in the most sophisticated restaurants. A short, sharp campaign to get every table server to ask 'And would you like a glass of fresh orange juice?' will produce immediate results, if you can present it as fun and challenging, rather than as a dreary chore. Upselling goes much further than asking rote questions, though. Table servers who genuinely understand and enjoy the products the restaurant offers will, almost unconsciously, sell more of them.

The effect of a better average check is to improve profits, if all other factors remain the same. Overhead costs are not likely to increase significantly because the customer has a side order or another glass of wine with his or her meal. A table server looking after four people will not have a great deal more work to do if all four guests are tempted to order a dessert. Yet this could easily add $26 to the table account, multiplied by the number of tables served that evening. A better average check has the tendency to go straight to the bottom line, so it is a potent tool for improving overall profits.

CHAPTER SUMMARY

Modern information systems generate a huge amount of data on sales patterns, percentage costs, average check and other indicators. To the professional Food and Beverage Manager, these are valuable measures of performance, and they will be checked frequently to monitor the food service operation. They are not, however, an end in themselves. Such indicators point to a need for specific adjustments. Skilled managers will have a good understanding of what factors may cause poor results, and a whole range of practical solutions at their fingertips.

The Food and Beverage Manager must understand the importance of correct stocktake procedures, in order to guarantee reasonable accuracy of the base data. He or she will be conversant with the relationship between food cost, beverage cost, anticipated cost and anticipated revenue, and will have a clear understanding of how labour cost and average check can affect profitability.

REVIEW QUESTIONS

1 What three methods may be used to value goods recorded during a stocktake?

2 What factors may cause a high food cost percentage?

3 Your menu features roast leg of lamb, served every day. You purchase rolled boneless leg (RBL) of lamb for this dish, and use it for no other item on the menu. Given the following data, calculate the anticipated cost of RBL lamb for the month:

Average price per kg as purchased	$6.40
Average trim weight per kg (fat, scraps)	nil
Average cooking loss per kg	120 g
Portion size, cooked	200 g
Portions sold last month	1085

4 What dangers are involved in a low stock-turn ratio?

5 What is an anticipated revenue test?

6 The year-to-date figures for the Central City Hotel show that sales revenue is pretty much on track, but labour cost is well above budget. What steps would you suggest to bring it back into line?

CHAPTER TEN

SANITATION
AND
SAFETY

Basic principles of food service
sanitation

Pathogenic organisms and other
sources of contamination

Controlling foodborne illness

The sanitation plan and the health
inspector's visit

Occupational health and safety laws

Fire safety in hotels and kitchens

The unspoken agreement

Customers entering a restaurant, café or hotel will have certain expectations that the restaurateur or hotelier is obliged to meet. They expect to be treated politely, to enjoy reasonably comfortable surroundings, to be able to order a range of food and drinks, and to consume them in safety. They will make an immediate judgement on the first three elements, and leave if the welcome or the surroundings do not suit them. Safety, on the other hand, is more difficult to judge. Customers have no alternative but to trust the restaurateur to handle food correctly, so that what is served is wholesome, uncontaminated and safe to consume. They presume that the restaurant is kept clean, safe and adequately protected from fire and other dangers. The restaurateur can train staff to be welcoming and polite, and offer an interesting menu. The hotelier can see to it that the furnishings and décor are attractive and in good repair. Both of them have an obligation to see that safe procedures are followed in food handling, work practices and general sanitation, thus keeping their side of an unspoken agreement with the customer.

Unfortunately, food service safety and sanitation is not seen as the glamorous end of our profession. It is often the last item on the mental agenda—far less interesting a subject than promotion of the latest wine list, the Chef's new menu or the refurbishment of the lounge bar. Nevertheless, a sound working knowledge of the subject is an essential qualification for a professional Food and Beverage Manager, and in many countries a restaurateur must demonstrate a formal qualification in food sanitation before being granted a licence to operate a restaurant. Public health and safety regulations are becoming more rigorous every year in Australia, so it will pay to know what constitutes good practice. The cost of altering or rebuilding an unsuitable facility can be high, but it pales in comparison to the cost of a lawsuit, should careless practice result in an injury to a customer or an employee.

Foodborne illness

There is probably no other subject pertaining to the restaurant business that attracts so much enthusiastic, and ill-informed, comment from the general public than the subject of food 'poisoning'. Almost everyone has at least one story to relate of an illness contracted after eating something at a restaurant or café. While there are dozens of factors that can produce the symptoms the public associates with food poisoning, the average person will almost inevitably blame the last thing he or she ate at a restaurant for the problem. Even the most hygienic food service operation can be unfairly accused of causing illness, and there is no effective comeback for the restaurateur: if the customer says he became ill after eating your food, there is almost no way of proving that it *wasn't* your food that caused the illness. The only option, then, for the food service manager, is to ensure that it is extremely *unlikely* that a customer should suffer a foodborne illness after eating at your establishment. To accomplish this, you will need to understand where foodborne illness comes from and how it can be controlled.

Pathogenic organisms

A pathogenic organism is one capable of producing disease in another living organism. We are surrounded by a whole host of pathogenic organisms in the natural environment. Some of these organisms cause illness in humans; some do not affect us at all. Of the ones that do affect us, a handful are commonly carried in food, and it is this group that most concerns the food service operator.

Chemical contamination

Few people would be unaware of the concern with which the general public regards chemical contamination in food. Pesticides, heavy metals, certain preservatives, artificial flavourings and colourings have all come in for severe criticism. Restaurant patrons object strongly to ingesting unwelcome chemicals with their food, and some of these chemicals may cause illness.

Physical contamination

The presence of broken glass, a bottle top, a piece of wire or a rubber band in a serving of food is obviously distressing for diners, even if they do not suffer a direct injury from it. More importantly, such an occurrence indicates a failure in safe food handling, and the restaurateur must suspect that other dangers are also going undetected.

Pest contamination

Like pathogenic organisms, pests have a strong instinct to reproduce, and the combination of a ready food supply and a suitable environment makes the restaurant kitchen or store-room attractive to a variety of insects and rodents. Not only can they cause direct damage, but pests also harbour pathogens which may, in turn, infect food.

The sanitation program

Since these sources of foodborne illness are more or less present everywhere, the food service manager must design a system that prevents contamination, controls the growth of pathogenic organisms and promotes safe handling. There is an important distinction to be made between 'clean' and 'sanitary'. 'Clean' refers to the visible condition of the dining room, equipment, storage areas and food handling staff. 'Sanitary' refers to the absence of dangerous contaminants, whether visible or invisible. A good sanitation program aims at controlling contamination, using chemical, environmental and practical means to deliver a safe product to the customer.

There may be some reluctance to admit that food contamination is a problem, particularly from food preparation staff who take pride in their work habits and professionalism. Unfortunately, foodborne illness is not restricted to small, dirty, poorly-run restaurants on the wrong side of the tracks. Some of the most serious outbreaks of foodborne illness in Australia have happened in large, carefully-supervised catering and food processing operations. No kitchen is immune from the host of dangerous organisms carried in from outside sources every day. Some people believe that, as more convenience foods and portion-controlled foods come on to the market, safe food handling will become easier. This is a dangerous fallacy: partially-prepared foods often require stricter handling practice than fresh, unprocessed foods.

The first step is education. All food handling staff (including bar staff and service staff) should be aware of the basic theory behind food sanitation. The worst enemy is ignorance; thousands of food handlers in the industry endanger themselves and their customers simply because they do not know what constitutes safe practice.

Bacteria, viruses and fungi

Bacteria are the most numerous and widely distributed forms of life on earth. They are present in water, in the air, in the soil, on the skin and in the intestinal tracts of insects and animals (including humans). Even in the deepest caves and the most remote areas on the planet, bacteria thrive and grow. These single-celled oganisms are immensely adaptive, and can live and reproduce in environments that would kill a human within hours. Given suitable conditions their reproductive cycle is explosive, and a single bacterium can produce billions of its own kind in less than 24 hours. Faced with such a formidable form of life, it is just as well that most of them are benign, and even helpful, to humans. The human digestive system could not function without the presence of beneficial bacteria in the intestines. Many of the foods we eat require bacterial action to grow, so our dependence on these microscopic organisms is complete.

Because they are so small (a typical bacterium is less than one-thousandth of a millimetre long), they are impossible to see without a microscope. Therein lies the problem for the food service operator, because not all of these animals are friendly. Some of them cause serious—even deadly—illness in humans, and it is these few that we are concerned about.

Bacteria are, like other living things, sensitive to their environment; and while they are highly adaptable, their growth may be contained by controlling temperature, moisture, acidity and the availability of oxygen in their immediate surroundings. Many bacteria can be killed or severely retarded by the absence of water, by a highly acidic environment, or by direct heat. This explains why early humans, long before they discovered bacteria, learned by trial and error that drying, salting, pickling or cooking food could preserve it from decay.

Types of bacteria

Clostridium perfringens This is sometimes referred to as 'the fridge bug', because of its tolerance of low temperatures. It causes abdominal pain, diarrhoea and nausea, usually from 8 to 22 hours after ingestion, and is generally regarded as a mild, but very common, foodborne pathogen. Found in soil and dust, and in the intestinal tracts of humans and animals. Commonly carried into kitchens with fresh vegetables. Highly temperature resistant, *C. perfringens* forms spores that can survive boiling, and will grow in the absence of oxygen.

Staphylococcus aureus 'Golden staph' is a very fast-acting pathogen, causing vomiting, cramps, diarrhoea and nausea within 1 to 6 hours after ingestion. The principal source is humans (40 to 50 per cent of the population may be carriers without suffering illness), especially those with open cuts, infections, abrasions, coughing, sneezing, pimples or skin irritations. It grows well in moist, high-protein foods, particularly meats and dairy foods. Tasteless, odourless and temperature tolerant, it is unpleasant but seldom deadly.

Salmonella There are several varieties, including the highly dangerous *S. typhii* (the cause of typhoid fever); others are less dangerous and rarely fatal. Symptoms include headache, fever, vomiting and abdominal cramps, usually appearing 6 to 48 hours after ingestion, but persistent over 2 to 3 days. Sources: shellfish, poultry (especially chicken), eggs, sausages, any uncooked meats, faeces spread by humans, flies or rodents. Destroyed by temperatures above 60°C. Commonly spread by cross-contamination.

Clostridium botulinum The cause of botulism, a serious disease with up to 65 per cent mortality, this organism is fortunately very rare in food service operations. It causes vomiting, abdominal cramps, acute distress and progressive respiratory paralysis, appearing 12 to 36 hours after ingestion. Anaerobic, *C. botulinum* grows in the absence of oxygen, particularly inside poorly processed tins of fish and other low-acid foods. Notably dangerous in home bottling or canning, it promotes visible decay and foaming, blown tins. Small amounts can be deadly: do not taste suspect foods. It is destroyed by high temperature.

Shigella This produces the disease known as dysentery. It is fairly rare, but implicated in shellfish poisoning due to polluted water. Humans are also a prime source, and faeces transmitted by flies, roaches and rodents. Symptoms are diarrhoea, cramps and fever occurring 12 to 36 hours after contact. It can be serious; fatal in rare cases. Controlled by water purification and careful hygiene in food handling, the organism is destroyed by boiling.

Viral infections

Viral disease is not commonly transmitted by food, because viruses are seldom able to survive for long outside the human body. Of some concern to the food service operator are the several viruses that cause hepatitis, a serious disease which may be carried by shellfish harvested from polluted waters. Because they are often consumed raw, oysters are the main culprit. Government inspection of oysters and other shellfish is quite strict, so purchases from licensed seafood wholesalers can usually be presumed safe. Under no circumstances should shellfish be purchased from any other source. Direct human-to-human transmission of viruses is possible in the food service industry, but human-to-food-to-human transmission is rare.

Organic toxins

Isolated cases of foodborne illness are attributed to toxic contamination from biological sources. Freshwater or saltwater fish affected by algal blooms may be dangerous, but the most common problem (although it is itself rare) is ciguatera toxin, found in the flesh and internal organs of some tropical fish, notably red bass, mackerel and other large Barrier Reef predators. A residual toxin, it accumulates in the food chain from its original source, a kind of alga growing on coral. Large fish from tropical waters must always be suspect, but occurrences are rare and usually affect anglers who consume a large amount of flesh from one contaminated fish. The effects are unpredictable, but essentially neurological: dizziness, double vision, extreme sensitivity to touch and breathing difficulty. Symptoms appear 2 to 12 hours after consumption. The toxin is odourless and tasteless and is highly resistant to heat, so cooking is not an adequate precaution.

Parasites

Here, the principal source of concern to the food service manager is the organism *Trichinella spiralis*, a tiny worm found in the flesh of domestic and wild pigs. It causes trichinosis, an unpleasant illness in humans. Symptoms appear 2 to 28 days after consumption of contaminated meat and include vomiting, nausea and abdominal pain, followed by fever. Even commercially produced pork carries some risk, but fortunately the parasite is easily killed by proper cooking. Pork should always be cooked to an internal temperature of 75°C, or until the meat turns completely grey. Sausages made with pork meat carry the same risk, so thorough cooking is the rule.

Fungi

Fungi are not animals, but plants, and include the whole family of edible mush-rooms, as well as yeasts and moulds. Cultured yeast is regularly used to make bread, cakes, beer and wine. Wild yeasts are always present in the air and account for much food spoilage, characterised by bubbling (CO_2 gas), a sour smell, and a vinegary or alcoholic taste. Yeast grows in the same temperature range as bacteria, and prefers moist conditions. It is easily killed by boiling and is toxicologically harmless, but may leave a tainted taste in food. Some mushrooms are highly poisonous, but this need not concern the food service operator who purchases edible fungi from recog-nised growers. Moulds, on the other hand, are a concern, because they will grow in a wide range of conditions, from cool and dry to warm and moist. Moulds are unsightly, and some are suspected to be mildly carcinogenic. They also may pro-duce infections of the sinuses or the skin, and are generally to be avoided. Any food showing signs of wild mould infection should be discarded. Ground spices exhibit-ing a rank, musty smell are also suspect.

Methods of control

Temperature control

Temperature control is the most important method of controlling bacterial growth. Most dangerous bacteria are held in check by low temperatures and destroyed by high temperatures (though there are notable exceptions). Freezer temperatures (−10 to −20°C) will slow bacterial growth almost to a standstill and will kill some of them, but not all. Cold-room temperatures (0 to 10°C) will slow bacterial growth, but do not stop it. A holding temperature of 70 to 80°C for hot food will stop growth and kill many bacteria, but not all of them. Cooking temperatures (100°C and above) will kill most bacteria, but may not destroy dangerous toxins. The danger zone, in which bacteria grow explosively, is between 15 and 60°C. In this range, a single bacterium can become a serious hazard in a few hours. Note that if food spends any time at all in this temperature range, bacterial growth will occur. If the food is later cooled, the bacteria do not die; they simply stop growing. So food safety is a function of temperature multiplied by time. From this, we get the industry rule 'Keep cold food cold, hot food hot, and do it quickly'.

Remember that a safe temperature means a safe temperature in all parts of the dish concerned. If a large container is used, the centre of the food may remain hot long after the surface appears to have chilled. Agitation is important to ensure rapid, even cooling or heating. This is why defrosting meats or fish at room temperature is so dangerous: by the time the core is defrosted, the skin of a chicken, for instance, has been at room temperature for a long time. Defrosting food in a coldroom ensures that the outside of the food never rises higher than the 0 to 7°C ambient temperature. It is slower, but much safer.

Temperature control is not completely effective, because bacteria are remarkably resilient. Some types form temperature-resistant spores, which easily survive freezing to −20°C, and may survive boiling at 100°C. When the food moves into the danger zone again, the bacteria will regrow. Most bacteria produce some form of toxin, which may be far more resistant to heat than the bacteria themselves. Thus, a food heavily contaminated by bacteria can remain dangerous even after the bacteria have been killed.

A case in point

Dora, a breakfast cook at the City National Hotel, had studied sanitation during her apprenticeship, but that was a long time ago, and no one on the management staff seemed overly concerned about it. Dora normally worked without help until the lunch shift started at 11.00 a.m., and she had devised a few short-cuts to make her job easier. After breakfast, she was responsible for preparing the soup of the day and setting up the lunchtime salad bar. On this morning she was running behind, and decided to re-use yesterday's beef and vegetable soup, rather than make a new batch. She took a container of it from the coldroom, put it in the bain-marie and turned it on at 10.00 a.m., in plenty of time to get hot by 12.00. Dora got the salads out of the fridge, then noticed that she was short of coleslaw, and had to go and make some. It took some time, but she still managed to get everything out on the salad bar in time for service, and got ready to go home. Just as she was leaving, the restaurant manager came in to say that a man had called to complain that his whole family had been ill after eating lunch at the restaurant the previous day. Dora left the lunch cooks to deal with that. After all, it was nothing to do with her.

In the above example, it is not surprising that foodborne illness has been reported, and there is probably much more of it going unreported. The breakfast cook's handling of temperature control is terrible, and without any effective supervision it may not even come to the attention of the Executive Chef. The soup which had been saved from the previous day might have been safe in the coldroom, but when it was placed in a cold bain-marie to heat up, it would spend at least 120 minutes in the danger range of 10 to 60°C—long enough for explosive bacterial growth. Bains–marie are designed to keep hot foods hot, not to heat them. The salads that were left on the bench at a warm room temperature might well have included mayonnaise-based sauces, diced meat and other protein-rich foods: perfect media for more bacterial growth. Putting them in a chilled salad display later would do nothing to control toxic contamination. With no input from management, other than to pass along a complaint, this is a disaster waiting to happen.

Cross-contamination

The single most common cause of bacterial infection in the food service industry is cross-contamination; that is, contact between a food that is unsafe and one that is presumed to be safe. The best example is contact between raw foods and cooked foods. All raw foods, including such innocuous ingredients as parsley and lettuce, must be considered bacterially 'hot', since they have undergone no cooking at all from the fresh state.

When cutting boards, knives, bowls and serving platters are used to process or serve food, they must be sterilised between uses. A chef portions a raw chicken (a very common source of staph bacteria) on a cutting board, then gives it a perfunctory wipe with a wet cloth before dicing the ham for a ham salad. The ham is cross-contaminated with live bacteria. Because the ham salad will not subsequently be cooked, and may spend time in the temperature danger zone, it is an unacceptable risk that your customers would not take if they were aware of it. Raw meat, contaminated with a small amount of clostridium bacteria, is stored in a coldroom for tomorrow evening's banquet. A busy table server goes into the coldroom for butter portions and does not notice when he jars the tray, causing a splash of meat juice to fall into a bowl of chocolate dessert mix. Later, the chocolate mousse is piped into glasses and left at room temperature on the buffet for more than two hours. By the time it is consumed, it is badly contaminated with clostridium and may cause everyone who eats it to become ill. To prevent cross-contamination, all containers should be covered; fresh and cooked foods should be kept separate; equipment should be sterilised (usually by machine dishwashing) between uses; and staff should be trained in safe practice.

A case in point

In an actual case reported in North Queensland, a group of tourists who had eaten at the same restaurant all became ill within 12 hours, exhibiting classic signs of foodborne illness. A Health Department check of the premises showed a reasonable standard of sanitation and cleanliness. Tests returned from the laboratory, however, revealed a sample batch of tabouli salad to be seriously contaminated with E. coli bacteria: almost certainly the cause of the illness. A check with the supplier tracked the parsley used in the salad back to an organic farm where dilute animal sewage was used as a fertiliser. The grower presumed that the parsley would be thoroughly washed before use; the restaurateur presumed that it was safe as delivered.

Personal hygiene

With humans as the principal source for a number of dangerous bacteria, (notably staphylococcus, shigella and clostridium) it must be obvious that good personal hygiene is vital in any food-handling role. Employees must wash their hands frequently, particularly after using the bathroom, changing clothes, handling money, smoking, sneezing, handling raw food or carrying boxes. Hair restraints are important, and plastic gloves are called for in some applications. Note that any staff member who has a chest infection, an open sore or rash, an itchy scalp, dermatitis, severe acne, sneezing or coughing cannot safely handle food, and should be put on other duties until recovered.

It is the manager's responsibility to see that handwashing and changing facilities are provided and used. There should never be a shortage of toilet supplies, and it is vital that clear rules of sanitation are posted, training given and reviews conducted to see that safe standards are maintained. This is a basic duty of care; the manager who fails to take this responsibility seriously is far more culpable, in law and in practice, than the employee whose error caused an outbreak of foodborne illness.

Sterilisation

Contamination in the food service environment is almost continuous, and it cannot always be controlled by safe food handling and temperature control. Used utensils, dirty plates, soiled preparation areas, insects, rubbish bins, empty packages and people are all sources of dangerous microbes. Some items will be passed through an automatic dishwasher, where a combination of effective detergents and a high-temperature rinse (usually above 80°C) will give reasonable protection. But the dishwasher will not solve all of our problems. This is where chemical control becomes important, and familiarity with the various types of cleaning and sanitising chemicals is required.

Soaps and detergents contain surfactants which help to loosen fats and grease, allowing dirt to be washed away in water. While this does a good job of physical cleaning, it is does not make things sanitary, or free of bacterial infection. To sanitise something is to kill all or most bacteria present, and for this job we need a bacteria-killing agent such as chlorine, iodine or quaternary ammonia. Iodine is seldom used these days, but chlorine is still an important chemical in municipal water treatment and in some cleaning applications. Quaternary ammonia and its derivatives are most often used in food service, because they are stable chemicals, are relatively safe to handle and have good bactericidal power and good rinsing qualities. A consultation with your local government Health Department and with a reputable chemical supplier will indicate which compounds are best for which applications.

Just as important as selecting the right chemicals is training the staff who will use them. Product identification, correct strength, correct application and length of time allowed for effective sterilisation are all points that should be covered repeatedly with food-handling and cleaning staff. Good chemicals are expensive, so this may be seen as a cost control exercise as much as a sanitation program.

Pest control

Pests do obvious damage to food supplies by chewing holes and depositing eggs, urine and faeces directly into food meant for consumption. This would be bad enough, if they did not also carry a wide range of pathogenic organisms that cause food-borne illnesses. The two major problems are insects and rodents. Insect control begins with screening to prevent access, and removal of the food supply. Foods must be kept in sealed, insect-proof containers and spills must be cleaned up immediately. Cockroaches are unsightly and regard almost anything as food, including soap, candles, built-up grease behind stoves and soiled linen. Rodents will gain access through remarkably small gaps, and are much more aggressive than insects about chewing their way into food containers, so paper sacks and hessian cannot be considered safe storage for flour and vegetables.

In commercial food service there is no substitute for a professional pest controller, who will inspect the premises, identify the signs of infestation and advise on methods of control. A variety of chemical baits and poisons are used which require very careful application and well-trained operators. Under no circumstances should you allow untrained people to use toxic chemicals around food or food equipment. No matter how smartly the stores and kitchen are kept, pests will be introduced every day from outside sources. Therefore, a continuing, frequent maintenance program is a necessity, and should be built into the budget for overhead costs. A continuing control program is not an excuse for careless food handling, however, because poor sanitation may result in serious infestations which even the professionals cannot eradicate.

A customer only has to sight one cockroach, running across a wall in the dining room, to form an extremely poor opinion of a restaurant's hygienic standards. It is almost impossible to change that perception once it is formed, and the customer is more than likely to spread the news to a few friends. Money spent on pest control is money well spent.

Physical hazards

A piece of plastic in the Caesar salad or a rubber band in the cheesecake may be deeply embarrassing, but is essentially harmless. A piece of broken glass in the dessert or a sliver of wire in a cocktail is a more serious danger. All of these may be traced to unsafe practices in the kitchen, the pantry or the bar. Training is part of the answer. Food and beverage staff who are constantly in a rush and put under pressure by inadequate skills or inadequate equipment, will make mistakes frequently. The correct method of disposing of packaging materials and the correct procedure for a broken glass in the bar are habits that must be drilled into people until they become second nature, even in the middle of a rush.

The experienced manager will also take practical steps to prevent accidents: wire wool scourers should be completely banned from any food or beverage preparation area. Glasses should never be stored near or above the ice bin. If a glass or bottle is broken near an ice well, the ice must be discarded and the bin cleaned completely. Any staff member wearing a finger bandage must also wear a protective glove or finger dock, which should be supplied.

The health inspector

The arrival of the inspector from the local Health Department is all too often viewed by the restaurateur or hotelier as an unwelcome intrusion. Faced with a discourteous—even hostile—greeting, the public health inspector must feel that the job is hard enough without having to deal with a defensive manager. In fact, all of us expect certain minimum standards of cleanliness and safe food when we dine out or buy food from a shop, and we expect the government to protect us by enforcing food safety laws.

It is only fair, then, that your food service operation should measure up in the same way. Your customers are, after all, relying on the same guarantee. A visit from the health inspector should be welcomed by any manager who takes seriously his or her responsibility to the customer. A trained health inspector can identify storage problems, unsafe handling practices or inadequate equipment which may be overlooked by staff who work in the same location every day. A unbiased, independent look at your procedures by a qualified professional will help to identify those areas that most need attention, which staff need training, and what major improvements might be included in next year's budget.

Many health inspectors in Australia face the very difficult job of bringing a wide range of food service facilities up to the minimum safety standards, often working with people who have little or no professional training. The café owner who does not see any reason why a chicken sandwich should not be left at room temperature all afternoon may find it hard to take advice, and will probably never be convinced. So when a health inspector visits a hotel, restaurant or club and receives a pleasant, professional reception from the F&B and the Executive Chef, it will be that much easier to build a good working relationship based on a common aim: the service of safe food.

Preparation for a health inspection is a good spur to supervisors and staff to have all areas, including the bars, checked for tidy storage, clean surfaces and equipment. For this reason alone, it is worth inviting the local health inspector along for regular checks. Stock should be inspected for use-by dates, open boxes should be discarded, and loose food stored in closed containers. Check coldrooms, freezers, automatic glasswashers and dishwashers for correct operating temperatures, and test some sample foods for internal temperature in storage.

When the health inspector arrives, encourage your staff and supervisors to ask questions and discuss procedures with him. This promotes knowledge of what is, after all, a technical subject. Let it be known that you take safe food handling seriously, and you will have won half the battle. Some local authorities offer short courses for food handlers at the local TAFE college. These should be a standard requirement for supervisors and section managers.

Occupational health and safety

Commonwealth and State legislation covers a wide range of requirements for employers and employees in the area of occupational health and safety (sometimes referred to as OHSA legislation). Federal programs such as Worksafe Australia seek to standardise these health and safety laws across the country, but each State administers its own Act and regulations. These lay down important requirements for employers, including those in the hotel and restaurant industry, to promote safe work practices and safe workplaces for all Australians. Essentially, the obligation rests with the employer to provide the proper facilities, equipment and protection to safeguard people from injury while they are working. Worker's Compensation, a government-supervised insurance scheme, has always provided for employees injured on the job; but OHSA legislation goes further, seeking to prevent accidents rather than simply compensate for them.

In practice, regulations may require the employer to supply protective clothing (gloves, eye protection, dust masks and the like) for certain jobs, particularly when fine particles (such as flour) or dangerous chemicals (including many cleaning products) are used by employees. The employer is also required to provide a safe working environment. In kitchens, bars and restaurants, which are already hazardous environments, inspectors will pay close attention to proper ventilation, non-slip floor surfaces, safe traffic flow and safety guards on dangerous equipment such as slicers, and make regular checks to see that potentially hazardous electrical equipment such as microwave ovens are in safe working order. Regulations may also cover safe procedures, including the maximum time an employee may operate certain equipment and maximum loads to be lifted by hand.

Occupational health and safety legislation is not a set of recommendations; it is the law. Should an employee suffer any work-related injury, whether acute or chronic, these laws make the employer liable for compensation, which can be substantial. The Food and Beverage Manager must be conversant with the requirements of local OHSA legislation, and bring to the attention of the General Manager or the owner any condition or practice that may be in violation of the law. Advice about how the law applies to your operation can be obtained from your local Workplace Standards Authority, Department of Employment or Occupational Health and Safety Office, or direct from the National Occupational Health and Safety Commission in Canberra. Several industry associations produce guides to the law as it applies to the hotel and restaurant industry.

Fire safety

Fires in hotels are particularly devastating for several reasons:

- high occupancy of the building compared to a shop or a factory
- multi-storey construction, which makes rescue difficult
- guests who are unfamiliar with the building layout and exits
- highly flammable furnishings, including plastics and synthetics
- the chimney effect of lift shafts and stairwells
- many sources of ignition, including smoking, kitchen and electrical.

When a fire is well established in a hotel building, more people are likely to die from inhalation of fumes than from direct heat or falling from windows. The furnishings of a modern hotel contain many materials which produce poisonous fumes when heated or burned, including synthetic fibres, polyurethane foam, plastics and paints. Add to this the fact that many guests will be panicky, unsure of where the exits are or what to do, and that corridors may be completely obscured by smoke, and you have a recipe for serious injuries and loss of life.

Adequate fire safety systems designed into the building are the responsibility of the architect and expert consultants, but operational fire safety is a another matter, and it does fall within the scope of the Food and Beverage Manager. Kitchens and restaurants are particularly dangerous sources of fire, and it is obviously important that fire systems, including extinguishers, alarms and emergency lighting, are kept in good working order. All fire exits should be free of obstructions or rubbish, and kept accessible at all times. Electrical equipment, including thermostats and wiring, should be inspected regularly by a qualified electrician and repaired promptly if a problem is discovered.

More important still is training the food and beverage staff in correct procedure, should a fire be detected or a fire alarm tripped. This should include training in hand-held fire equipment, procedure for reporting a fire that cannot be controlled, and safe practice when dealing with electrical equipment, deep fat fryers, toasters and the like. All staff should know what their role is when a fire alarm sounds. They may be assigned to help guests leave the building, to turn off gas, electricity or ventilation systems, to check parts of the building for evacuation, or simply to leave the building and assemble outside in a specified location for a head count.

A fire safety audit, conducted by the local fire brigade accompanied by the Food and Beverage Manager, should be conducted every six months at a minimum.

CHAPTER SUMMARY

There is an unspoken agreement with any guest who uses a restaurant, club or hotel that his or her safety will be adequately protected while on the premises. It is the responsibility of the management to see that this agreement is honoured. In the Food and Beverage department, this responsibility covers more than one area.

Food hygiene is necessarily a technical subject, which requires a working knowledge of microbiology and safe food-handling practice. A professional Food and Beverage Manager is expected to be conversant with these matters, and able to plan an effective system of checks and inspections to see that food is being safely stored, prepared and served. Working with the Executive Chef, the F&B must set up a sanitation program which includes training food handlers in the correct use of equipment and chemical controls, proper temperature control and safe storage procedures.

In addition, the Food and Beverage Manager has a responsibility to protect employees from unsafe working conditions or practices, ensuring that obligations under the Occupational Health and Safety Act are met.

While fire safety involves many other departments of a large hotel or club, the F&B will take a particular interest in the restaurants, bars and kitchens to see that fire prevention and control systems are in place and tested.

REVIEW QUESTIONS

1 What is a pathogenic organism?

2 Food can be regarded as safe if it has been stored overnight in a commercial coldroom. True or false?

3 What temperature range can be regarded as the 'danger zone' for bacterial growth?

4 Why is it dangerous to defrost frozen meats at room temperature?

5 Describe cross-contamination in a commercial kitchen.

6 What are the two most important steps the food service manager can take to prevent pest damage and contamination?

CHAPTER ELEVEN

RECRUITING AND MANAGING STAFF

Staff management and strategies for recruitment and retention

Interviewing skills and reference checks

The induction process

The concept of 'spin', or self-confidence

Handling poor performance, and the use of negotiation to improve performance

The essentials of management

The basic theory of management is that you can accomplish far more by working through other people than you can ever hope to accomplish by yourself. As Food and Beverage Manager your job is to train, motivate, guide and reward a large group of table servers, bar staff, stewards, supervisors, banquet staff and cleaners. Your goals are to provide high-quality food, drink and service to your customers in comfortable surroundings, and to return a satisfactory profit on the department's operations. To satisfy these aims, you must have a group of enthusiastic people around you who are working towards the same goals.

Most of us in the industry have listened, at one time or other, to a manager or supervisor who complains bitterly about the laziness, incompetence and lack of motivation of his staff. This is nothing more than a sad reflection on the incompetence of the manager, not the staff. If anyone is responsible for the general atmosphere in the workplace and for the commitment of each employee to provide excellent service, it is the manager himself.

Some managers fail to grasp these fundamentals. On the one hand, they will readily blame their staff for mistakes; on the other, they will refuse to accept responsibility for their own actions. Without direction and leadership, any organisation will slip into apathy, neglect and conflict. It is the manager's role to lead, to inspire, to cajole, to correct, to do whatever is necessary to achieve the goal. The manager who spends her time watching her back, scheming for advancement or competing for status, has missed the point: real security and recognition are based on success, and success is based on the people who work for you.

Firefighter or leader?

The inexperienced manager, full of enthusiasm and eager to succeed, often makes a show of how many hours he works and how many difficulties he has to cope with. In the jargon of management theory, this is a 'firefighter' manager, who rushes from one place to another putting out 'fires' as they arise. This habit conveys a certain sense of importance, as the manager bustles about answering emergency calls, rushing to the scene, making hasty decisions and telling all who will listen to him about his enormous work load. Unfortunately, the 'firefighter' has yet to learn the first rule of management: we accomplish more when we work through other people.

Consider the very different style of the experienced manager. This manager's organisation is built on a team of highly-skilled people, each one of whom is capable of dealing with operating problems competently and quickly. Emergencies seldom occur. Minor 'fires' are put out at the source and do not require the intervention of the senior manager. This state of affairs is not a lucky accident. The senior manager has worked for a long time, planning how things will be done, forecasting where and when resources will be needed, training and encouraging people to become self-reliant and backing them up when they need help.

A quick test to see which style of management is employed in any organisation is to ask what would happen if the senior manager were suddenly called away for a month. If everything would crash into chaos within the week, then we have a 'firefighter' manager who has failed to build a workable team. If the organisation would continue more or less as usual, tended by a competent team of second-level managers and staff, then the senior manager has done the job well. In management, as in other fields, less is often paradoxically more.

Staff development

If you understand that building a trained, self-confident and committed staff is your primary job, then two other problems that beset the industry will be addressed at the same time.

First, Australia suffers from a continuing shortage of skilled hospitality staff. For all the efforts of our TAFE colleges, hotel schools and traineeship programs, the industry continues to grow much more quickly than our ability to supply trained staff to operate it. This means that the manager who establishes an organised and efficient staff training program will be taking steps to ensure that her own establishment will not have to compete on the open market for skilled staff, and that the staff she has will want to stay with an organisation that offers further training. Moreover, the atmosphere created by a manager who is devoted to the development and success of her staff means that staff turnover will be reduced. People are generally happier and more stable in a job that provides challenge, interest and a sense of involvement in decision-making.

Second, the general trend of labour legislation over the past decade has been to increase the rights of the employee to the point where it may be extremely difficult to sack an unsatisfactory worker. Labour laws are, perhaps understandably, weighted in favour of the employee. It becomes all the more important, then, to select staff carefully and to cultivate an atmosphere in which even a mediocre or inexperienced employee can be encouraged to succeed. The old-fashioned notion that management can 'give the fellow a go, and if he doesn't cut it, sack him' has long since been laid to rest by punishing compensation claims and damaging labour disputes.

If any further evidence were needed to prove that investment in a skilled and stable staff is a priority, one could look at the financial realities of hiring staff. A new employee represents a number of costs to a hotel, club or restaurant. There is the cost of advertising to find the person, and a further expense in management time to interview, evaluate and check references. Another supervisor or employee must spend time explaining the operation to the new staff member; there are often uniform costs; and finally, there is a hidden cost in the low productivity of that employee until he or she is fully trained. Industry estimates of the total cost of hiring a new casual table server vary between $1000 and $2000 per employee, and may well be higher. High staff turnover, then, is not just an inevitable problem in the industry—it is a damaging cost that can easily destroy a modest profit.

If a restaurant owner considers buying a new piece of equipment (a computerised cash register, for instance), he will shop carefully for the best unit at the best price. The high initial cost is regarded as an investment in better productivity or control, and it will be amortised over a number of years. The unit would be carefully maintained and serviced to protect that investment. A piece of equipment that cost an operation $20 000 per year in interest charges and operating costs would be chosen very carefully indeed. Yet, as has been pointed out,* some managers will hire an employee who costs much more than that in wages and benefits, on the strength of a cursory interview and reference check.

Recruitment

The traditional methods of staff recruitment in the hotel and restaurant industry are word-of-mouth, newspaper advertisement, employment agency and internal promotion. Each one has its pros and cons. A good Food and Beverage Manager will use all four to find the best people for the job. In a large operation, you may be assisted by a personnel or human resources department. Even if this is the case,

*in *Cost Management* by Morrison, Ruys and Morrison

careful monitoring of the process by the Food and Beverage Manager will be necessary to avoid letting a good prospect slip through the net.

Word-of-mouth

In any city or medium-sized town, it is entirely likely that food and beverage staff from several different restaurants or hotels will know each other and possibly socialise together. This provides access to a useful pool of experienced staff, which the manager may draw upon to fill a vacancy. In its favour, this method offers a kind of pre-screening, as applicants may already know something about your conditions, duties and rates of pay as well as the type of business your establishment operates. A well-run organisation may develop a good reputation and enjoy the enviable luxury of a steady stream of applicants who would like to join it. A good employee who introduces another will usually have some investment in seeing that the new person succeeds, which may make the induction and early training phases somewhat easier. To its detriment, this method of recruitment offers the manager little control over what is said or promised, so a new applicant may have unreasonable expectations of pay or conditions. Neither is it reliable, since there is no telling how many contacts may be made, or how long it will take to fill a vacancy. In rare cases, a dishonest employee may recruit another dishonest employee, creating a more serious problem for the management.

Newspaper advertisement

There are more vacancies filled by this method than any other, and it remains the traditional first line of enquiry in the industry. Here the manager will have to weigh up costs and benefits between national, trade and regional newspapers, and make a careful decision about the wording of the advertisement. There are certain legal constraints on this wording, with which the manager should be familiar. It is illegal under current anti-discrimination laws (with certain special exceptions) to specify the age, race, sex, ethnic background, physical attributes or marital status of the applicants you wish to interview. It is quite legitimate, however, to specify experience, qualification, time in trade, language ability, special skills or hours of work, as long as these represent no infringement of the industrial award or industry agreement governing the job.

In its favour, the newspaper advertisement reaches a wide audience, providing excellent coverage of possible employees. Staff living in other parts of the country may get your local newspaper to see what employment opportunities are available. Compared with other methods, newspapers are quick, and the wording of advertisements may be changed daily according to need. Against this is the possibility that the newspaper casts too wide a net: you may be paying for circulation which does not actually do you any good. There may be a large number of replies to a general employment advertisement, which will mean increased work for the manager or Personnel department, who will have to sift through dozens of unsuitable applicants to find one person.

The most effective newspaper advertisement is the one that offers the most information. You should be as specific as possible about the attributes of the person you are looking for, within the constraints of the law.

Branford Beach Inn
requires a
Cocktail Bar Attendant

Applicants must be experienced (minimum 3 years) in cocktail preparation, bar service and stock control. We require a good standard of presentation and customer skills, and the ability to work shifts including weekends and public holidays. Previous references are required.

Excellent conditions, award wages paid and uniform provided. To arrange an interview, telephone Mr David Kerris on 2333 3456 between the hours of 2.00 p.m. and 4.00 p.m. on Thursday, December 21. Interviews will be held on Saturday, December 23.

Figure 11.1   Employment advertisement

In Figure 11.1 detailed requirements for a cocktail bar attendant have been given, without transgressing anti-discrimination laws. The minimum standard of experience has been specified and the applicant informed that references will be required. By determining a particular time to receive telephone enquiries, the manager has avoided interruptions over several days from applicants calling for more information. When the manager takes the calls, he will be able to concentrate on a specific set of questions and offer personal interviews only to those enquirers who seem to fit the qualifications. These interviews will be scheduled at 15-minute intervals on Saturday morning.

Employment agencies

The Commonwealth Employment Service (CES) and private employment agencies exist to match applicants with job vacancies. Some managers discount the use of the CES, in a mistaken belief that they will not find the person they are looking for through a public service. In fact, the CES can be extremely useful, but the manager must invest some time on the telephone describing the exact qualities being sought. CES interviewers are skilled at determining who may suit a vacancy, as long as they understand clearly what is required. Any likelihood of having 'borderline' applicants sent along for an interview is offset by the fact that the service is free to the employer. In some cases, the CES may advise on various government subsidies available to encourage employers to hire people who are at some perceived disadvantage (the long-term unemployed, the disabled, Aboriginal people, Torres Strait Islanders, unskilled youth). These should not be seen as a 'bonus' for the employer: generally, they are intended to compensate you for the cost of extra training or accommodation that the disadvantaged person may require. The decision to hire a particular individual should always be based on the potential that person has to become a valuable member of the staff, not on the amount of money offered as an inducement.

Private agencies usually offer a service paid for by the employer. Having done a search for suitable applicants, the personnel agency will advertise, conduct interviews, check references and screen applicants until it is ready to put forward the person they believe most suited to the vacancy. In return for this work, the agency will charge a finder's fee, commonly based on a multiple of the employee's weekly salary or a percentage of the yearly salary. This fee will vary greatly according to the difficulty of matching an applicant to the job, and should be negotiated before the agency is commissioned to find the right person. Private agencies may also help with temporary staff to cope with a special event or a short-term vacancy. This need may sometimes be met by the local TAFE college or hotel school, whose students need work experience. A close connection with the teaching staff at these establishments will prove useful to the Food and Beverage Manager.

The advantages of using public or private agencies is that much of the work is done for you. You may need only interview two or three applicants to find the right person for the job. The disadvantage is, of course, that the finder's fee may be substantial, and must be added to the normal costs of recruiting a new staff member.

Internal promotion

Some companies follow a strict policy of internal promotion, in the belief that the best qualified people for the job are already working for them. The investment in training time is likely to be much less than for a person new to the organisation. Internal promotion may be effectively used to boost staff commitment, if a clear path of advancement is offered as part of the general conditions of employment. As manager, you are likely to know a great deal about the employee's temperament, ability and level of skill, thus eliminating some of the guesswork inherent in hiring new staff.

There are some dangers in this method of staff selection, however. There may be a temptation to promote people as a reward for services rendered or time served, rather than choosing the best person for the job. This pattern is known as the 'Peter Principle'.* According to this principle, managers in any organisation tend to rise

---

* from *The Peter Principle* by management theorists Lawrence J. Peter and Raymond Hull

to their level of incompetence by promotion, then go no further. The cumulative effect on the organisation is to ensure that all responsible positions are occupied by incompetent people—clearly a recipe for disaster. There may also be a tendency to presume that the newly-promoted manager or supervisor will train herself, a dangerous assumption that would not usually be made with a new employee. Promoted staff members may find it difficult to adapt to new responsibilities, not least because other staff may be reluctant to regard them in the light of their new position.

As long as the Food and Beverage Manager retains a clear and objective view of the qualifications for the job, and understands that well-planned and well-supervised training is required for any new position, internal promotion may be effective. It presumes, of course, that new employees are brought into the organisation at entry level to replace those promoted.

The interview

Well-developed interviewing skills will prove invaluable for the professional Food and Beverage Manager. You must be comfortable with telephone and personal interviews, and have some skill at reading between the lines of a written application. Familiarity with professional qualifications (including overseas qualifications) will also be useful, particularly if you are recruiting chefs, *sommeliers*, senior restaurant staff or managers. The goal is to learn as much as possible about the prospective employee in the shortest possible time.

The telephone interview

This is the manager's most useful tool for separating likely candidates from a large field of applicants. Telephone contact is efficient and brief, and wastes little of the manager's or applicant's time if it is conducted properly. The best way to plan a telephone interview is to prepare a 'script', or short reminder list, of the questions to be asked. If this is typed on a sheet of paper with space left for notes, then photocopied, it will serve as an excellent reference. A possible script for the advertisement in Figure 11.1 is given in Figure 11.2.

The name and telephone number are taken first, so that the applicant can be reached again in case of a disconnection or another call. Asking for the address allows the manager to evaluate speaking voice and telephone poise, which may be important for the job. The arrangement of the script is from the specific to the general, so that you need not waste time with an applicant who is unqualified. If the reply is 'No, I'm not experienced with cocktails, but I would like to learn', the manager has the opportunity to terminate the interview with a polite 'I'm sorry, but that is a requirement for the job. Thank you for calling, and do keep an eye on the paper for other bar positions we may advertise.'

Name:

Telephone number:

Address:

Are you fully trained in cocktail preparation?

Where were you trained?

How long have you been a cocktail bar attendant?

Have you any problem with shift work, including late nights and weekends?
Any regular commitments—social, family or sport?

Do you have your own transport?

Are you working now? How long a notice would you give your present
employer?

If you are not employed, who was your last employer? Your supervisor's
name? Telephone number?

How long did you work there? What were your duties, exactly?

Who was your employer before that? Your supervisor's name?
Telephone number?

Are you physically able for the duties involved? Have you ever claimed
worker's compensation?

The hours of the job are . . .

The wage per hour is . . .

Overtime is paid at . . .

The uniform is provided, but you are expected to provide . . .
(shoes, belt, etc.)

Do you have any questions about the job?

Are you available for a personal interview at . . . on Saturday?

Comments:

Figure 11.2 Telephone interview script

The script specifically avoids questions that may indicate possible discrimination. Applicants are not asked for age, sex, marital status or race. Questions are asked to determine the applicant's willingness to work the necessary hours, and very specific questions are asked about previous employment, since the next step for the manager will be to check references. Anyone who has genuinely worked for another organisation should be able to provide a telephone number and the name of a supervisor or manager. You manner should be serious and businesslike: you are interested in facts at this point; personal evaluation will come later. The question about fitness is legitimate, since a disabled person may still be physically capable. (A person with an artificial leg, for instance, might cope perfectly well with this job.) The question about worker's compensation is designed to alert the manager to an employee with a history of injuries or chronic health problems. The applicant is read the basic terms of employment and given an opportunity to decline if they do not suit. If, by this point, the applicant still sounds like a reasonable prospect, a personal interview is scheduled at an agreed time.

The point of this process is to identify possible candidates quickly, and to decline anyone who does not fit the bill. A caller who could not provide references, for instance, or who mentioned important sporting commitments on weekends, might be politely thanked, but would not be offered an interview. This would take perhaps two or three minutes, compared to a time-consuming personal interview.

The reference check

At the end of the allotted time for telephone interviews, no more calls are accepted. The manager begins the most crucial part of the screening process: the reference check. Failing to do this check promptly is foolish in the extreme, since there is no better source of information about an employee than his or her former employer. This is not to say that every bit of that information will be reliable (memories may be vague, the employer may have been primed, some people will offer no comment), but the chance of obtaining good information is so high that the telephone call is worth it. Some managers object to the cost of an interstate or international call: this would seem ridiculous, since the call is unlikely to cost more than ten dollars, and a bad employee can cost more than that by a factor of 1000. To do a reference check, the manager calls the number given (it may be necessary to look it up) and identifies himself:

'This is David Kerris, Food and Beverage Manager at the Brandon Beach Inn. I'm calling for a reference check on a former staff member. Is Tina Kern there, please? I have a young woman by the name of Sharon Temis applying for a job as a cocktail bar attendant here at the Brandon Inn. She tells us she did the same job for you between March of last year and the present. Can you confirm her employment dates? What were her duties? Was she punctual? Did she have any learning difficulties? How did she get along with other staff? Can you tell me why she left? Would you re-employ her?'

The person at the other end is thanked, and the second reference call is placed. This one may be more revealing than the first, since the temptation for the applicant to exaggerate or conceal information becomes stronger with the passage of time. The same method is used to find someone who remembers the employee, and can comment on her performance. In the case of a key supervisory position, this process may be extended to the third or fourth reference, in reverse chronological order. Notes are taken on the original interview form, for use during the personal interview. It is not useful to 'surprise' the applicant with information received from a former employer; it is enough to note it and compare it with what the applicant says.

Obvious danger signs are misinformation: lying about what duties were performed, or how long the employment lasted. Unfavourable comments about a former supervisor or company may point to a chronically discontented employee. Reference checks that reveal a problem, such as dishonesty or repeated lateness, should not be discussed unless all other criteria are in favour of hiring the person. In this case, the negative report should be offered in a neutral tone of voice for comment. Sometimes a frank explanation will be given, and a decision can be based on that.

The personal interview

Equipped with the original record of the telephone interview and the results of the reference checks, the manager can approach the personal interview with confidence. The time allotted to the interview should be uninterrupted, so it is wise to place a hold on any calls during this time. The applicant should be made comfortable in a quiet place. A small amount of social chat may put the applicant at her ease, so that the requirements of the job can be explained. Try to avoid hackneyed questions such as 'Do you think you are suited to this job?' or 'What makes you the best choice for the position?' These seldom elicit more than vague generalisations that the applicant thinks you want to hear. It is far more revealing to ask specific questions about the duties of the job. A bar attendant might be asked to describe how to make a piña colada, or the correct procedure for ringing off a till. A supervisor might be asked to describe how she would handle training a new table server, or deal with a serious customer complaint.

The applicant should be given plenty of uninterrupted time to reply to these questions. Deliberate pauses, in which the manager says nothing, may be used sparingly to encourage the applicant to say more. Avoid taking too many notes while a person is speaking. Body language, poise and self-confidence will offer more clues to the applicant's personality than a long list of pseudo-psychological questions. You may expect the interviewee to be nervous; the trick is to allow her to relax and talk freely, for that is when people reveal most about themselves. The applicant who remains tongue-tied and uncommunicative may not cope well with the customer-intensive nature of the industry. The opposite type, the applicant who can hardly stop talking through nervousness or otherwise, may be easier to train and adapt to the requirements of the job.

The interview should be brought to a distinct end. The manager may ask if there are any more questions about the exact details of the job. The applicant should be thanked and told when a decision is likely to be made. You should reassure the person that she will be contacted whether she is successful or not, by a certain time and day. With a few minutes to make notes on the interview sheet, you are ready for the next interview.

The follow-up

After due consideration (and possibly further reference checks), the best person for the job can be selected. The call should be made promptly after the decision, and the offer of employment made. Once it has been accepted, all the other applicants who attended personal interviews should be telephoned, with a polite message thanking them for applying, informing them that the position has been filled and inviting them to apply again when another position is advertised. It is not good policy to promise to retain an application on file, unless a specific time period (say, four weeks) is agreed. Leaving an open date means that the applicant still thinks she is under consideration long after the file has been discarded, and an out-of-date file will, in any case, be of limited use to the manager. It is better to encourage unsuccessful applicants to apply again when a new vacancy occurs. Failure to notify job applicants of the result promptly is both arrogant and rude, and will do the reputation of the manager and the establishment immeasurable harm. For this reason, unsolicited applications should not be accepted on a routine basis, since each one accepted will require a reply. Callers should be informed that the company's policy is to advertise specific jobs, and accept applications only for those jobs.

Staff induction

Strategies for effective staff training will be discussed in the next chapter, but it is appropriate to mention induction procedure here, since it is very closely related to recruitment procedure. Induction is the process by which a new employee is introduced to the organisation, made to feel welcome and prepared for initial training. People seldom forget their first few days on the job, and in this crucial period many basic opinions are formed about the organisation, the style of management and the commitment to quality service. If the induction process is handled well, a new employee is quickly ready to learn routines and duties. If it is handled badly, the employee may spend weeks feeling as if he or she is not quite part of the team.

The key is information: it is essential to answer all the new employee's questions promptly and accurately.

The current fashion for 'mission statements' is perhaps a bit overdone, but there is value in stating clearly what the operation seeks to achieve. In a fast food restaurant this might be to serve consistent quality food quickly, and to offer pleasant and efficient service to the customer. In a fine dining restaurant the objective might be to serve superior quality food and wine in very comfortable surroundings, with careful attention to the customer's enjoyment of the meal and the service. It is usually possible to state these goals in a sentence or two, and this should be introduced at an early stage in the induction.

After this is made clear, the employee will have a host of queries, voiced and unvoiced, about how she is expected to work and where, who she will report to, when she will be paid and how, the hours of work, location of supplies and so on. These queries are best handled by means of an induction checklist, which the supervisor or manager moves through in an orderly fashion, confirming that the employee understands each point before moving on to the next. Information covered should include:

- the name and title of the person doing the induction
- a description of the induction process and how long it will take
- names and titles of immediate supervisors
- names and titles of senior management
- where personal effects can be safely stored
- location of the toilet and changing rooms
- general hours of work and breaks
- uniform issue and minimum grooming standards
- rate of pay, bank details for payment and tax declaration form
- day and time pay will be available
- any other paperwork required by the employer
- meal arrangements
- procedure for sick calls, emergencies and first aid
- fire alarms, equipment and fire drill procedure
- required safety equipment and procedures
- location of the principal workplace and property tour
- introduction to other staff.

At this point the employee should be given an opportunity to discuss what has been covered, ask more questions, or get more detailed information. This is an important point in the induction, and should not be hurried. Once the checklist and discussion have been completed, the new member of the team will go on to learn specific duties and methods of work.

It is worth noting that the person who covers this checklist will have created a kind of bond with the new employee. In the event of a question or problem, the new staff member is quite likely to return for advice to the person who first introduced her. Some senior managers prefer to cover this checklist themselves, to create an early sense of trust and approachability.

Staff management

The concept of 'spin'

The employee who is self-confident, well-trained and satisfied by his work is the same person who offers the best quality of service, the best productivity and the strongest capacity to handle the varied demands of a busy food and beverage operation. When a staff member is unsure of himself, feels threatened by his supervisors or is asked to do work beyond his ability, it should come as no surprise that his quality of work will be low. Some management writers have likened this principle to the spin of a top: a fast-moving top, with plenty of momentum, can handle several bumps and changes of surface without slowing down noticeably. A slow-moving top, on the other hand, is easily pushed over and stopped by the slightest touch. This is a valuable metaphor for the way people work. The more 'spin' that can be given to an employee, the more useful contribution can be expected of him.

Certain actions tend to increase a person's self-confidence and ability. These include completing a task well and quickly, a compliment from a guest, recognition for a new skill obtained, thanks from the manager for a job well done, a cheerful working atmosphere, a sense of involvement in the way things are going, and genuine responsibility for a part of the operation. These are potent tools the manager can use to develop a strong, confident and successful team. The manager may not be able to control guest compliments (though she can see that every one of them is widely publicised), but she can certainly control all of the rest.

Other actions tend to decrease a staff member's 'spin' and must be carefully controlled. These include reprimands for poor-quality work, nagging by a supervisor, a feeling of frustration caused by petty rules, rudeness from a manager, harassment, a public dressing-down in front of other staff, criticism of manner, appearance or speech, suspicion, fault-finding or blame for a guest complaint.

As managers, we will be most successful by working through other people. Other people will be most successful if they are self-confident. It must be obvious, then, that any action which increases a worker's 'spin' is good management practice, and any action that reduces it should be avoided. Yet, in thousands of workplaces around the country, managers behave as if the opposite were true. Some managers are arrogant and fault-finding, are dismissive of other people's opinions, keep their employees in the dark, give compliments grudgingly and rarely, and are quick to assign blame when things go wrong. It is little wonder that their operations suffer from high staff turnover, poor customer satisfaction and an unpleasant atmosphere.

Increasing 'spin'

It is not enough to believe in this simple premise (that staff with high morale do better work); it is necessary to practise it constantly. A cheerful greeting by name, for everyone who works for you, is a beginning. Regardless of the pressure of the moment, the manager must be unfailingly polite in his dealings with customers; his staff deserve the same. When an employee has done a difficult job, a brief and sincere acknowledgement from the boss will be remembered for weeks. It should never be patronising, false or effusive—a simple 'thank you' is often enough. A successful hotel or restaurant does not survive by lurching from one crisis to another. Many people have to do repetitive jobs well to ensure that quality standards are met. A good manager seeks out those people daily, and offers small compliments or encouragements. You might mention to the gardener that the flower display looks particularly good today, or compliment the cashier on the neatness of his books. A table server polishing cutlery might be encouraged simply with a smile and a wave. Complimenting one employee in front of another is particularly effective. The cynic will say that this model of a manager drifting through the day dispensing sweetness and light is unrealistic, and will vanish when the action gets tough. The cynic misses the point: the experienced manager takes every opportunity to increase 'spin', because he knows he can count on it just when it is needed most.

If there is a danger in this practice, it is that your encouragement may become insincere or perfunctory. It is important that you identify real accomplishments, and comment on those, rather than give out blanket compliments without a genuine reason. Staff generally respond well to hard facts and figures: the highest number of covers served for the week, the best average check, the fastest turn-around of a banquet room. A compliment to professionalism and skill is highly valued, and encourages your staff to meet bigger challenges with confidence.

Dealing with negative behaviour

There will inevitably be times when a staff member has failed to achieve the required standard. This might be because of a genuine mistake, a lack of attention, a clumsy action, carelessness or lack of skill. Other more serious problems might be chronic lateness, unwillingness to take direction, contempt for the customer or management, disruptive behaviour, harassment of other staff, sloppy presentation or dishonesty.

If the Food and Beverage Manager is committed to building an effective and well-motivated staff, she must also realise that allowing poor behaviour or standards to pass uncorrected will seriously undermine this effort. It will be necessary for her to act just as promptly to correct negative behaviour as she did to encourage positive behaviour.

The first step in this process is to discover what negative behaviour occurred. Often, it is not the employee in question who can best answer this. The manager should ask brief, factual questions of other staff and supervisors to get an idea of what the problem is, gathering as much information as possible before planning a solution. There is no less inspiring a sight than a manager who goes off half-cocked to confront an employee, having heard only half the story. The point of speaking to an employee who has a problem is not to chastise or abuse him, but to correct the behaviour. To do this, you will need all the facts at hand so that you are ready to present a 'get-well plan'.

For minor infractions or mistakes, you will be concerned to correct the behaviour with minimum loss of 'spin'. The correct approach is to speak to the employee casually (not, that is, at a formal meeting in your office, but somewhere in the workplace) and explain that the behaviour (a late arrival, a mistaken order) caused a problem. You may explain briefly how the behaviour affected other staff, and ask for a commitment that the action will be done the right way next time. If the staff member wishes to explain how the mistake happened, allow him to do so, but keep it brief and focus on a successful outcome, such as how it can be prevented in future. Do not allow the discussion to become an extended gripe about work conditions, other staff or outside commitments. If the employee insists that there is a lot to talk about, agree on an appointment in your office at another time. If you can obtain a promise of a quick solution, thank the employee and finish with a positive comment to the effect that you still have confidence in him, and consider the matter closed.

More serious misconduct, or a chronic problem, should be acted upon immediately it comes to your attention. Once again, gather your facts and work out your proposal for a get-well plan before asking the employee to meet you in a private office away from the workplace. Make an effort to understand how the employee feels about this meeting. She may have a deep grievance, or feel a sense of injustice. There will be some fear of dismissal, often masked by aggressiveness or denial. The employee may be eager to drag in a list of complaints against other staff, or a set of excuses relating to outside circumstances.

This meeting must be handled very carefully. You have an investment in this person, in terms of training and experience, which should be protected. You want to solve the problem with the least possible damage to her self-confidence, so that she can be reinstated as a successful part of the team. If you are tempted to consider dismissal, you must keep in mind the legal and financial implications of such a decision.

The goal is to get the employee to acknowledge that her performance or behaviour has not been up to standard, then to negotiate a deal with measurable results. There will be a strong temptation to wander off the subject, discussing anything but the employee's behaviour. This must be resisted, if you are to avoid a damaging and ultimately pointless exercise. Keep the discussion confined to behaviour on the job, and firmly refuse to be drawn into discussion about other staff, the employee's home life, your own performance as a manager, or any other subject but the one at hand. Do not drag in past performance or previous reprimands, unless these are directly related to the deal being negotiated. You want to set a goal, and a given time frame, which the employee agrees to achieve. If the employee is successful, this will lead to full reinstatement as a valued member of the organisation. If the employee is unsuccessful at the first goal, another one will be negotiated and the process tried again. You will be careful to document the discussion and the outcome agreed upon. Both parties will sign this agreement and retain copies. A word of encouragement ends the meeting; you both expect that the negotiated deal will be fulfilled.

This method has been proven successful in many organisations, since it is based on negotiated agreement between people with an equal stake in the outcome. It is based solely on desired behaviour on the job. It is not punitive, nagging or personal. You will need to ensure that your supervisors understand this policy, believe in it and implement it. There is no point in negotiating a solution with an employee, only to have another supervisor treat him as if he were under suspicion, on probation or likely to fail.

A case in point

James S. was a very good supervisor with a small problem. Though he was well-organised, good with customers, cool under pressure and highly skilled, he did not suffer fools lightly. If a new table server was clumsy at wine service, or unsure of the correct way to write a docket, James was more inclined to take over and do the job himself, rather than train the new staff member to do the job correctly. James thought that if a person called herself a table server, she ought to know what she was doing. After several complaints from restaurant staff about David's abrupt manner and intolerance, the Food and Beverage Manager invited David in for a meeting.

David was at first defensive about his level of skill, and criticised the Personnel department for sending him untrained staff who were supposed to be experienced. The F&B emphasised that David's skills and value to the organisation were not in question: it was simply his behaviour towards service staff that needed adjustment. The manager suggested a simple training scheme, which would allow

David to teach advanced service skills to a small group of restaurant staff twice a week, and agreed to a small increase in labour hours. David agreed to moderate his behaviour and concentrate on lifting the skills of those around him. Both agreed to a review after six weeks. The Food and Beverage Manager followed up the meeting with a written note of the points discussed and the agreement reached.

CHAPTER SUMMARY

The professional Food and Beverage Manager realises that his or her success depends almost entirely on the quality of the staff. To find these people, recruit them, introduce them to the organisation and encourage them is a primary role of the manager. The manager must be familiar with the various methods of recruitment, the most efficient way to conduct interviews, and the obligations an employer has to those who are seeking a job. The induction process is a very important step in bringing a new employee onto the team, and should be carefully thought out. Building employee self-confidence and motivation is equally important, so the manager should understand the concept of 'spin' and be able to cultivate it. Corrections to the way an employee does his work must be handled objectively and fairly, concentrating on behaviour only, encouraging the staff member to retain his self-confidence. A negotiated 'get-well plan', with measurable goals and an agreed time-scale is the best way to accomplish this.

REVIEW QUESTIONS

1 Newspaper advertisement is a traditional way or recruiting new staff. Give some advantages and disadvantages of this method.

2 What essential information should the manager seek in a preliminary telephone interview?

3 What is an induction checklist?

4 What actions can the manager use to increase an employee's 'spin', or self-confidence?

5 Describe a plan of action for dealing with an employee's persistent lateness.

6 What are the ingredients of a successful 'get-well plan'?

CHAPTER TWELVE

STAFF TRAINING

The role of training in effective food and beverage management

Apprenticeships and traineeship programs

Types of training, their application and effectiveness

How to assess training needs and evaluate training outcomes

Meeting industry needs

A great deal of attention has been paid to the subject of training in recent years, for two reasons: a shortage of skilled staff in certain industries (notably the tourism industry) and a rising unemployment level. Training is seen as the answer to both problems. The intention of government legislation and some industry initiatives has been to take people off the unemployment roll by giving them marketable skills in growing industries. Worthy as this intention is, it does not always solve the immediate problems of the working manager, who needs skilled staff on the payroll now. In many cases, managers will find it more effective to train the staff they already have, rather than wait for government and the labour market to catch up with demand. Unfortunately, training is like advertising: you can spend a great deal of money on it for little measurable result. It is important to understand how training fits into an overall management plan for a food and beverage operation.

The benefits of training

If you can create an organisational culture that encourages life-long training, and promote the idea that a professional hotelier is a highly-skilled individual with a wide range of talents, then you will by default create interest in the profession. The 19-year-old female table server who takes a job in the coffee shop may not be aware that the hotel industry has a much better than average record for promoting women to the highest levels of management. The breakfast cook may not know that executive chefs are among the highest-paid professionals in the country. The school leaver who takes a job as kitchen porter could, one day, become a top-flight restaurant manager, given the right training and experience. Our industry has many disadvantages (unsociable hours, heavy commitment) but it also offers some of the best conditions and most challenging work available in the private sector. Add to this the opportunity for travel and the high salaries commanded by the top professionals in the field, and you have an attractive package. Training is the key, and the sensible manager makes sure that his staff are aware of the connection.

The opportunity to improve professional skills and aim for a more responsible position is a powerful motivator. Even in a modest restaurant operation, there is scope to obtain training and experience that will broaden future career prospects, including the possibility of opening one's own restaurant. If you can convince your staff that training and practice lead directly to advancement, then you will create an atmosphere in which people actively seek to improve their skills and knowledge. The benefit for the food and beverage operation is obvious: motivated people do the best work.

When a manager takes an interest in the career advancement of an employee and offers suitable training, a clear message is given that the employer cares about the individual and wants her to succeed. This can often be a more powerful inducement to loyalty than a pay increase or a longer holiday. As the employee masters new skills, the organisation benefits from a more productive and capable worker, trained for the exact conditions in which she works.

Boredom is a factor in some entry-level jobs, simply because our industry requires many things to be done over and over again. It would be a rare individual who gets much job satisfaction from polishing the cutlery, or sweeping the floor for the twentieth time this week. However, the storeman who is stacking and counting tins for most of his working day may be encouraged to do the job well if he is also being trained to operate a sophisticated computerised stock-control program twice a week. The table server might be interested in an opportunity to learn cocktail preparation, and the dishwasher might be studying night auditing in her spare time. As long as the training offered conveys some benefit for the hotel, club or restaurant (such as the employee having an opportunity to use the skill in future) then it can be a powerful incentive to the worker, with little disadvantage for the employer.

How training can fail

Since training has become a buzz-word in the hotel industry, there is some danger that management will presume that all training—any training—is a worthwhile goal in itself. This is an expensive mistake, because training takes up time, resources and money. If it does not provide a measurable result by improving the quality of product or service; if it does not generate better staff loyalty and a lower staff turnover; then it can be a waste of money.

The most common complaint heard in the industry is 'Yes, we offer them good training, and as soon as they've completed it, they leave'. Simply training people does not mean that you have won their hearts and minds. If the working conditions are poor, management is careless and rewards are low, you will not retain staff just by teaching them how to fold napkins or by showing them a video on work-place safety. The most effective way to use training is to make it part of a general program to improve the way your staff work. The employee who identifies a particular skill that she needs to reach the next level of her career, and requests training in that skill, will be far more committed than a staff member who is simply told to attend a program in which she has no interest.

The proliferation of industry training programs has led to a wide offering of courses in the field of general psychology, often described as 'management skills', 'team building' or 'personal development'. While these may have some entertain-ment value, they suffer from several disadvantages. They are often regarded as some-thing of a staff holiday, the lessons learned are seldom retained for long and they offer no hard qualification that the employee can later use for career advancement. A genuine desire to improve the 'quality of life' within an organisation is better advanced by developing good managers and supervisors, who can practise what they have learned every day.

In an interesting industrial experiment a few years ago, the Australian Govern-ment attempted to compel employers to spend money on training by introducing a 'Training Guarantee Scheme'. This scheme required employers to spend a certain percentage of their total payroll cost on training, or forfeit that amount to the Gov-ernment. The scheme was not a success, because throwing money at training is not an effective way to manage it. Training costs must be controlled like any other cost in the food and beverage operation: the benefit must be measured against the expense.

The most skilled and experienced chef is not necessarily the best person to offer training to other chefs. To have knowledge is one thing; to be able to impart it is quite another. The skills required to pass on information efficiently, and have the student retain it, are rare enough; finding them in a person who is also an experi-enced hotel professional is difficult. Fortunately, these skills can be developed, and the first step in a good training program is often to train the trainer. TAFE colleges, hotel schools and some universities offer short courses aimed directly at this require-ment, which are essential for people within your organisation who are regularly called upon to train other staff.

Types of training

Apprenticeships

Staff training is not something that has sprung up in the past decade; it has been going on ever since hotels and restaurants opened their doors to the public in the 17th century. As long ago as the medieval trade guilds, training was organised, con-trolled and paid for in cash or in labour. The echo of these early training schemes is still with us in the form of the apprenticeship, now mostly confined in the hotel industry to the training of chefs and pastry-cooks. In return for a certain number of years' labour at reduced wages (and often no wages at all), the apprentice cook was attached to a master chef, who agreed to pass on the secrets of the trade. When the apprentice chef had completed his indenture to the master, he was tested on his newly acquired skills and granted admittance into the guild if he was successful. A modernised version of this system is still used in many countries. Aspiring chefs (male and female) contract to work for an employer for less than the normal wage for a set number of years, in return for training in their profession. In Australia and New Zealand, this working experience is usually complemented by time spent at the hotel school or TAFE college, where technical instruction is given in a classroom setting. The arrangement is strictly controlled by an apprenticeship board, which will eventually grant the formal qualification when the apprenticeship is completed.

Traineeships

Hotels and restaurants do not run on chefs alone, so a wide range of other skills must be taught to restaurant staff, bar staff, receptionists, cashiers and kitchen hands. Since these jobs are not provided with formal apprenticeships, other types of training exist. In some cases, formal traineeships are arranged with the Department of Employment, Vocational Training and Industrial Relations (DEVETIR). These traineeships usually involve some time spent at the local TAFE college or other recognised training facility. Allowances or subsidies may apply, to compensate the employer for the fact that the trainee will spend some weeks of the year away from the workplace. If properly administered, these schemes can provide an excellent framework for training a new employee, with a recognised qualification at the end of the program. Some hotels and companies offer 'in-house' traineeships designed to train young managers, who will spend some time in each of several departments.

Apron training

Perhaps the most common method of training in the industry is the least reliable: a system known colloquially as 'apron training'. This is no more than introducing a new employee to an old employee and giving instructions that the new person be 'shown around, shown what to do'. While the new worker will be doing something within an hour or two, there is no guarantee that it will be productive work, and it may be some time before the new worker feels confident that he knows what is expected of him. The disadvantages of this system are many: bad habits are passed on, there may be no explanation of quality standards, and there is no check to see that the new person has gained all the skills he will need. This system creates isolation from management, confusion, stress, unfair presumption that the new employee is competent, unreliable customer service and rapid staff turnover. The system is so bad, in fact, that it is a wonder it survives at all in the industry, but it is alive and well in many otherwise well-run establishments.

Apron training is simply lazy management. If the new employee can be parked somewhere out of sight to cope as best he can, then the manager can return to his office and get back to studying a report that indicates a dangerously high labour cost. Part of a new employee's training can certainly be delegated to other staff, but it must be to a purpose and a plan. The new employee needs to feel that his supervisor or manager is taking an active interest in how quickly he fits in. The supervisor should make frequent checks to see and record what skills have been learned, and to answer questions about the right method, the right equipment and the required standard.

Operations manuals and written instructions

Some successful food and beverage operations rely heavily on written training manuals and notices, particularly in the fast food industry. Here consistency is extremely important, and the supervisor may be dealing with unskilled and inexperienced labour. The theory is that, by writing everything down in simple language, often accompanied by illustrations and diagrams, new employees are constantly guided by an unchangeable set of rules. This system has been proven highly effective in the fast food industry and in some parts of the hotel industry, such as housekeeping. Even in sophisticated restaurant operations, menu photographs, table set diagrams, wine-matching charts and reminder lists are commonly used. The advantage of written procedures is that they are fixed; they do not rely on interpretation or memory in the same way as verbal instructions do. They may be displayed prominently in back-of-house areas, so that an employee who has forgotten a particular garnish or table setup can check the correct method without the embarrassment of asking a supervisor for the second or third time.

Written instructions are particularly appropriate for machinery and safety systems. A checklist on the side of an automatic dishwasher will enable anyone with reasonable literacy to operate the machine safely. A piece of equipment that is used rarely (say, a fire appliance) should have brief, clear instructions which can be read and understood quickly in an emergency.

Programmed learning is the term used for the type of study that allows a trainee to learn at her own speed, but does not allow progress to the next level until the current one has been mastered. Some excellent programmed learning manuals have been prepared* to provide staff with the opportunity to master a difficult subject (such as wine knowledge, advanced food preparation or management studies) at their own pace.

---

* Usually by the larger multi-national hotel corporations, for internal use.

Written instructions and manuals have some obvious limitations. Literacy may be a problem, or staff who speak a language other than English.* Fixed instructions may not be of much use when an unusual request or situation presents itself. More confusing still, the accepted standard may have drifted significantly since the manual was last revised, so that the new employee can be confused by written instructions that describe one method, when a totally different method altogether is actually being practised. The greatest disadvantage of written training materials, though, is the cost of preparing them. Writing clear instructions is a very specialised skill, as is the preparation of clear diagrams. Both should be left to professionals, for all but the simplest applications.

Supervisor training

Training in a particular area by the supervisor can be very effective, since the supervisor is close to the subject and has an inherent interest in making the new employee productive in the shortest time. This method still requires management, however. The supervisor should be given a clear set of guidelines to ensure that each point is covered, and a record should be kept of exactly what the new employee has been taught. An assessment should be made at each stage, so that the employee is declared competent before progressing to the next stage.

The supervisor must be provided with adequate training materials and sufficient time to devote to the training process. It may be useful in some cases to schedule several staff members for an introductory session. Wine service, banquet operations, bar setup or cashier's procedures are often handled in this way. This will improve the efficient use of the supervisor's time, and provide a pool of trained staff who may be called upon at need.

In-house training sessions

Following on from training given by a supervisor, it may be useful to schedule training sessions out of ordinary working hours for subjects that require more in-depth instruction. Handling customer complaints, writing rosters, planning a wedding reception and introducing of a new procedure are examples of subjects that may best be presented in a formal training session.

It is important to schedule these training sessions only for those staff who are ready to learn and use the information presented. The temptation to send everyone along, on the presumption that it will do them some good, is a mistake. The larger group may not be immediately interested in the subject, making it harder

---

* A famous example occurred at New York's Waldorf Astoria Hotel when a new general manager was appointed. He discovered that all the hotel's operating manuals and instructions were written in English, while more than 70% of the staff used Spanish as their first language and read English with difficulty. The manuals were translated immediately.

for those who do need the information to get the most out of the time allotted. There is no harm in creating the impression that special training sessions are for a select few, who are being groomed for more responsibility and possible promotion. Attendance at a training session should be earned, and recognised as an accomplishment in itself.

The person who gives such a training session must obviously be competent, have the necessary skills to present the information cogently and clearly, and be ready to answer specific technical questions without hesitation.

Specialist trainers

In some cases, the subject will be best covered by an outside consultant, selected for his or her in-depth knowledge of a particular field. An expert in computer software might be called in to teach a small group the operation of a new POS system, or a specialist wine lecturer invited to teach advanced wine knowledge to staff in the fine dining room. An instructor from the St John Ambulance Brigade might present an emergency CPR course for a wider group, or a representative from the coffee supply company be invited to demonstrate the correct operation and maintenance of a new espresso machine.

In each case, the Food and Beverage Manager should discuss the presentation with the trainer in advance, confirming what information will be presented and at what level. A quick run-through will call attention to any areas the F&B considers most important, and prevent incorrect procedure being presented to staff. A convenient time and a suitable venue should be agreed on as well as the fee, if any, that will be charged. Once this preparation is complete, the Food and Beverage Manager can draw up a list, in consultation with supervisors and department managers, of the staff who would most benefit from the training session.

Outside training courses

It is quite common in the public service, and in some large hotel companies, to send the staff member to the training course rather than bring the training course to the staff. This may be for reasons of efficiency (a large number of people attending from different locations) or facilities (sending a bar manager to the brewery for training on beer reticulation systems). Since sending a staff member to a course often involves significant transportation, accommodation and tuition costs, this type of training is usually restricted to senior staff.

In the area of hotel and restaurant management, there may be courses offered by the local TAFE college or university which will benefit supervisory staff who are being prepared for promotion. Where a staff member can make a good case for the application of a particular course to his or her duties, the manager should lend a sympathetic ear and consider offering complete or partial sponsorship. Other possbilities are adult education courses at TAFE or the university, which are often quite reasonably priced and conveniently scheduled. This kind of investment is made, not just to improve the skills of the employee, but also to demonstrate an active commitment to his career and to build loyalty.

Tertiary study

Several universities offer degree courses in tourism or hotel management, suitable for those who wish to pursue a long-term career in the industry. Such a degree is an excellent qualification when competing for a sought-after position, but it does not usually provide an automatic entry to middle management. Students are often frustrated to learn that several years' practical experience, often in entry-level jobs, is still required after graduation.

When an employee is serious enough about career development to undertake part-time tertiary study leading to a degree in hotel management, tourism studies or business management, the employer will do well to encourage it. The company may consider a partial scholarship, or assistance in the form of time off for examinations, allowance for study load and possibly career guidance.

The manager should be familiar with tertiary course offerings available in the locality and by correspondence. If an employee shows interest in pursuing a formal career in hotel management, the information should be current and close to hand.

Cross-training

One area sometimes overlooked in a large operation is the opportunity for cross-training. That is, an employee working in the Stewards department may have a keen interest in computers, and would appreciate a chance to learn the operation of the stock control system. Casual banquet staff may jump at the chance to learn table cooking in the restaurant, or a cashier to take a turn behind the cocktail bar. Managers who regard this as a waste of precious time, or think it too much trouble to arrange, do not understand the valuable effect it can have on team-building. In our industry, it is all too easy for people to retreat within the limits of their job. The grill cook may be intolerant of special guest orders, until a spell on the poolside barbecue puts her in direct guest contact for a month or two. The table server who is careless about writing legible dockets may reach a new understanding after two weeks' experience on the cashier's desk.

Cross-training has other effects, of course. In an emergency, it can be extremely useful to have a cashier who knows how to make cocktails and a banquet server who can step in to help the restaurant staff. The chance to learn how another department works, with a change of surroundings and duties, can often revitalise an employee who is beginning to get bored, or give a developing supervisor a sense of how the whole interrelated machine works. Cross-training between departments in a large hotel is even more valuable, creating friendships and connections that short-circuit the normal hierarchy and promote fast and flexible customer service.

Assessing training needs

The key to using training efficiently is to understand what is needed and by whom. If customer complaints make it clear that there is a problem with the efficiency of breakfast service in the coffee shop, this is not the time to devote all your attention to a new course in selling skills for the restaurant staff. The coffee shop problem should be addressed first to see if training can help. There may be a need to train supervisors in better service planning, or to teach the breakfast crew a more efficient way of dealing with orders. There could be a bottleneck at the cashier's desk, because an inexperienced cashier has not had enough training in the fast handling of breakfast bills. Training may not be the whole solution (there could be an equipment problem, insufficient seating or overbooking from the front desk), but it will almost always help.

An operating department that has chronic problems can be identified by guest comments, by its performance under pressure, by reports from other departments, by talking to supervisors or simply by working in that department to assess its efficiency. If the Stores department has repeated problems—running out of stock, late delivery to the kitchen and bars, poor reporting—then it is the responsibility of the Food and Beverage Manager to do something about it. Rather than descending on the department, issuing a lot of orders and adding to the confusion, the sensible manager will work with the stores staff for a few days to identify how training or retraining might improve performance. The next step is to decide what kind of training is needed, and assemble the resources to deliver it. If the problem is traceable to sloppy paperwork, a brief session for all stores staff on the correct procedure may be enough to solve it. If the problem stems from an employee who is not sufficiently trained to handle the job asked of him, then individual training may be required.

Training needs can also be assessed on an individual basis, continually. The good manager always has a mental file of each employee's abilities, potential, previous experience and aptitudes. It is your job to make sure that all staff are offered suitable training at the appropriate time, to keep their interest, develop their skills and contribute to the overall efficiency of the department. This requires a genuine interest in the welfare of every person who works for you, an interest that will not go unnoticed by your staff and will, in any case, make you a better manager.

If you continue to take further professional training yourself, you will set an example. You want to promote the idea that training is valuable and continues throughout the career of a professional hotelier. There is no better way to demonstrate this than to practise it. Industry associations, management organisations, TAFE colleges and universities offer a wide range of professional development courses that may be applicable to your job. Taking one or two of these every year will allow you to see your own organisation from the outside, and remind you that management is an art and a science that can be learned and practised and refined without limit.

Evaluating training

No professional would spend a large amount of money on print advertising without checking the newspaper or magazine to see if the advertisement appeared. Nor would you purchase an expensive dishwashing machine without calling around a few times to see it working. If you authorise spending on training, you have a vested interest in checking whether it works. Unfortunately, training is not something we can put on the loading dock scales or measure in a numerical report. Training is carried around inside the heads of the people who work for you, so you must measure it by indirect means.

If the training given is in a practical and easily demonstrated skill, you might simply ask for a demonstration. If a new computerised ordering system has been installed and the restaurant staff have been trained in its use, you can ask each table server to demonstrate his or her ability to enter an order accurately and prepare a bill using the new machine on a 'dry run'. If a new chef has been given the job of setting up the luncheon buffet, you may visit it several times in a week to check consistency, presentation and quality. A few minor lapses can be put down to inexperience, and gentle corrections made. If there are more serious gaps in performance, then you may have to reassess what kind of training was given and by whom.

Some training outcomes are more difficult to measure. If a training course for supervisors is presented, aimed at improving their people-management skills, it might be some time before there is any noticeable change in the way they work. The test will come when a supervisor is required to handle a thorny staff problem, or an unexpected rush puts that department under pressure. It is important to record what training has been given and to whom. A note on each staff member's employee file, indicating that he or she has attended a particular course, is a beginning. You will also need to review—after 30, 60 or 90 days—the overall effect of the training course. These comments can be recorded in a training planner, which is nothing more complicated than a week-at-a-glance diary. In it, you schedule training sessions, note who attended them, record who gave the training and later add comments on the results. This training planner will become a valuable tool for measuring the cost and the benefits of different kinds of training, and planning next year's training budget.

If an employee is sent at the company's expense to a recognised course offered by an educational institution, a certificate of successful completion can be added to that employee's file. It will also be wise to assess the employee's performance after the course to measure how useful the course has been, and to indicate the employee's suitability for further training. If specialist trainers are brought into the establishment, you will need to check their credentials, ask for references from other organisations who have used their services, and establish at the outset what the training goals are and how they will be measured.

CHAPTER SUMMARY

Training is an investment in the smooth operation and quality of service in any food and beverage operation. The aims are twofold: to improve the efficiency of the organisation and to encourage the professional development of each staff member. The benefits for the organisation are a more competent and loyal staff and better service to the customer. The Food and Beverage Manager must be familiar with the different types of training, and take responsibility for planning the overall departmental training program.

Since training is a cost, it must be intelligently controlled to derive the maximum benefit from every dollar spent. To this end, the manager should be aware of the pitfalls of inappropriate training and be able to assess training needs correctly and measure the results gained from each training initiative.

REVIEW QUESTIONS

1 Explain the difference between an apprenticeship and a formal traineeship.

2 'Apron training' is still common in the hotel industry. Explain what it is, and what disadvantages it has.

3 How can a manager assess the training needs of an operating department?

4 How does cross-training benefit an organisation?

5 What methods can be used to check the effectiveness of training?

CHAPTER THIRTEEN

MANAGEMENT STYLE

Management styles and the developmental stages from new supervisor to professional manager

Methods of work, understanding systems and training strong second-line managers

The qualities of the professional manager

Finding a successful style

'Management style' is the term used to describe the way in which a manager does his or her job. There are almost as many management styles as there are managers, but they can be grouped into general categories based on how the manager handles the key functions of the role: planning, forecasting, cost control, leadership, staff development, marketing and customer relations. In the hotel and restaurant industry, we suffer from a higher-than-average rate of 'burn-out' among middle management staff. Part of the explanation is that the industry allows a wide variety of management styles to flourish, many of which are seriously unsuited to the business of running a hotel, club or restaurant.

The manager of a large retail shop may be obsessive about staying on duty every hour that the shop is open, easily running up a total of 60, 70 or 80 hours a week. An hour or two after the shop closes its doors, however, there is little practical reason for the manager to stay there, so she goes home. The same compulsion to stay on duty in an international hotel, which operates seven days a week and 24 hours a day, will rapidly lead to exhaustion. The owner of a small manufacturing business in a country town might run his business like a sweatshop, managing by threat and intimidation, because his employees have little choice but to put up with it. The same management style in a large city club would lead to crippling staff turnover and, quite possibly, industrial action or compensation claims.

The manager who sees her department as a stepping-stone to advancement, at the expense of the people who work for her, will spend more time playing politics than building an effective team. The autocratic manager behaves as if his staff are there to take the blame for whatever goes wrong, and manoeuvres to credit himself with any success. The ineffectual manager is constantly complaining about the difficulty of running a department with untrained staff, demanding customers and inadequate equipment. All of these styles can be found in the hotel industry: the only thing they have in common is that they do not work for long.

A professional manager is someone who has acquired, by long practice and experiment, a management style that is successful in terms of customer satisfaction, staff morale, profitability and personal achievement. She does not drive her staff; she leads and encourages them. She understands that forecasting and planning are the principal functions of management, and that too much time spent doing things restricts the amount of time left for thinking about what is to be done. At the same time, she realises that time spent isolated in an office, far from the working environment, diminishes her ability to control, direct and guide the operation effectively.

Developing management skills

Good managers are trained, not born. Some train themselves; others are lucky enough to find someone who will help them avoid the major pitfalls along the road. The process begins whenever an employee is singled out for promotion to the first level of management: the working supervisor.

The new supervisor

It is common enough for a senior manager to keep an eye on the most adept table server, the fastest bar attendant or the most capable chef. When the time comes to appoint a new supervisor, this person is the most likely candidate and may be offered the job. Since the offer is seen as welcome recognition for hard work and an opportunity for advancement, it is seldom declined. Unfortunately, the necessary training for the employee's new role is often overlooked, on the presumption that he already knows what he is doing. Cast into his new duties with little preparation, the new supervisor has a host of difficulties to overcome. There may be some resentment from staff who only last week regarded the new supervisor as 'one of the crew'. The new supervisor will have to establish a measure of authority if others are to take directions from him.

With a lot more responsibility on his shoulders, the supervisor has little time for planning, because there is far too much work to do. Eager to prove himself able for the new job, he doubles his efforts and begins to work longer hours, staying with the job for 'as long as it takes to get it done'. So good is he at the technical aspects of the job that he often finds himself working hard while other staff stand around watching. He offers them a challenge to keep up with him, confident that he can lead them by example. In line with his new position, he begins to take an interest in measurable results, such as the number of covers served, the total takings in the cocktail bar or the wage cost results for the month. When an unexpected rush occurs, he can be seen flying from one place to another, calling for all hands on deck and maximum effort.

By setting a furious pace, he finds that some of his people are unwilling to keep up, and staff turnover begins to rise. Finding new people is an unwelcome chore, and he is inclined to start six new table servers in the hope that one of them will be good enough to keep on. There may be some paperwork to be taken care of, but he regards it as a nuisance. The real work is out there on the floor, making sure that things are running well. If he is asked what plans he has for his section, his most likely reply is 'I'll think about that once we've got through this rush'.

The dangers here are obvious: there is little or no control being exercised beyond getting through the day. Burn-out is a distinct possibility, unless the new supervisor can get past the point where he believes he must do everything himself. A suggestion that there may be a better way to do things is often met with dismay; after all, isn't he working hard enough already? Emergencies and unexpected changes are still dealt with in 'firefighter' style, rushing to correct problems as they arise. Rising staff turnover is a hidden cost that can quickly cut into departmental profits, and it will do nothing to make the new supervisor's job any easier. With no special training in how best to approach the new job, the same person who was once the best table server on the restaurant staff has become the weakest member of the management team.

The experienced supervisor

If the new supervisor is able to survive the difficult readjustment to a management role, some new habits will emerge. With some experience under his belt, the supervisor begins to see a little further ahead and makes the first important step towards real managerial skill: he begins to delegate some tasks to reliable staff members. At this point no real responsibility is delegated, but the supervisor will assign a list of jobs that can be done to help get things organised. Short-term planning may begin at this stage, with some forward thought given to which people will be needed, when they should be on duty and what roles they will fill. The supervisor begins to take an interest in forecasts to help him in this task.

A keener interest in financial results may emerge, but the labour cost figures at the end of the month will still probably come as a surprise. The supervisor has not yet learned to adjust rosters accurately to achieve a budget. At the moment it is enough to see that all shifts are covered and that everyone has turned up for work. He is becoming aware of the price of supplies and overheads, takes more care to avoid waste, and is more scrupulous about requisitions, quizzing his staff about what they are ordering and why. He regards paperwork as a chore, but realises it is necessary to run the organisation, so he will often stay late to complete a roster or fill out a report.

On the floor, the supervisor has learned that doing everything himself is not the answer. He makes sure to chase up each one of his staff, to ensure that they are doing some work. No one is left standing around without a job to do. If the restaurant is quiet, he will assign staff to polish cutlery, clean out store cupboards or fold napkins. He is beginning to identify his best people, to rely on them for some help and make sure that they are given the most favourable shifts. Staff turnover may still be higher than he would like, but experience has taught him to screen job applicants more carefully, so as to avoid a constant round of training new people only to have them leave a few weeks later. Still, he is often heard to say 'If you want a thing done right, you might as well do it yourself'.

The experienced supervisor is completely functional at this point, and will probably cope with a sudden rush or a shortage of staff without throwing in the towel. He is tired, though, because he keeps nearly all of the responsibility to himself and puts in very long hours. Burn-out is still a danger, especially when the supervisor reflects on how easy things were when he had only himself to look after.

The emerging manager

A combination of experience, learning from other managers by example and possibly doing some study of management theory allows the experienced supervisor to develop into a real manager. At this stage, the emerging manager begins to see patterns in the way things happen. He becomes interested in the prevention of problems before they occur, rather than rushing to fix them. Forecasting is now more important to him, and he seeks out the information that will allow him to plan a week or two in advance. He has made the connection between accurate information and efficient operation, has started to make his own forecasts and has set some of his own departmental goals. He is pleased when his system works, and proud of the improvements he can achieve in cost control and productivity. If the supervisor has not already had a promotion to manager, he is certainly in line for the next vacancy that presents itself.

The manager now understands that delegation means more than simply handing someone a list of jobs to be done. He begins to rely on a small group of assistants who can be trusted to handle real responsibility. His first tentative experiments with this idea seem to work, and his staff respond well to the idea. He no longer finds himself chasing people to make them work, because staff morale is improving and turnover is dropping. The new manager has come to appreciate the value of training, not just as a good idea in theory, but as a practical solution to operational problems. He is ready to take advice from some of the people who work for him, in order to improve the way the system works. An unexpected benefit of these new developments is that he is now able to work somewhat shorter hours, confident that, during quiet periods at least, the place will look after itself without his constant presence.

The manager begins to establish good relations with other operating departments, at first because he needs their help, and later because he understands that his own operation is part of a larger whole. As a result of this, he begins to see that other department managers are under exactly the same sort of pressure, but that some cope with it better than others. He takes an interest in what methods these successful managers use, and will adopt whole systems if they seem useful to his operation.

With a more stable crew, the manager is now able to be more selective about the staff he employs. A warm body and a heartbeat are no longer enough; he is looking for people with the right combination of skills and personality to fit into the team. He takes an active role in recruiting new staff, screening them carefully and choosing the right people. He has learned that a thorough induction makes people productive much faster than simply throwing them into the deep end to see if they sink or swim. If he is asked at this point about his plans for the department, he will be able to outline a few good training ideas, suggest some useful rearrangements to the way things are done, and provide a list of new equipment he would like to see included in the next year's budget.

At this point, the department head knows that she has a competent manager in the making. There are still many skills to be developed, but the basic ideas are there. Further management training would be appropriate before the next promotion is considered. This is a time for consolidation of the new manager's abilities and for some experience to be gained. The manager will now be readily approachable, and will appreciate being taken into confidence about future plans and marketing initiatives. His opinion should be sought on new developments that will affect his area.

The experienced manager

The principal area of progress here is the cultivation of a group of second-line supervisors, who are for all practical purposes running the operation. Trained, given real responsibility and encouraged to succeed, these supervisors are not only capable of running the department in the absence of the manager; they are also directly involved in the setting of departmental goals. The manager has now gained real control over his operation by allowing himself the time to understand whole systems and plan far in advance. During peak periods, the manager will probably be on the floor, but will not have to give directions or stand in for line crew; he will be free to study how the machine functions, noting those areas that could still use improvement, and planning how that improvement might be achieved. He is openly enthusiastic about his department and his crew, and welcomes new challenges.

The experienced manager sees his role as setting policy (with the participation of his supervisors), monitoring results (profitability, cost control and customer satisfaction) and forward planning. He is completely conversant with the standard indicators, and does not have to wait until the end of the month to learn what his labour cost percentage is: his own information system can tell him that on a daily basis. He is taking an increasing interest in marketing and pays close attention to what sells, what contribution margin is achieved and what the average customer spends. He does not just wait for results, but has full command of how sales projections, cost control and budget targets can be influenced by operational decisions.

Staff morale is high; so is productivity. Relieved of the pressure of running the operation, the manager now takes an active interest in the success of each person working for him. He has learned how to use responsibility to develop staff confidence, and keeps a constant eye open for potential supervisors. He has developed the knack of gaining and retaining staff loyalty, and very rarely has to correct behaviour; his staff do it themselves. Staff turnover is now low and stable, and the manager has delegated screening to his supervisors. They have been well trained in recruitment, interviewing techniques and induction, and are quite capable of evaluating whether an applicant is likely to be a successful addition to the team. Even training has been delegated. The manager has identified those members of the crew who are best with new employees, and encourages them to perfect their own skills by teaching them to others. His role in staff development is to train new managers, a task he enjoys and does well.

Clearly, this is an able and confident manager, who has the full support of the people working for him. His department is likely to be profitable, and guest comments will reflect an efficiently run and professional operation. The manager has grasped the essentials of quality management and is enthusiastic about developing new talent. Promotion to greater responsibility is likely, since he has demonstrated advanced management skills and has already trained several possible replacements for himself.

The professional manager

At this level, the manager is almost completely concerned with the development of people in order to achieve corporate goals. The professional manager may have little or no involvement in production, but he does have a very active role in setting standards of quality and customer service. His principal task is to recruit, develop and guide other managers, who are in turn responsible for the various areas of operation. This is the role of a general manager in a large hotel. He (or she) will lead a group of people who work with him rather than for him. He has a proven track record of inspiring good people to pursue excellence, and having the wisdom to let them get on with it. He will rarely admonish anyone on his team, since he has learned that self-motivation is the most powerful tool at his disposal. By recognising and rewarding success, he appeals to the natural competitiveness that lies within every successful manager.

His understanding of financial controls is sound, and he has a keen appreciation of the fact that it is easier to increase profits by improving productivity and controlling costs than by pursuing market share at any price. He is conscious of return on investment and the obligation a company has to its shareholders and directors.

The professional manager keeps himself well-informed on the market—not just as it is now, but as it will be in five or ten years. His planning is long-range, and he is careful to involve all of his department managers in the process, both for their specialist knowledge and for their commitment to goals they have helped to set themselves. He has long since learned that people will work hardest when they have a personal and professional stake in a company's success.

Freed of involvement in the production process, he is able to concentrate more attention on the customer. He is likely to spend a good deal of his time talking to individual and corporate customers, gauging their degree of satisfaction, listening to comparisons with the competition, and tracking emerging trends in the industry. He encourages his staff to be customer-oriented, and gives them the resources and back-up they need to provide extraordinary service.

By this time, the professional manager is completely at home in his role, and will take on more ambitious projects as they come up. He concentrates on producing results, and the bottom-line profitability of his operation proves that he can achieve them. He may progress through the corporate hierarchy of a large company towards a senior management post, or start his own company. Given some familiarity with the product and the market, the professional manager is qualified to take on a similar role in nearly any industry.

In summary

Every manager should be able to see himself or herself in one of these categories, and understand that the pressures of the job are not unique to anyone's particular situation. Managing people is not easy: it takes a great deal of patience, determination and endurance. Some managers will succumb to burn-out before they are able to reach the next level, but will stay in their job because it provides reasonable conditions and rewards, or else will leave the industry to try something different.

Qualities of the professional manager

Whether managing the food and beverage department of a large hotel, operating a busy gaming club or running a successful restaurant, the professional manager exhibits a number of key qualities. These go beyond good operational planning and technical skill into the realm of personality. These are not just commendable traits; they are essential tools for success in any managerial role.

- **Bearing** is the term given to a combination of traits including personal grooming, good manners, politeness under pressure, seriousness of purpose and the
quality of your speech. At one end of the scale is the pompous manager, who
comes across as self-indulgent, vain and pretentious. At the other end of the
scale is the crass, loud, vulgar person who has great difficulty convincing anyone that he is, in fact, the manager. Your intention should be to strike a middle
note: your bearing should be dignified without being self-important, your speech
careful and your manners excellent. You will dress well to set an example for
the people who work with you without being vain about it, and maintain your
personal grooming meticulously. You will be giving people directions that have
the force of an order. That authority is carried with you even when you are
making a joke, so take care that you do not damage it by careless speech or an
overly 'matey' tone of voice. You should avoid coarse language, because you do
not know who may be offended by it, and be careful of sexist or racist speech.
Both of these are ill-mannered, and may actually be illegal. No story does the
rounds of your staff more quickly than a description of your behaviour when
you have had a few drinks. Though you may be in the business of serving alcohol,
it is a very bad idea to consume it while you are on duty, or even on the premises.
Join people for a drink if it is appropriate, but stick to mineral water or a soft
drink.
- **Courage** may seem an old-fashioned term, but you will need it to make difficult decisions, take calculated risks and go against the tide when necessary. The
manager who always takes the least controversial line and the safest option will
never excel. This quality applies to your dealings with staff, customers and your
own superiors. If an employee has done something clearly wrong, do not hide
behind a written memo or a notice on the wall. When you have all the facts of
the matter, go directly to that person and tell him what it is that concerns you.
You will gain a reputation for honesty and plain dealing that will benefit you
immeasurably. In an extreme case, where dismissal is the only option, you must
be prepared to do it cleanly, dispassionately and promptly. If a customer has a
complaint, you will let your supervisors handle it in order to develop their own
self-confidence, but if they are clearly out of their depth, you will not avoid
the matter. When a direction or policy issued by senior management creates a
problem for your operation or your staff, you must be prepared to go and argue
your case clearly and effectively.
- **Decisiveness** is the opposite of indecision, and it is a quality much appreci-
ated in a manager. This does not mean that you should make decisions hastily
or without a full understanding of the facts—quite the opposite. When a decision
is called for, you will go after the information you need to make it, then lose
no time about giving an answer. Some inexperienced managers hedge their

decisions, for fear of making the wrong one. Others will insist that a policy is adhered to, even when it is obviously not the right one. Both habits lead to a lessening of your authority and reputation as a manager. You may be asked for a fast call; that is part of the nature of the business. You must learn to gather information quickly and accurately, and be ready to admit it when your decision goes the wrong way. You will occasionally wear a little egg on your face, but your average will improve with experience, and people will respect you for your ability to get it right more often than not.

- **Dependability** means simply that if you say you will do a thing, you will do it, however inconvenient or difficult it proves to be. A promise to a staff member to look into a holiday request may be the least critical thing on your job list today, but it is right at the top of that employee's concerns, and you will not improve your standing in her eyes if you forget about it. If you promise a guest to arrange a reservation for him and then fail to do so, you damage not only your personal reputation but that of the establishment as well. Some promises are specific; some are implied. You may not specifically tell your staff that you will arrange for their wages to be paid promptly this week, but it is assumed that you will. Any failure to do so is seen as a lapse in your dependability. One conclusion you may draw from this is that you should not offer promises lightly. Whatever you agree to do becomes a guarantee that you will do it, so beware of promising what you cannot deliver. It is better to be frank and say 'I'm sorry but I just won't be able to do that today. Can I get someone else to help you, or can it wait until Monday?' rather than lightly promise and then fail to deliver.

- **Endurance** is a professional qualification in our industry, which can see the restaurant just as busy at 10.00 p.m. as it was at 6.30 a.m. You must be able to keep up the pace, since the people who work for you are relying on your ability. This means, paradoxically, that you should not be on duty all the time. One of the most valuable lessons a manager can learn is to pace himself and take time off as soon as it becomes possible. This has two effects: it means that you can be refreshed and operating at full efficiency when you are on duty, and it delivers a clear message of trust and confidence to your second-line supervisors, who will look after the place while you are away. Inevitably, the 14–hour day will come up occasionally, but even in this case, the ability to pace yourself will have a great impact on the quality of your work and your decisions. There is no more pointless exercise than the habit of staying on and on, long after you have ceased to be useful on duty. Managers who have this habit imagine that they will be seen as tireless and hard-working; what the staff and customers actually see is someone who is drawn and half-exhausted all the time.

- **Enthusiasm** is perhaps the most difficult of all qualities to cultivate. There is a certain superficial appeal in the cynical remark or the world-weary attitude.

Unfortunately this is cumulative, so that when an energetic response is required, it may be very difficult to arouse. A good manager understands that enthusiasm for quality, for guest service and efficient operation is a delicate plant that needs nurturing. A positive attitude, a habit of accepting challenges willingly and the capacity to 'talk up' your staff will be rewarded with a healthy atmosphere that motivates people to do their best. Negative comments about guests, about other staff members or about senior management may grab a little attention, but they are in the long run destructive to your reputation. An unflattering remark about another manager will eventually rebound, and the listener will be left with a nagging doubt as to what you might say about them, out of their hearing. Few of us are blessed with an unfailingly positive outlook, but the experienced manager is able to control her demeanour when on duty or talking to other members of the staff or management.

- **Integrity** is the quality that assures the people you work with that you can be counted on to do the right thing. Honesty is a large part of it, especially in an industry in which the temptations are many and varied. It is impossible to expect perfect honesty from the bar staff handling cash, if the bar manager regularly serves drinks to his friends without payment. The manager must be scrupulous in observing the rules, if he wants the rules to be observed by the people who work for him. Integrity also means that your actions will be constantly examined for evidence of slyness, deceit, self-serving, laziness or immorality. There is no habit that is not eventually discovered in the self-contained world of a large hotel, so you will do well to behave in an empty room as you would before a crowd of people. The manager must be a paragon of virtues: any failing you allow yourself is interpreted by your staff as licence to do the same thing and more.

- **Good judgement** means that, when you are called upon to make a difficult decision, your actions will be widely accepted as just and fair. This is most important when dealing with people, especially if an argument or disagreement is involved. The correct method is the same one used on a grander scale by a court: you should listen carefully to both sides of a story, allow each person involved to speak his or her whole case, call for more information if you need it, give your decision and explain how you arrived at it. This need not be excessively formal or long-winded; the whole procedure may take ten minutes, if the disagreement is simple and requires a quick resolution. The obvious pitfalls to avoid are: showing unfair prejudice against one side or the other, making an over-hasty decision before you have all the facts, refusing to make a decision altogether because you do not wish to upset anyone, or imposing your authority unnecessarily on a situation that would have worked itself out. Good judgement is also called for when planning what work is to be done, when it will be done, by whom and in what order.

- The power of **loyalty** cannot be underestimated, and it is a quality that is both given and received. When people work for you, they give up a small part of their own self-determination and allow you, as manager, to make decisions for them about what is to be done. The unspoken agreement is that you will take responsibility and defend their interests and well-being when required. To ask a person to do something, then stand back when things go wrong as if it were none of your affair, is to violate the basic trust that you have been given. Loyalty in the other direction means that your staff will follow your directions even when they are not entirely sure you know what you are doing. This kind of loyalty is earned by proving many times over that you will stand by them, that you are genuinely concerned for their welfare and that you will not ask them to do anything that you do not believe is right. This kind of close-knit interdependence is the most powerful bond that a manager can create. It should never be abused, because it has the ability to move mountains.

- **Tact** is a keen sense of what should be said and what might be better left unsaid. It springs from a sound understanding of other people's feelings, and it is an extremely useful quality in the hotel and restaurant industry. If a staff member appears for work looking dirty and dishevelled, a loud reprimand in front of other staff may cause that person to do something about his appearance, but it will leave a deep resentment that will inevitably come to the surface some time in the future. A quiet word and some help obtaining a fresh uniform will achieve the same result without embarrassment. Tact is essential when dealing with guests, and the ability to gently influence a guest's behaviour without giving offence is highly regarded in a professional hotelier.

- **Appreciation** is the ability to recognise the accomplishments of other people and reward them with an open hand. This does not mean that you have to be constantly presenting people with awards, bonuses and trophies. It simply means that a good manager provides his or her staff with plenty of feedback (and in particular, positive feedback) every day. There is nothing an employee enjoys more, in the workplace, than being recognised for doing a good job. Even the least skilled worker has something she does well, if it is no more than keeping her area tidy or completing a simple job on time. A word or two of unexpected compliment from the manager can have an extraordinary effect on that person's pride and self-esteem. Bigger accomplishments deserve bigger rewards, and many companies organise employee awards on a monthly or yearly basis. The danger is that this sort of recognition can become insincere or routine, which devalues it in the eye of the recipient. The most effective appreciation is still personal: a genuine 'thank you' from the manager is a powerful incentive.

If all of this sounds somewhat old-fashioned in an age that seems to reward aggression, greed, ruthlessness and ambition, the fact is that it still works. An aggressive manager may frighten his staff into doing something, but they will do it only as long as they remain frightened. A dishonest or unfair manager will have to deal with more dishonesty and suspicion all around her. Whenever you are given the responsibility to lead a group of people, they will respond best and longest to the qualities that they admire, and offer freely much more than they are asked for.

CHAPTER SUMMARY

Management can be described both as an art and as a science. As an art, it relies on intuition, talent and practice. As a science, it can be studied, analysed and dismantled into its component parts. Management style is the way in which individual managers choose to do their work. Some styles are more effective than others, and the professional manager is always seeking to learn better techniques.

The development of a manager can be seen as passing through a series of stages, from the new supervisor coping with the abrupt change from an employee's role, through to the highly skilled and experienced manager who is capable of running complex organisations. As skills are acquired in planning, forecasting, staff development and leadership, the manager begins to understand that management is a profession in itself. In order to succeed at this profession, a good manager needs certain qualities that will inspire people to work with him and for him. These qualities can be identified and cultivated to further improve managerial skill.

REVIEW QUESTIONS

1 What difficulties can be anticipated for a staff member promoted to supervisor?

2 What characteristics would you expect to see in a developing supervisor?

3 How can a manager achieve decisiveness without making hasty errors?

4 What does dependability imply in a professional manager?

5 What is a 'firefighter' in management jargon?

6 Burn-out is a constant danger in hotel management. How can it be avoided?

BIBLIOGRAPHY

Commonwealth of Australia. *Alcohol Misuse and Violence: An Examination of the Appropriateness and Efficacy of Liquor Licensing Laws Across Australia*, Tim Stockwell (ed.), Australian Government Publishing Service, Canberra, 1993.

Karass, Chester Louis & Glasser, William. *Both Win Management*, Ty Crowell Co., New York, 1980.

Kivela, Jacksa. *Purchasing for the Hospitality Industry*, Edward Arnold (Hodder & Stoughton), Melbourne, 1989.

Morrison, Paul, Ruys, Hein & Morrison, Brian. *Cost Management for Profitable Food and Beverage Operations*, Hospitality Press, Melbourne, 1994.

National Institute for the Foodservice Industry. *Applied Foodservice Sanitation*, 2nd edn, William C. Brown Co., USA, 1978.

Peter, Dr Laurence J. & Hull, Raymond. *The Peter Principle*, William Morrow & Co., Inc., USA, 1969; paperback edn, Souvenir Press Ltd, London, 1994.

INDEX